PRAISE FOR
*AN AFRO-INDIGENOUS HISTORY
OF THE UNITED STATES*

"Dr. Mays brilliantly makes accessible the knowledge of how Native, Black, and Afro-Indigenous communities, under the oppressive projects of settler colonialism and white supremacy, have navigated points of tension and harm, while simultaneously revealing instances when we've resisted by way of solidarity and allyship. Ultimately, he reminds us that both the 'Indian problem' and the 'Negro problem' are, in fact, a white supremacist problem."

—MELANIN MVSKOKE, Afro-Indigenous (Mvskoke Creek) activist

"Framed as an answer to questions in Mays's life as well as in his scholarship, this is a startlingly ambitious and deeply engaging study. Refusing to separate two sprawling, interconnected stories but respecting the integrity of each, Mays changes also the whole story of US whiteness as a system of thought and power. A perfect book to be read in classes or given to friends who want to understand the mess we are in and the resources of those who resist."

—DAVID ROEDIGER, author of *How Race Survived US History*

"This is a bold and original narrative that is required reading to comprehend the deep historical relationship between the Indigenous peoples who were transported from Africa into chattel slavery and the Indigenous peoples who were displaced by European settler colonialism to profit from the land and resources, two parallel realities in search of self-determination and justice."

—ROXANNE DUNBAR-ORTIZ, author of
An Indigenous Peoples' History of the United States

"Only twenty years ago, Kyle Mays's voice wouldn't even have passed through academia's and media's gatekeepers. The fact that a voice like this can be heard today and tell his own story is unexpected great news for America . . . and it's just the beginning."

—RAOUL PECK, director of *I Am Not Your Negro*
and *Exterminate All the Brutes*

"A bold, innovative, and astute analysis of how Blackness and Indigeneity have been forged as distinct yet overlapping social locations through the needs of capital, the logic of the nation-state, and the aims of US empire. While we know that slavery and settler colonialism are intricately linked, Kyle Mays uniquely demonstrates that the afterlives of these two institutions are also linked. They provide the land, bodies, and capital for 'newer' systems of bondage to flourish, such as mass incarceration. You will never think of the peoples' history the same way after reading *An Afro-Indigenous History of the United States*."

— ROBIN D. G. KELLEY, author of *Freedom Dreams: The Black Radical Imagination*

An
AFRO-
INDIGENOUS
HISTORY *of*
the UNITED
STATES

An AFRO-INDIGENOUS HISTORY *of the* UNITED STATES

KYLE T. MAYS

ReVisioning American History

BEACON PRESS,
BOSTON

BEACON PRESS
Boston, Massachusetts
www.beacon.org

Beacon Press books
are published under the auspices of
the Unitarian Universalist Association of Congregations.

25 24 23 22   8 7 6 5 4 3 2 1

This book is printed on acid-free paper that meets the uncoated paper
ANSI/NISO specifications for permanence as revised in 1992.

Text design and composition by Kim Arney

Beacon Press's ReVisioning American History series consists
of accessibly written books by notable scholars that reconstruct
and reinterpret US history from diverse perspectives.

An earlier version of a portion of chapter 4 was previously
published as "Transnational Progressivism: African Americans,
Native Americans, and the Universal Races Congress of 1911,"
American Indian Quarterly 37, no. 3 (2013).

Library of Congress Cataloging-in-Publication Data
Name: Mays, Kyle, author.
Title: An Afro-Indigenous history of the United States / Kyle T. Mays.
Description: Boston : Beacon Press, [2021] | Series: Revisioning American
history | Includes bibliographical references and index.
Identifiers: LCCN 2021020880 (print) | LCCN 2021020881 (ebook) | ISBN
ISBN 9780807006993 (paperback) | ISBN 9780807011713 (ebook)
Subjects: LCSH: African Americans—Relations with Indians. | African
Americans—Race identity. | Indians of North America—Mixed descent. |
Indians of North America—Ethnic identity | United States—
Race relations. | United States—History.
Classification: LCC E98.R28 M39 2021 (print) | LCC E98.R28 (ebook) |
DDC 973/.0496073—dc23
LC record available at https://lccn.loc.gov/2021020880
LC ebook record available at https://lccn.loc.gov/2021020881

To Liseth, El Don, ChiChi

CONTENTS

AUTHOR'S NOTE

I AM WRITING this book for at least three reasons. First, because of my personal identity: I am Black and Saginaw Chippewa. Second, if I am to imagine a new world, one that brings an end to a world that hates Black people and reproduces antiblackness and white supremacy, and a world that erases Indigenous people and reproduces their dispossession through settler colonialism, I intend to tell some histories that have been ignored at best or made invisible at worst. Third, there is a deeply intellectual component rooted in my interactions in graduate school.

When I visited a prospective graduate school, I met with an infamous Black studies professor in his office. When I told him that I was interested in doing research on the links between the American Indian Movement and the Black Panther Party, he scoffed, saying, "There's no relationship." Beyond the fact that he was at worst lying and at best very misinformed—I believe he knew of some of these histories but, because of his "hotepness"—he didn't want to discuss the importance of Black and Indigenous solidarity. (By "hotep," I mean the hyper-masculine Black male who has an ahistorical, Afrocentric conception of himself; refers to men and women as "kings" and "queens"; and basks in their alleged connection to ancient Africa and all of its glory.) He had no basis for that claim. I was also upset that he so easily dismissed my research idea. However, since that time, I've learned that Black *and* Indigenous people continue to produce similar responses as that Black studies professor. As an Afro-Indigenous person, I also know that there is a crucial need for a book that considers the history of Afro-Indigenous struggles, their interactions throughout US history, and how that particular relationship is the foundation for our new sphere of freedom. For me, it is essential that I include Black and

Indigenous people in our collective understanding of liberation. I want to recover some lost histories to show that Black and Indigenous peoples' histories are tied not only to enslavement and dispossession but also a struggle for justice. The journey has entailed many diverse challenges, all while Black and Indigenous peoples have sought belonging and freedom in a country that continues to say, "We don't want you."

How does one begin to write a large book on the topic of intersecting Black American and Native American cultures, histories, and peoples? As a Black and Saginaw Anishinaabe person from Michigan, I begin with my story. My mom is Black American and was raised in Cleveland, Ohio; she is a descendant of enslaved people from South Carolina on her father's side. Her grandmother came to Cleveland, Ohio, in the mid-1930s from Fayetteville, Georgia. My dad is Black and Saginaw Anishinaabe, and raised in Detroit and Lansing, Michigan. His grandmother, my great-grandmother, Esther Shawboose Mays, came to Detroit in the spring of 1940 from the Saginaw Chippewa reservation. She married a Black American man, Robert Isiah Mays, and his family was from Tennessee. They produced nine Afro-Indigenous children. Her children were very active in both Detroit's Black and Indigenous community struggles from the 1960s through 1990s. This activism culminated in my aunt Judy Mays founding the Medicine Bear American Indian Academy—a Detroit Public School with an all–Native American curriculum, designed for Black and Indigenous as well as Latinx students. Medicine Bear was the third public school in the US to have been created with a Native American curriculum. Importantly, the school would not have been created without the advocacy of Black politicians in Detroit.[1]

I come from two different communities. However, I would be remiss not to acknowledge that my Black ancestors came from Indigenous peoples. I don't know the particular tribe; that information was lost because of slavery. I know about the Indigenous heritage of only part of myself. While it might be impossible to find out my personal African Indigenous heritage, I can at least acknowledge the larger history of Indigenous Africans, my heritage.

A major focus of this book is not only to analyze Black American and Indigenous relationships but also to recover and acknowledge the Indigenous roots of people of African descent. I am not claiming that those people are indigenous to what is now the United States, nor do I think Black folks should be so invested in what would be the equivalent of a white nationalist project such as the United States. We should be more visionary than that. However, US Indigenous peoples should also help think through the antiblackness that exists in their community and how they might, as Canadian Indigenous (Mississauga Nishnaabeg) writer and musician Leanne Betasamosake Simpson suggests, make room for Indigenous people on their land.

When I have traveled the country to discuss my research, I often get two versions of a comment or question about identity. First, a person of Black American ancestry might share that they have Cherokee blood in them, maybe Blackfeet. Or, someone, usually a young person, will ask me how I deal with being both Black and Indigenous. I tell them that, for me, it wasn't a contradiction being Black and Indigenous. While others questioned me, my family didn't question or police my identity.

I did experience an instance of being questioned by others—or identity policing—when I was a graduate student, attending an academic conference. I was at the hotel lobby, recognized a peer from my own graduate institution, and saw that they were with a group of other Native people. I'm sure I gave everyone some dap (exchanged a fist pound greeting), and then one of the people, from a Southwestern US tribal nation, asked, "Why are you wearing those earrings?" I replied, "'Cause I like them." They responded, "Where did you get them?" "From a powwow," I snapped back, after quickly concluding that they wondered why a Black person had adorned themselves with "Native" earrings. This antiblack exchange made me angry, if not insecure.

Still, I never felt comfortable in my intellectual knowledge of Black and Indigenous relations until graduate school, because it was there that I was able to delve into the research and really read. I carved out time to think about my identity and how I wanted to help change the intellectual game of how we approach Afro-Indigenous history. Graduate school offered me five years to reflect on myself and learn how to be me—my full Afro-Indigenous self.

My quest in this book is to recover histories, reorient our understanding of historical events and peoples, and project what a present and future idea of Black and Indigenous solidarity might look like. We need a new way of talkin' about these relationships.

In documenting encounters between Black and Indigenous peoples, I have focused the majority of my examples in this book in unexpected ways and places. In fact, the whole book could be considered unexpected. I challenge the very notion of what we "know" about these relationships. I am only mildly interested in writing about the relationship between, for example, the Five Tribes and enslaved Africans, though I'm sure that's what many will expect. The topic of enslavement and dispossession in the nineteenth century dominates the books on African Americans and Native Americans. However, if we are to build a shared Afro-Indigenous future on stolen Indigenous land and recover the Indigenous roots of the ancestors of stolen Indigenous Africans, then it will require we find underexplored histories, rethink "accepted" histories, and survey solidarities and tensions—and also imagine how the world might look after white supremacy and settler colonialism have been dismantled.

I have not written this book as a historical narrative, where the author's voice is almost entirely mute. Throughout the pages I offer commentary here and there so that you, dear reader, and I can have an in-text conversation.

—KYLE T. MAYS, PHD
Atlanta and Los Angeles

An
AFRO-
INDIGENOUS
HISTORY *of*
the UNITED
STATES

INTRODUCTION

*Thousands of volumes have been written about the historical
and social relations existing between Europeans and the Native
Peoples of the Americas and between Europeans and Africans, but
relations between Native Americans and Africans have been sadly
neglected. The entire Afro-Native American cultural exchange and
contact experience is a fascinating and significant subject, but one
largely obscured by a focus upon European activity and European
colonial relations with "peripheral" subject peoples.*

—JACK D. FORBES (Powhatan-Renapé
and Lenape; cofounder, D-Q University)[1]

AFRO-INDIGENOUS HISTORY

I have been writing this book my whole life. I do not mean literally
writing every word for thirty-plus years. It began long before me.
What do you imagine when you think of Afro-Indigenous history?
You might be more familiar with the term "Black-Indian" or "Afro-
Native."[2] I use the term "Afro-Indigenous" to mean both the intersecting relationship between Black American and Native American
peoples and those who identify both as Black and Indigenous. Related
to the terminology question, I am also writing this book because of the
myths that exist about Afro-Indigenous histories and peoples.

The first myth that people think about when they consider Black
and Indigenous histories is the Cherokee enslavement of African peoples. Yes, that happened, and that is perhaps the dominant discourse
when we think of African American and Native American intersecting
histories.[3] However, there is much more beyond that particular history. Others might mention the Buffalo Soldiers; yes, that did happen.[4]
But again, there are histories beyond the nineteenth century.

The second myth is that there are very few reasons to compare
Black and Indigenous peoples' experiences in the United States. The

saying goes something like this: Blacks fight for civil rights and natives struggle for tribal sovereignty, nothing more, nothing less. For instance, in the late Patrick Wolfe's book *Traces of History: Elementary Structures of Race* (2016), the Australian anthropologist and ethnographer traces how white settlers reproduced different forms of colonialism and hierarchies in settler societies such as Australia and the United States. He sees the African (American) and the Indigenous experience in the United States as inherently different. Wolfe wrote, "A relationship premised on the exploitation of enslaved labour requires the continual reproduction of its human providers. By contrast, a relationship premised on the evacuation of Native peoples' territory requires that the peoples who originally occupied it should never be allowed back."[5] According to this logic, Black Americans were exploited for their labor and Indigenous people were exploited for their land, and these two distinctions define their unique political struggles. As a result, there is no need to compare their experiences. By extension, one might surmise from this that there is no need to find alliances in the fight for social justice to end antiblackness and Indigenous erasure. Nothing could be further from the truth.

Finally, I hope to unpack that, for people like me, there is little representation with respect to Black and Indigenous peoples. We often have to choose between one identity or the other, depending on the circumstance. That is unfair, even tragic. Our histories are important, and deserve to be told, in a parallel and systematic way. The Standing Rock Sioux resistance against the Dakota Access Pipeline, the Black Lives Matter Movement, the poisoned water in Flint and water shutoffs in Detroit, and the murders of Breonna Taylor and George Floyd have created a renewed sense of urgency to understand how these different histories and peoples have related to each other, and how they will continue to relate in the future. These movements did not emerge out of nowhere, which suggests that there is a longer history of solidarity that I hope to recover.

RECONNECTING DISCONNECTED HISTORIES

In 1920, Carter G. Woodson, "the father of Black History," wrote, "One of the longest unwritten chapters in the history of the United States is that treating of the relations of the Negroes and the Indians."[6]

More recently, 2011 MacArthur "genius" grant awardee Tiya Miles and scholar Sharon P. Holland note, "Pain and loss. Slavery and land. These terms map onto and move through one another as perhaps the primary concepts in Afro-Native Studies."[7] The relationship between African and Indigenous peoples can be understood in three words: collaboration, conflict, and controversy.

From the time that Europeans kidnapped Africans and brought them to North America in the late sixteenth century, the destinies of Europeans, Africans, and Indigenous peoples would forever be changed. The introduction of Africans as exploited people on Indigenous land set the stage for the exponential growth of capitalism. It is important to reiterate and state this clearly: the foundations of the United States, its current power and wealth, were built on enslaved African labor and the expropriation of Indigenous land. The US democracy that some uphold as the greatest political system since sliced bread has failed to live up to its claims of being a liberal democracy. Instead, it is foundationally an antiblack and anti-Indigenous republic. According to political scientist William Galston, liberal democracy has four components: republican principle, democracy, constitutionalism, and liberalism. He defines "republican principle" as popular sovereignty. People legitimate the government. "Democracy" means that all citizens have equality, and the structure of the government is inclusive citizenship. "Constitutionalism" means that the structure of the government exists in written form, a document like, for example, the US Constitution. Liberalism centers on people's individual rights and privacy. Thus, liberal democracy combines all these elements, though popular sovereignty is limited.[8] US liberal democracy has been "living beyond its means" since the beginning.[9] The Founding Fathers have built debts that they or contemporary white Americans will never be able to pay off.

Enslaved labor and the expropriation of Indigenous land were central to US wealth. For example, in the historiography of the antebellum period in the American South, scholars typically write first of the removal of Native people as a jumping-off point for the exploitation of enslaved Africans, which subsidized the development of modern capitalism.[10] However, as historian Claudio Saunt argues, "the flow of financial capital that created and sustained the empire of cotton directly underwrote the dispossession of native peoples in the south."[11] Though other forms of exploitation have occurred since the original dispossession and enslavement, such as the ever-growing US military industrial complex, which has emerged in nearly every part of the world, these two structures, together, formed modern capitalism. Moreover, the other slavery—the enslavement of Indigenous peoples—was also a central part of the United States' development. In historian Andrés Reséndez's award-winning book, *The Other Slavery* (2016), he argues that Europeans enslaved between 2.5 million to 5 million Indigenous peoples.[12] Although Indigenous enslavement did not measure in scale to African enslavement, as Reséndez argues, it shared with the other system at least four features: "forcible removal of the victims from one place to another, inability to leave the workplace, violence or threat of violence to compel them to work, and nominal or no pay."[13] This set of facts should allow us to trouble the simple distinction that "Africans were enslaved and Indians either died off or were dispossessed and confined to reservations."[14] History is much more complicated, and it is crucial to think further about how these histories interact.

However, it is tempting to focus almost solely on how Black and Indigenous peoples collaborated to resist European domination—such as the founding of Maroon communities. This is romantic at best, and ignores the fact that these two groups were not natural allies. Maroon communities were a group of Africans who escaped enslavement, and often found ways to resist being recaptured by living with one another out of plain sight. Perhaps the most well-known Maroon community in the US was a group of Africans who escaped slavery and lived with the Seminoles.

Yet, it is important not to romanticize these relationships. For instance, even the telling of Bacon's Rebellion in 1676 reveals a different history. Let me offer a brief history. William Berkeley, the governor of the Virginia Colony, denied Nathaniel Bacon the authority to lead soldiers to kill and murder Native Americans in Virginia so that they could occupy land. Bacon, who got caught up in his feelings, decided to take his soldiers and challenge the authority of Berkeley and attack the "enemies," who were the Susquehannock. Bacon and his henchmen attacked the Susquehannock, then they burned down Jamestown. They drove Berkeley back to England, and halted tobacco production for a year. The traditional narrative suggests that the rebellion that occurred in Jamestown was a moment of class solidarity between Black and white people, many of whom were indentured servants, fighting as a part of Bacon's militia. In reality, however, the rebellion was really rooted in white settlers' desire for land, and they wanted to kill Native people to get it.[15] In the aftermath, twenty-three people were hanged, and racial lines between Blacks and whites were hardened. Bacon's Rebellion was not about the overthrow of capitalism but about landownership for lower-class white men like Bacon.[16] Another possible narrative, the more accurate one, is that Bacon was decidedly anti-Indigenous, as white men, the landowners and the landless, wanted Indigenous land.

There are some who argue that the Africans who participated also acted with anti-Indigenous animus. However, that reading flattens the fact that oppressed Africans had their own motives for their freedom. As historian Vincent Harding notes, "Although the motives of Bacon and many of his white comrades now appear ambiguous, and there was unmistakable anti-Indian racism and much greed for plunder mixed in, the available evidence nevertheless indicates that blacks in the rebellion believed themselves to be fighting for their freedom."[17] Bacon's Rebellion is the perfect opportunity to discuss the tensions between not only whites and Blacks and whites and Natives but also between Blacks and Natives.

The accepted Afro-Indigenous histories are centered on African enslavement and Indigenous dispossession. In historian Roxanne Dunbar-Ortiz's award-winning book, *An Indigenous People's History of the United States* (2014), she writes, "The history of the United States is a history of settler colonialism—the founding of a state based on the ideology of white supremacy, and the widespread practice of African slavery, and a policy of genocide and land theft."[18] Importantly, Dunbar-Ortiz's definition of settler colonialism carefully includes the enslavement of Africans as one of the two parallel projects in the formation of the United States. In this sense, blackness, or the Black American experience, is central to also understanding how settler colonialism built this nation and impacted Indigenous peoples. However, while it was not the intent of her work, we forget that the African peoples were in fact Indigenous peoples who were violently ripped from their homelands. The ancestry of Black Americans, or the descendants of the enslaved, may not originate in North America, but they are Indigenous. They are what historians Sidney Lemelle and Robin D. G. Kelley have called "'New World' descendants—the daughters and sons of Africa."[19]

It might seem controversial to call Africans and their descendants' Indigenous peoples, but it is not. To reclaim, insofar as we can imagine, the Indigenous roots of Africans in the diaspora is neither an attempt to replace Indigenous peoples of the US nor to act as settlers in some real or imagined return to Africa, as previous generations have done. However, we do have to account for the fact that, besides some cultural remnants that were able to survive historical erasure, Africans living in the US, because of enslavement, were stripped of their heritage. As Cedric Robinson notes in *Black Marxism: The Making of the Black Radical Tradition* (1983), "The cargoes of laborers also contained African cultures, critical mixes of cosmology, and metaphysics, of habits, beliefs, and morality. These were the actual terms of their humanity."[20] Africans did not just lose their indigenous practices and beliefs, even after enduring the incomprehensible horrors of the slave trade. Robinson continues, "These cargoes, then, did not consist of intellectual isolates or deculturated Blacks—men, women, and children separated from their previous universe. African labor brought the past with it, a past that had produced it and settled on it the first elements of consciousness and comprehension." Even something as simple as West African techniques for rice cultivation are an example of indigenous knowledge transferal, and these were a major contribution to the US colonies and throughout the Americas.[21] So, who exactly was Robinson referring to? Perhaps we could look to the acclaimed poet Phillis Wheatley, the first woman of African descent to publish a book of poetry in prerevolutionary America. Or we can look at Olaudah Equiano, who wrote the first African-authored narrative describing the horrors of the slave trade. These were two Indigenous peoples stolen as children from their homeland and marked as enslaved. It is thus not surprising that the roots of whiteness have sought to eradicate the African past, and to create a hierarchy of difference rooted in white supremacy.

To understand how racial hierarchies have contributed to the formation of US society and how the political structure came to be, we have to go back to their roots. As legal scholar Cheryl Harris argues in her influential article "Whiteness as Property," the foundations of race in the United States, especially whiteness and property, were developed through both the enslavement of Africans and the dispossession of Indigenous peoples.[22] It is important to understand how the white settler state helped construct the image of Black and Indigenous peoples in ways that allowed them to continue to be dehumanized and treated as separate political, economic, and social structures.

An Afro-Indigenous History of the United States explores how Black and Indigenous histories have intersected in important ways; this intersection helps us better understand the broader contours of US history. It examines the links, both solidarities and tensions, between people of African descent and Indigenous people in the United States. This book argues that the twin oppressions of antiblackness and settler colonialism have been a central site through which racial and gender formations have occurred in the United States. Moreover, it demonstrates how Black and Indigenous peoples, in spite of presumed differences—that is, the different ways they were treated by the settler state—have sought solidarity with each other. They have always sought to disrupt, dismantle, and reimagine US democracy; they have even sought to radically transform how this society operates.

In using a phrase such as "radical transformation," I don't intend to focus on political violence and more volatile means of resistance. Nor do people only protest, for instance, at the point of production. There are many forms of resistance, and Black and Indigenous people have used a variety of tactics. They have used movement to new geographic spaces, new ways of communicating with one another, counter language; they have attended congressional hearings, participated in rallies, written poetry and other forms of literary production, all to demonstrate that they were sick and tired of being sick and tired of colonialism and white supremacy.[23] They have always resisted in little and subtle ways. As Kelley notes, "While the meaning and effectiveness of acts differ according to circumstances, they make a difference," and "daily acts of resistance and survival have had consequences for existing power relations, and the powerful have deployed immense resources in response."[24]

Black people have, in many ways, sought to belong within, outside, and next to US democracy. Black belonging in this society has really been about imagining home and longing for a return home, or at least trying to create home. Black folks have found numerous ways to try to do that. They have used Black nationalism, which was a call for the US government to give them land as compensation for their enslaved labor. Before the ratification of the Fourteenth Amendment, some claimed that being born in the US afforded them citizenship.[25] Some have even sought to return to the homeland of their ancestors, one generation removed and, later, several generations removed. Black people in the United States and throughout the diaspora have been forced to pursue this path because they were forcibly removed from their homeland. Some might believe that Black people seeking belonging in the US nation-state and showing patriotism is an expression of some blind allegiance to the democratic project, or worse, to whiteness.

Kelley argues that the history of Black folks has been about movement both "real and imagined." Black people have always desired freedom through their movement to a new place to call home, in order that they may belong. While Black folks might no longer be imagining an exodus to Africa, the term has "always provided black people with a language to critique America's racist state and build a new nation, for its central theme wasn't simply escape but a new beginning."[26] But what is home and how has history disrupted people of African descents' conception of home? It is hard to say. But are we to tell the descendants of those ripped from their homeland, whose ancestors' blood exists in the soil, that this isn't their home? People of African descent have a responsibility to think about their relationship to this indigenous place, and what their responsibility might be going forward to Indigenous nations. By the same token, Indigenous people of what is now the United States, I would argue, have a responsibility to their Black relatives. What that responsibility looks like will depend on a particular Indigenous nation's protocols—and they shouldn't be afraid to adopt new protocols. However, it is something that we need to think about collectively, for the purpose of our shared futures. And this book is my attempt to recover histories, rethink older histories, and contribute to the future of these people.

Indigenous peoples have desired to live freely as sovereign people, right next to the US nation-state. Indeed, the basis of the legal and political relationship of the United States with tribal nations—treaties—is rooted in tribal nations' ability to exist as sovereign entities alongside the United States. However, this relationship has been unequal at least since the 1830s.[27] It is an unequal relationship, but Native people hold treaties as sacred. It is *the* defining political feature that distinguishes Native people from other oppressed groups. In addition to seeking their sovereignty, Indigenous peoples have sought ways to survive the genocide and changing nature of the US nation-state.

Just as Black folks have always fought to belong in spite of the many forms of white supremacy that they have encountered, Native people have continued to survive their supposed disappearance. Anishinaabe writer Gerald Vizenor argues that Native people continue to survive in spite of colonization and erasure. Using the term "survivance" to describe Native peoples' persistent resistance to colonization, he writes,

> Native survivance is an active sense of presence over absence, deracination, and oblivion; survivance is the continuance of stories, not a mere reaction, however pertinent. Survivance is greater than the right of survivable name.
>
> Survivance stories are renunciations of dominance, detractions, obtrusions, the unbearable sentiments of tragedy, and the legacy of victimry. Survivance is the heritable right of succession or reversion of an estate and, in the course of international declarations of human rights, is a narrative of native survivance.[28]

Native peoples' survival and thriving right along the continued operation of the US nation-state is remarkable. They have used the law, warfare, writing, and other acts of resistance to challenge their colonial condition. As Indigenous peoples have asserted survivance, Black folks have asserted their belonging. In this way, the fact that both have survived violent forms of the US settler/white nationalist project and have attempted, at times together and at other times separately, to make the principles of US democracy work is remarkable. Black belonging and Indigenous survivance remains central to how they have survived and will continue to do so into the future.

THE STAGES OF AFRO-INDIGENOUS HISTORY

An Afro-Indigenous History of the United States is transnational. While the majority of these stories take place on occupied Indigenous land (the US), there are other moments that happen in places as far as London. Chapter 1 discusses the lives of Africans and those we would consider Afro-Indigenous in prerevolutionary America. People like Phillis Wheatley and Paul Cuffe, the former kidnapped and enslaved at an early age, and the latter, born to an Indigenous mother and African father, created an Afro-Indigenous modernity in prerevolutionary America, in an attempt to assert the humanity of people of African descent. I argue that we should rethink how we view the early Indigenous Africans, and acknowledge that they maintained at least some of their Indigenous heritages. In chapter 2, I look at the ideological foundations of US democracy through some of the foundational documents such as the *Federalist Papers* and the Constitution, and through some of the important thinkers, like Thomas Jefferson and Alexis de Tocqueville. I also critically explore how these documents were fundamentally anti-Black and anti-Indigenous. Chapter 3 explores the long nineteenth century, and how Black and Indigenous peoples used a variety of methods to resist dispossession and enslavement. It also shows how some participated in the larger discourse of US democracy, by challenging it and imagining how it could be better.

Chapter 4 analyzes the development of Black and Indigenous internationalism during the Progressive Era, demonstrating how they forged an idea of themselves beyond white supremacy and settler colonialism. Chapter 5, set during the post–World War II period, considers how Black American civil rights leaders viewed Indigenous peoples and struggles, and how, for the most part, they attempted to understand Indigenous struggle as something to learn from. At other moments, however, some erased the history and present reality of Indigenous peoples. Chapter 6 looks at the relationship between Black Power and Red Power during the 1960s and 1970s. Exploring key moments of resistance, including the Black and Red Power Movement, the Poor People's Campaign, and Wounded Knee, this chapter makes the case that Black Americans and Native Americans often forged ideological alliances in the pursuit of freedom.

Chapter 7 looks at the relationship between Black and Native people in the realm of popular culture and discourse, breaking down ideological debates about, for instance, the relative toxicity of the N-word and R-word, and thinking critically about debates regarding cultural appropriation. It also explores where, in spite of popular belief, Black

Americans often demonstrate some consciousness on issues facing Indigenous people in popular culture. Chapter 8 offers an analysis of Black Lives Matter, Native Lives Matter, and policing. In the wake of the murders of Breonna Taylor and George Floyd, in March and May of 2020, respectively, I argue that we need both movements, as both are helpful in trying to imagine a world outside of policing. I conclude the book by discussing how a Black and Indigenous future might look beyond settler colonialism and white supremacy.

One of my favorite writers, Leanne Betasamosake Simpson, writes in *Islands of Decolonial Love*, "We're all hunting around for acceptance, intimacy, connection and love, but we don't know what those particular medicines even look like so we're just hunting anyways with vague ideas from dreams and hope and intention."[29] If you're a non-Black or non-Indigenous person, keep this in mind. We just want freedom. We don't want to die at the hands of police brutality. We are tired of living in a state of fear because we don't belong. Above all, I want people to pick up this book and be angry in the spirit of Audre Lorde.[30] Lorde taught us that being angry at oppression is just as normal as any other emotive forms of expression. I want you, dear reader, to pick up this book and acquaint yourself with new characters and histories, to think differently about well-known figures and old documents, and to either continue dreaming and building a world outside of white supremacy and settler colonialism, or begin thinking about it. We have to dream and build at the same time. We will win; we must.

CHAPTER ONE

INDIGENOUS AFRICANS AND NATIVE AMERICANS IN PREREVOLUTIONARY AMERICA

TYPICALLY, WHEN WE THINK OF Africans arriving on the shores of what would become the United States, we see them through the lens of their condition of bondage in 1619. We see them as Black. As a result, we tend to assume that whatever identity they had, because of the Middle Passage, was ripped away, never to exist again. They were no longer Indigenous. We also fold them into the project of US democracy.

For instance, some Indigenous people on my social media accounts took issue with "The 1619 Project," published by the *New York Times Magazine* and headed by investigative journalist Nikole Hannah-Jones. The project's aim is to observe the "400th anniversary of the beginning of American slavery." It seeks to reframe the country's history, understanding 1619 as our true founding, and placing the consequences of slavery and the contributions of Black Americans—as patriots—at the very center of the story we tell ourselves about who we are.[1] A variety of writers and artists also document the foundational role that African enslavement played in the development of the US nation-state. Moreover, they make the case that Africans and their descendants remain the exemplar of US democracy and patriotic ideals. That is, if the founders could not follow the democratic principles they laid out, surely Africans could. In the introduction, Hannah-Jones writes, "Without the idealistic, strenuous and patriotic

1

efforts of black Americans, our democracy today would most likely look very different—it might not be a democracy at all."[2] Such a statement is obviously needed.

Some established (mostly white male) historians did not agree with some of the "historical facts" in "The 1619 Project" and made that public. While we might quibble with some of the historical interpretations in the project, the onslaught of criticisms aimed at Hannah-Jones—from conservatives and liberals, and Donald Trump—seem over the top. Hell, Trump, at the White House Conference on American History on September 17, 2020, went so far as to say that "The 1619 Project" is "toxic propaganda, ideological poison" that if not abolished will "destroy our country."[3] We know of his (white supremacist) agenda. But what about the historians? Is one reason some historians didn't like "The 1619 Project" because they have a beef with journalists? I've heard since graduate school that journalists aren't *real* historians (as if historians don't produce bad history). I also wonder if people felt some type of way because she's a Black woman journalist. I'm not calling anyone racist and sexist, but, well, you know, she is a Black woman who has and continues to do a helluva good job challenging the nation to consider that maybe this democracy ain't all that! Some took issue with the framing, including whether or not the US is, in fact, a democracy.

On August 15, 2019, an Indigenous person tweeted—and later deleted after backlash—"I acknowledge the need for projects like "The 1619 Project." But who are we willing to forget in order to be remembered?" They continued, "The Iroquois Confederacy/Haudenosaunee, founded in 1142, is the oldest living democracy on earth. Erasing one doesn't make the other more visible."[4] Terri Hansen, a Winnebago journalist, confirms this account, writing, "The Iroquois Confederacy, founded by the Great Peacemaker in 1142, is the oldest living participatory democracy on earth."[5] There might be validity to this claim, especially in regard to understanding the roots of democracy in what would become the United States. However, we could also quibble with the whole ideological roots of democracy, and to say "oldest living democracy on earth" might be a stretch. The earth is a large place, and what might be a democracy in the eyes of some might not be in the eyes of others. In fact, given the problems that Black and Indigenous peoples continue to face in the US, is this a democracy? On the other hand, I don't know why we would want to link an Indigenous conception of democracy with one founded on dispossession and enslavement—even if the colonial settlers did co-opt it.

It is true that Indigenous people are often erased in discussions of history and memory. That is the work of settler colonialism in the US. Even more, people see Indigenous people as having vanished; that's why we have mascots and other forms of racism that are unique to Native people. Mascots perpetuate the idea that Indigenous peoples are either all dead or frozen in time. Therefore, they exist only as a caricature. Indeed, as Philip Deloria reminds us, the US nation-state's very identity is constructed through "playing Indian."[6] However, I would pose this question: What if we remembered that those Africans forced to come to the British colony of Virginia were, actually, Indigenous people? How would that help us think differently about early Atlantic encounters between Indigenous peoples from the African continent and those in North America, and beyond? Finally, are we to ignore that other societies, including African ones, may have had forms of "democracy," perhaps even better than what we would consider democracy today? I will leave this question for others to research.

My goal in this chapter is to provide a few examples of these early indigenous encounters, arguing that enslaved Africans did not lose their ideas of what it meant to be Indigenous. Instead, I place them within a world where they maintained their idea of democracy while also being forced to come to terms with the condition of their blackness.[7] Furthermore, I argue that we should, as best as we can, take seriously the trauma of what the transatlantic slave trade did to Africans. How did they cope with their new condition in a new place? We can only answer this question with the limited historical data that we have. I don't mean to suggest that people of African descent are the First Peoples of this land; that is erasure, and a form of anti-Indigenous rhetoric that hoteps tend to perpetuate. I am interested in acknowledging the history of enslaved Africans, and asserting their humanity in its fullest.

Considering the trauma of enslavement, we uncritically assign the mark of enslavement to African peoples. We forget or minimize that these people carried with them their language, cultures, histories, and relationships. In rethinking how we view Afro-Indigenous history in the United States, we first need to recall that Africans forced to come to this country did not racialize themselves as Black in their homelands;

they had their own indigenous roots and tribal beliefs; they were connected to lands, customs, and cosmologies. They were Indigenous.

To write about an Afro-Indigenous history of the United States is also to understand that encounters between Indigenous people in what became the Americas and Indigenous Africans were what amounted to a chance meeting between a variety of Indigenous groups, forced into contact because of capitalism and colonialism. And while we can debate whether those African descendants maintained specific tribal identities, what is not debatable is the fact that customs, traditions, languages, and their remembrances of land—the fundamentals of a people—remained. As W. E. B. Du Bois notes in *Black Reconstruction in America*, "In origin, the slaves represented everything African." They came from "the Bantu tribes from Sierra Leone to South Africa; the Atlantic to the Valley of the Nile; the Nilotic Negroes and the black and brown Hamites, allied with Egypt; the tribes of the great lakes." These Africans "brought with them their religion and rhythmic song, and some traces of their art and tribal customs."[8] And so, it is here where I begin to trace how white supremacy forced these two groups into contact with one another, and where the tensions and possibilities of Afro-Indigenous solidarity emerged.

I begin with the history of Olaudah Equiano, Phillis Wheatley, and Paul Cuffe. Using their work, I explore how they constructed their relationship to place, and suggest that, in addition to reading each as a representative voice of Black people, we should also reframe their condition as African Indigenous peoples. Even beyond them, it should not be surprising that Africans, especially in the late eighteenth and early part of the nineteenth centuries, maintained some Indigenous knowledges about their cultures and histories while also forging early conceptions of Pan-Africanism.

Historian Sterling Stuckey explains that enslaved Africans who had arrived through the Middle Passage did not just forget their Indigenous roots. From death ceremonies to connecting with the ancestors in the spirit world, those connections were not erased among the enslaved Africans. Stuckey writes:

> During the process of their becoming a single people, Yorubas, Akans, Ibos, Angolans, and others were present on slave ships to America and experienced a common horror—unearthly moans and

shrieks, the smell of filth and the stench of death, all during the violent rhythms and quiet coursings of ships at sea. As such, slave ships were the first real incubators of slave unity across cultural lines, cruelly revealing irreducible links from one ethnic group to the other, fostering resistance thousands of miles before the shore of the new land appeared on the horizon—before there was mention of natural rights in North America.[9]

In addition to a common identity, even during enslavement, they maintained cultural elements. We should assume that Indigenous Africans did not lose all manner of being Indigenous. Instead of determining what they lost, we would do well to consider what they kept with them, and how that persisted. In other words, what types of Indigenous African roots gained traction in the soil of other Indigenous peoples where they now tarried? One way that Indigenous Africans continued to resist their oppression was through writing.

OLAUDAH EQUIANO

There are familiar characters in US Afro-Indigenous history. Perhaps the first one we think of is Crispus Attucks. As in American horror cinema—well, it's a persistent urban legend in Black communities—he was the first person killed in the American colonists' fight for "liberty." But that was 1770. What about the years prior? We can begin with Olaudah Equiano. There remains great controversy about Equiano's *The Interesting Narrative of the Life of Olaudah Equiano, or Gustavus Vassa the African* (1789). In Vincent Carretta's biography, *Equiano, the African: Biography of a Self-Made Man* (2009), he argues, based upon two sources, that Equiano falsified his African origins. Carretta believes that Equiano was born in the Carolinas.[10] We should be careful about easily dismissing Equiano's or other enslaved Africans' birth claims. As historian Manisha Sinha remarked, "The places of birth of enslaved Africans were often misreported or assumed from their last known destination by persons doing the recording. The identity of displaced Africans was highly malleable and subject to arbitrary categorization by European authorities."[11] Equiano provides a window into the horrors of the slave trade. I am using Equiano's book to provide a window into his Indigenous roots.

Equiano was the first African in the West to describe the horrors of the slave trade to a large audience. In addition to telling us about the importance of slavery, he also allows for us to reconsider his Indigenous African roots. As Chima J. Korieth asks in the introduction of the edited volume, *Olaudah Equiano and the Igbo World: History, Society, and Atlantic Diaspora Connections* (2009), "What does Equiano's autobiography offer towards a reconstruction of the Igbo world and history? What does it offer in articulating Igbo history in an Atlantic context?"[12] I ask a different question: How does understanding Equiano's roots help us expand our idea of who was Indigenous in the early Atlantic world, and how did Indigenous Africans, marked by enslavement, understand their own Indigenous selves within this new, traumatizing context?

African literature scholar Maureen N. Eke argues that "because Equiano was aware of the various (predominantly negative) discourses about slavery and Africans during his time, he chose to re-imagine his community, to re-construct it, as it were, re-stitch, piece together anew, the Igbo (African) world in his narrative in order to counter the European 'othering' of Africans as a justification for their enslavement."[13] In other words, Eke does not assume that his autobiography is false. Rather, as part of the larger body of African diasporic writing, which utilizes the genre of autobiography to tell the world about the plight of the Black experience, Equiano was hoping to get some form of relief, or liberation, for his people, in order to be seen as human.

Equiano describes in his autobiography that he was born in the province of Eboe, located in present-day Nigeria, around 1745. Eboe was likely Igbo. His connection to place is important. He provides crucial information about social dynamics as well as the particular place from which he was kidnapped.[14] He describes in great detail the political life of his village. From marriage to food and cultural customs, he offers a window into the Indigenous lives of his peers. Throughout the first three chapters, Equiano makes several references to his "native African" peoples. He articulates how Africans continued to understand not only their particular Indigenous identity, but also how they related to other groups, especially through mutually intelligible languages.

After he was kidnapped from his homeland, he continued to identify as an Indigenous person, but also developed other relationships that expanded upon his identity. He writes, "From the time I left my own nation I always found somebody that understood me till I came to the seacoast. The languages of different nations did not totally differ."[15] In addition to describing himself as being "easily learned," he also writes that he acquired two or three different languages during his captivity. Because of the condition of enslavement, he was forced to learn different languages in order to communicate, surely as a way to meet basic needs, or perhaps to imagine how they could all collectively liberate themselves. We might call this dialogue a discourse of freedom. They were likely exchanging ideas in order to discursively think about how to gain their freedom. After all, language remains a central component of liberation in human history.

Upon entering the slave ship, he experienced horrors that we can't even imagine. The smell and sorrow that he experienced led Equiano to think, "I now wished from my last friend, death, to relieve me."[16] While death did not relieve him, he did experience some reprieve upon learning that some of his fellow Indigenous people were also suffering the same yoke of bondage. He asked them what would be their fate, and they responded that they would go to the white people's country and work for them.

It is through this relationship that we began to see how they constructed their sense of self through their enslavement. In other words, they gained another identity, that of an enslaved person versus one who is free. This does not mean that they lost their Indigenous identity; it just means they had to conceptually and materially come to terms with the conditions of their oppression.

I want to pause here and remind the reader that Africans did not get rid of their Indigenous practices and beliefs. I return to Cedric Robinson, who writes, "For those African men and women whose lives were interrupted by enslavement and transportation, it was reasonable to expect that they would attempt and in some ways realize, the recreation of their lives."[17] While we might wonder why Equiano would decide to go to England later in his life, I would contend that we don't really know the psychological impact that being kidnapped and transported as cargo to a whole new world would have on a person. I don't even know if we even have a vocabulary, a grammar to describe such terror that this historical event caused those who experienced it. I am amazed at the level of detail and pain with which Equiano wrote.

While some believe he made up his own history, I think we should embrace his literary genius, and never forget that his ability to recount these traumatic events in such detail demonstrates the inventiveness of this Black literary form in the face of trauma, and its resiliency over the centuries from the era of enslavement well into the present.

PHILLIS WHEATLEY

During every Black History Month in schools across the US, students surely celebrate the life and legacy of Phillis Wheatley. Wheatley, who was born in western Africa around 1753, is known as the first Black person and first enslaved person to publish a book of poetry. She was a literary genius. In Black queer writer Alice Walker's essay, "In Search of Our Mothers' Gardens," she rhetorically asks us to consider the potential of Wheatley: "What then are we to make of Phillis Wheatley, a slave, who owned not even herself?" Within the context of enslavement and gender discrimination, people like Wheatley were hardly able to utilize all of their gifts and reach the apex of their creative genius. Slave traders captured her and transported her across the Atlantic. She was purchased by John Wheatley to be a servant to his wife, Susannah. Although the property of John and Susannah's, she virtually replaced their daughter, who had died at the same age of Wheatley, who was seven at the time. They named her Phillis, after the ship.[18]

The Wheatleys taught Phillis, a child prodigy, to read and write in English, Greek, and Latin. That she learned to write in another language and spoke it fluently is pure, unadulterated Black Girl Genius. As African American literary scholar Henry Louis Gates Jr. observes, "Recall that this seven-year-old slave spoke no English upon her arrival in 1761, toward the end of the Seven Years' War—a global conflict between French and British imperialists and, in the US, a variety of Indigenous nations. By 1765, she had written her first poem; in 1767, when she was thirteen or fourteen, the *Newport Mercury* published a poem that Susanna Wheatley submitted on her behalf."[19] In 1773, as the American Revolution approached, and in the same year she published her book, *Poems on Various Subjects, Religious and Moral*, John Wheatley emancipated her.

Wheatley did not appear to write much about her origins in West Africa, and history does not reveal to us exactly where she was from her birth through the first several years of her life.[20] We could imagine she didn't write about her experience because the memories faded under the weight of the trauma of being ripped away from one's family and land. And in the only poem in which she refers to her predicament, titled "On Being Brought from Africa to America," which honors her Indigenous roots in Africa and as an enslaved person, she seems thankful for being given the opportunity to be brought from her "Pagan land" and taught the goodness of Christianity. However, she also makes sure to comment on how white people viewed Africans' "dark skin": "Their colour is a diabolic die." Yet, she reminds her peers, "Remember, Christians, Negros, black as Cain, may be refin'd, and join th' angelic train."[21] She challenged the white Christians to view Black folks as human beings, able to walk in the righteous path of Christianity. In addition to finding ways to challenge white Christians, she also communicated with Indigenous peoples, demonstrating some form of admiration, if not solidarity.

Wheatley was dedicated early on to the cause of ending slavery and offering a critique of the British colonists' ideas of liberty.[22] At the age of eleven, Wheatley wrote to Reverend Samson Occom, a Mohegan Presbyterian minister. She would write to him again almost a decade later, on March 11, 1774, stating that she was "greatly satisfied with your Reasons respecting the Negroes, and think highly reasonable what you offer in Vindication of their natural rights." Wheatley pointed out that freedom was an inherent right of people, writing, "In every human breast, God has implanted a Principle, which we call Love of Freedom; it is impatient of Oppression, and pants for Deliverance." She knew freedom, and it was taken away from her. It is no surprise that she held it close to her bosom. Freedom for her was an expression of love and a way of being. She understood even better than the colonists that the desire for liberty and an end to the brutalities of enslavement required an impatience in humanity's refusal to end it. She also commented on the contradiction that white people, seeking liberty for their freedom from Britain, would also continue to enslave Africans. She wanted to "convince them of the strange Absurdity of their Conduct whose Words and Actions are so diametrically opposite." She continued, "How well the Cry for Liberty, and the reverse Disposition for the exercise of oppressive Power over others agree." Perhaps an early example of signifying, which is a form of indirect critique found in African American Vernacular English, she ended her letter by stating, "I humbly think it does not require the Penetration of a Philosopher to determine."[23]

We don't know exactly why Wheatley wrote to Occom beyond showing him some love for his "obliging kind epistle." It seems to be beyond the realm of their shared Christianity. Perhaps, being an Indigenous African herself, she identified in some ways with the experiences of Native people in revolutionary America. As historian Sterling Stuckey notes, "What is true of black African culture is true of any culture rich in artistic and spiritual content: initiation into it in youth guarantees its presence in consciousness, and to a considerable extent in behavior, for a lifetime."[24] While she adopted a "Black" identity, in part because of the circumstance of her enslavement, she surely never gave up every component of her African identity, even as she was kidnapped and enslaved at an early age.

When Wheatley died, she was gravely ill. Perhaps she never really reached her true potential. As Alice Walker contends, "Had she been white, [she] would have easily been considered the intellectual superior of all the women and most of the men in the society of her day."[25] Wheatley was not only an African genius, but an Indigenous genius who, because of enslavement, was never able to really delve into the meaning of what it meant to be an Indigenous person in her poetry. It makes me wonder, what if she could remember her homeland, her customs and traditions? How would that have impacted her poetry? We will never know.

LUCY TERRY PRINCE

If Phillis Wheatley is the OG Indigenous African poet who came of age during the American Revolution, Lucy Terry Prince is the first one to rewrite the origins of Black poetry without a pen. Lucy Terry was kidnapped from West Africa when she was a young girl and brought to Rhode Island around 1730. She was purchased by Ebenezer Wells to be a house servant for his wife, Abigail Wells. From an early age, Terry learned from Abigail Wells how to read and write.

In 1756, Abijah Prince, Terry's love interest, purchased her freedom from the Wells. Shortly thereafter, they married. Abijah Prince, a free Black man, had come to Deerfield, Massachusetts, in 1746; he would go onto serve in the French and Indian War. They met in that year, but he did not want to marry her until after he purchased her freedom. They would go on to have six children.[26]

When she was about twenty-two years old and living in Deerfield with her owners, she heard of the murder of two white families on August 25, 1746. In an incident serving as precursor to the French and Indian War between Great Britain and France (also called the Seven Years' War), which included Indigenous nations fighting on both sides, a group of Indigenous peoples attacked the families. It is not known why, but it was likely retaliation for encroachment, or at least for some other killing that those settlers had carried out.

In response to these killings, and probably knowing the victims, Terry composed an oral poem titled "Bars Fight." It is both a memorial for those settlers who were killed, captured, and injured and a denigration of Indigenous peoples. It is not clear when she produced the poem, but it is very likely that she shared it shortly after her emancipation. It begins,

> *August 'twas the twenty-fifth,*
> *Seventeen hundred forty-six;*
> *The Indians did in ambush lay,*
> *The names of whom I'll not leave out.*[27]

She then lists the names of those affected. The poem was preserved orally until 1855, when Josiah Gilbert Holland published it.[28] It demonstrates the persistent narratives that settlers make in a society: when Indigenous peoples commit an act of armed struggle, it is a slaughter, but when white people do it, it is a great victory. It also illustrates the role of popular culture in passing down memorials of settlers. It is not surprising that she sided with whites. As a devout Puritan, she grew up in a town where describing Indigenous peoples as bloodthirsty savages was the norm.[29] Lucy Terry's poem, its subject an incident on the eve of the French and Indian War, was passed down several generations before the Civil War. It presents the complications of Indigenous Africans growing up in a society predicated on enslavement and dispossession.

Lucy Terry offers a cautionary tale. Although she was an Indigenous person, she was kidnapped and reprogrammed into a settler society that actively hated Indigenous peoples of the northeast. And she contributed to a narrative that memorialized the killing of Indigenous peoples. As historian Ibram Kendi writes in *Stamped from the Beginning*, "Racist ideas are ideas. Anyone can produce them or consume them."[30] If anyone can reproduce racist ideas, they can also replicate settler-colonial ideas about Native people, even other Indigenous peoples. Racist or settler-colonial ideas are not divorced from histories of violence. However, reproducing an idea is not the same as having the power to use a narrative in order to commit violence. Even today, Indigenous people become enraged when Black people discursively erase Indigenous peoples; however, discourse is connected to power, and Black people don't have the power to subjugate Indigenous peoples.

PAUL CUFFE

Perhaps one of the earliest examples of an Afro-Indigenous person who embodied and embraced both of his identities was Paul Cuffe. Cuffe was born on January 17, 1759, on Cuttyhunk Island, Massachusetts, to Ruth Moses, who was Aquinnah Wampanoag. His father's name was Cuffe Slocum. Slocum's African name was Kofi. According to Henry Louis Gates Jr., "Kofi is a Twi word for a boy born on Friday, so we know that he was an Ashanti from Ghana."[31] Paul Cuffe biographer Lamont Thomas notes that the Ashanti people enslaved Kofi at a young age. He was later kidnapped by Fanti slave catchers, who took him to the Royal African Company on the Guinea Coast. He reached Newport, Rhode Island, in 1728, and was purchased by Ebenezer Slocum, a Quaker.

In 1742, Slocum sold Kofi to his nephew, John Slocum. In 1745, Slocum freed Kofi, and a year later, Kofi married Ruth Moses, a Wampanoag woman.[32] We don't know why he married this Indigenous North American woman. Maybe he simply enjoyed her personality and found her extremely intelligent and attractive. Perhaps they just vibed. Or, in addition to those things, perhaps he saw that they shared similar cultural roots, and he wanted a partner he could raise children with who could also offer familiar ways of child rearing. We don't know. However, in the realm of these early encounters, there have to be a variety of contexts in which we understand how these Afro-Indigenous encounters occurred.[33]

What is significant is that Paul Cuffe (and his siblings) was not just an early example of an Afro-Indigenous person, even though that is often how he is cited. Importantly, he is an Indigenous person, from his mother's and father's sides. Although he embraced his blackness, or rather Africanness, we could imagine that his father shared with him not only the ideals of being a good Quaker, having been raised that way himself, but also some ideas of what it meant to be Ashanti, or Indigenous. We could not expect the elder Cuffe to have a fully developed sense of an Indigenous self since he was kidnapped as a preteen and brought to Massachusetts. However, he surely learned at least a few things, and passed them on to his children.

Although Paul Cuffe would refer to himself as "mustee," or part Indigenous, he seems early on to have asserted his Indigenous identity. Indeed, even later in his life, he would title his own book *Narrative of the Life and Adventures of Paul Cuffe, a Pequot Indian: During Thirty Years Spent at Sea and in Traveling in Foreign Lands*. Given the strong anti-Black sentiment in the late eighteenth century, it should not be surprising why Cuffe emphasized his Indigenous identity more often, especially early on, and would later fight to return himself and others to his father's homeland. He understood one aspect: that he was marked as Black. It seems that throughout his life, he vacillated between being African and Indigenous. Of course, his identity was shaped by antiblackness, and the prospects of living in a world that was both anti-Black and anti-Indigenous, but where the mark of blackness forced him to be seen a certain way.

Cuffe was instrumental in advocating for Black folks to travel back to Africa, particularly Sierra Leone. Why would Cuffe want to go back to Africa, given his mother's Indigenous roots? Quite simply, it was because of the anti-Black racism of the time. While Native people in the northeast were experiencing what historian Jean O'Brien has called "dispossession by degrees," as an Afro-Indigenous person, Cuffe was also dealing with racism toward Black folks as well. He experienced dispossession *and* the stigma of blackness.[34]

Cuffe was well known, even by the British. For instance, on August 2, 1811, the *London Times* documented Cuffe's travels from Sierra Leone. Traveling with a group of Black folks from the US, Cuffe arrived in Liverpool. At the age of fifty-six, the newspaper described him as solely Black and asserted that any success he had was attributed to coming from the white society of Massachusetts. The article alleged that after Cuffe read Thomas Clarkson's *Abolition of the Slave Trade* (1808), who was a staunch advocate of ending the slave trade in Britain, it stoked in him "all the powers of his mind to a consideration of his origin, and the duties owed to his people."[35] Importantly, Cuffe also imagined a world where Black and Indigenous peoples would live together. In 1817, he recommended that there be two Black nations. One would be in Africa and the other in the western part of the US. Cuffe, as someone who was Indigenous on both sides, could imagine a social and political world in which Black and Indigenous peoples could live free from the oppression of white society.[36]

What is important about Cuffe is that he tried to imagine a different life for his people. Though Black and Indigenous, he did not want to deal with the total climate of antiblackness, and therefore sought to return to the African continent. Though he might have had some settler-colonial ideas which he learned in the colonies—surely a part of his upbringing in colonial America—he desired to return to the land of his father. In the history of Afro-Indigenous peoples in the United States, he set the stage for other encounters going forward.

CONCLUSION

Cuffe, Equiano, Terry Prince, and Wheatley lived during an era of hardening racial lines between white and Native, Black and white. They lived in a world where their skin color marked them as fundamentally different, even as they possessed extraordinary abilities. Moreover, they were also forced to change their identities from whatever Indigenous ethnic group they identified with to that of being a Black/African person. Blackness became their condition, and the consequences of it they bore daily.

Indigenous writer Thomas King writes, "When we imagine history, we imagine a grand structure, a national chronicle, a closely organized and guarded record of agreed-upon events and interpretations, a bundle of 'authenticities' and 'truths' welded into a flexible yet conservative narrative that explains how we got from there to here."[37] In American history, we learn that the first person killed in the name of revolution was Crispus Attucks. His death in the Boston Massacre marks the beginning of the Revolution and, for some Black liberals, he is the quintessential example of Black patriotism, the first fallen star in the name of American Revolution. That is, Black folks have fought for this country—for democracy—and therefore deserve to be included into the democratic project, as citizens.

During Black History Month, we celebrate his death. What does his death symbolize? In the propaganda of US democracy, we have constructed Attucks as a person who died in the name of the American Revolution. Maybe he did die for that cause. However, as an Afro-Indigenous person, I feel it leaves me with many questions. What if he had his own motives? Maybe he was sick and tired of being sick and tired? Maybe he was sick of the oppression from the Brits and other white folks. What if Attucks wanted something more? What if we could reclaim his legacy for something outside of the triumph of US democracy? Still, this does nothing to tell us about the person. There is little evidence about his life, including if he was a mixed-race Afro-Indigenous person. According to historian Mitch Kachun,

> Attucks almost certainly interacted closely with all three groups, and his life experience . . . allowed him to see the best and worst of eighteenth-century America: the economic and social vitality of growing and prospering colonies, the oppression of racial slavery, the intermingling of diverse peoples and languages in bustling Atlantic seaports, the opportunities and dangers of life at sea, the fluidity of identity in America's formative era, and the new language of liberty and natural rights that came to define the idealistic new nation's sense of self.[38]

Attucks has a much more complicated history, and some historians question how much he was actually invested in the colonists' goals for revolution; some even refer to him as a thug.[39] According to Samuel Adams, the cousin of John Adams, who defended one of the British soldiers, Attucks's "very looks was enough to terrify any person, what had not the soldiers then to fear?" He also described him as demonstrating "mad behavior."[40]

The colonists immediately began to memorialize Attucks's death for their cause. Paul Revere created an engraving three weeks after the attack titled, "Bloody Massacre Perpetrated in Kings Street in Boston."[41] There is no denying that Attucks is a central part of our collective memory regarding martyrdom and American Revolution, and children will continue to be taught about his sacrifice for the revolution. If we continue to identify him as an Afro-Indigenous person, even if he was a "thug," perhaps we should reclaim him as an Afro-Indigenous fighter who wasn't so much invested in US democracy; rather, he was a person seeking basic human rights not for settler-colonial enslavers, but for African and Indigenous peoples.

What can we learn from these early encounters and examples of Afro-Indigenous peoples? First, we should remind ourselves that Native US people should also include Indigenous Africans in their understanding of who is Indigenous. Second, we should reorient our understanding of Indigenous encounters in prerevolutionary America. This has the potential of helping Black youth see themselves not outside of modernity, but squarely in it, with Indigenous roots, even if they can't necessarily go back to Africa and trace them. We also see the experiences of people mixed with African and US Indigenous roots who were considered Indigenous by some, but strongly identified with their African roots because of the rampant antiblackness. Finally, these experiences should help us understand that neither antiblackness in the form of enslavement nor Native dispossession were, by themselves, fundamental to US democracy. They were both tied together, foundational to how whites developed an idea of race and property, and how the US continues to be shaped today.[42] Without understanding both of these as white supremacist and settler-colonial projects, we will continue to have a distorted understanding of US history, and also have a severe lack in understanding our present circumstance, and how we gon' get free going forward.

CHAPTER TWO

ANTIBLACKNESS, SETTLER COLONIALISM, AND THE US DEMOCRATIC PROJECT

I REMEMBER READING Alexis de Tocqueville's *Democracy in America*, published in 1835, and the *Federalist Papers*, published in 1787, in the introductory course at James Madison College. JMC is a residential college at Michigan State University for students of liberal arts and public policy. Students and faculty consider it an elite institution on campus, where the nerdiest of nerds choose to subjugate themselves to (initially) low grades on the first quiz and paper, as well as the possibility of having a lower GPA. The Madison students were, at least when I went there, the "Madison All Stars," so named because of all of the activities they participated in, and how actively they worked in politics. I (still) love and hate the college.

Every first-year student is required to take the dreaded two-course sequence, MC 201 and 202 (Introduction to Public Affairs I and II). When I saw the syllabus, I wasn't nervous—I was terrified. It included *Democracy in America* and the *Federalist Papers*. I had vaguely read Federalist No. 10 in my AP US History course, but I didn't understand it. And now, being on the big stage of a university made me anxious, but I was determined to do well. To my surprise, the majority of the other students had read it. I was shocked. I was the only person of color in the class. Reflecting on where these students had come from, I should not have been surprised.

We first read the *Federalist Papers*, and I got off to a rocky start—earning the fantastic grade of 1.8 (out of 4.0) on the first quiz. Older students had told me that a low grade was normal, so I wasn't trippin'. Then, after reading the *Federalists*, we began reading *Democracy in America*. There was so much we covered in that long book, but very little time dedicated to it. One night while reading, I started perusing the rest of the book, ready to read something else because the shit I was reading was boring. I stumbled on passages about Black and Native people in the US, in a chapter titled, "The Present and Probable Future Conditions of the Three Races Which Inhabit the Territory of the United States." I stayed up and read that part instead of the assigned reading. It was fascinating. Tocqueville actually wondered what the future of Black and Indigenous peoples would be within the US? Reading that passage changed my life.

The next day, I asked my professor why we didn't read those passages. His response was something to the effect of "it's not that important." I was hella confused as to why we didn't read it. The purpose of the course is to introduce students to the political theory of (liberal) democracy, why it is important, and how it should shape our view on the US going forward. Even to this day, a colleague of mine who works in the college told me they still aren't reading that chapter.

I use this story to introduce readers into the theories and beliefs of several white men, one of whom was central to the United States' foundational political identity and theory, and another, though French, who offered a deep ethnographic reading of the United States. Importantly, these authors articulated a prevailing viewpoint of US democracy, one that would not include Black and Indigenous peoples. They didn't just offer political theories; they also offered ideas of racialization and belonging, which continue to influence how we view Black Americans and Native Americans in the present day.

The foundations of whiteness today are rooted in the twin oppressions of Africans and US Indigenous peoples. How we view race and, in the formative years of the United States, who can own and be property was rooted in these oppressions. As legal scholar Cheryl Harris writes, "Because whites could not be enslaved or held as slaves, the racial line between white and Blacks was extremely critical; it became a line of protection and demarcation from the potential threat of commodification, and it determined the allocation of the benefits and burdens of this form of property."[1] For Native people, property meant "white privilege through a system of property rights on land in which the 'race' of the Native Americans rendered their first possession rights invisible and justified conquest."[2] "White" meant property owner and human, "African and Indigenous" meant the opposite. And it wasn't just property that European settlers were creating. In the development of their governing ideology, they believed "that the preservation and enhancement of their own democratic institutions required Indian dispossession and the coercive use of dependent groups, most prominently slaves, in order to ensure that they themselves had access to property."[3] The core foundations of US democracy, and white people's strong belief in its possibilities were, from the beginning, based on the subjugation of Black and Indigenous peoples. Until we as a nation—and white people in particular—come to terms with this, we aren't ever really going to see any real changes.

The ideological roots of US democracy are rooted in whiteness. Whites believed that economic independence meant freedom and citizenship; it meant the continued expansion of US empire, the continued exclusion of Black and Indigenous peoples, and the continued immigration of certain European immigrants.[4] These were the wages of their idea of freedom and belonging. But there is a reason that, within this country, the ideological roots of words such as "freedom" have remained fundamentally different for different people throughout US history. Black people have sought to be free from the chains of enslavement and the stigma assigned to them. Indigenous peoples have maintained their sovereignty as a counter to the settler project of US democracy. And white people have desired freedom—the ability to be first-class citizens—through their ability to acquire property. Again, one could become a property owner through enslavement and Indigenous dispossession, both of which contributed to the development of white citizenship.

US DEMOCRATIC FORMATIONS

According to Haudenosaunee oral history, the founders of US democracy conceptually drew their ideas of a constitution from the Iroquois Confederacy. Although the evidence is scarce—and why Native people would want to align their conception of democracy with that of the United States is baffling—there is some evidence that at least partially illustrates this point. In 1754, Benjamin Franklin and Thomas

Hutchinson wrote the Albany Plan. This plan was designed to set- tle the relationship between the thirteen colonies. While they would each be independent, they would also be mutually interconnected in a large-scale sense, under the direction of a president-general and an- other council of leaders. The term they used for the latter was "grand council," which seems to be taken from the Iroquois Confederacy.

The United States Congress has acknowledged the impact. In the fall of 1988, in celebration of the two hundredth anniversary of the signing of the Constitution, during the 100th Congress, 2nd session, legislators passed House Concurrent Resolution 331. Its purpose, ac- cording to the text of the resolution, is "to acknowledge the contri- bution of the Iroquois Confederacy of Nations to the development of the United States Constitution and to reaffirm the continuing government-to-government relationship between Indian tribes and the United States established in the Constitution." In addition, the resolution highlights the influence that the concepts of the Six Na- tions had on the thinking of Benjamin Franklin and George Washing- ton. Finally, the resolution states, "the confederation of the original Thirteen Colonies into one republic was influenced by the political system developed by the Iroquois Confederacy as were many of the democratic principles which were incorporated into the Constitution itself."[5] I have heard that the ideological architects of US democracy formed at least part of their government structure on the Confeder- acy, but I was unsure. If I'm being honest, since they are historical enemies of my own people, and just to be petty, I wasn't inclined to accept that this was true! It still makes me uneasy that the Haude- nosaunee would want to highlight that the US founders took part of their ideas from them. I mean, if US democracy is at the very least a flawed system of government, if not fundamentally anti-Black and anti-Indigenous, why should Native people want to associate with it? Still, it surely pains some white folks to even read that their sacred idea of democracy was, in part, taken from Native people. It's okay, don't be so fragile.

THE *FEDERALIST PAPERS* AND *WHITE FRAGILITY*

In her book *White Fragility*, sociologist Robin DiAngelo argues that white people are inclined to believe themselves to be victims. She writes,

"The smallest amount of racial stress is intolerable—the mere suggestion that being white has meaning often triggers a range of defensive responses. These include emotions such as anger, fear, and guilt and behaviors such as argumentation, silence, and withdrawal from the stress-inducing situation."[6] White people are fragile. Their ego, built on the foundations of white supremacy, which allows them to automatically claim a type of personal innocence divorced from history and structures, can't even handle being called racist. The roots of antiblackness and anti-Indigenous sentiments predate the establishment of what would become the United States. However, they were codified in some of the sacrosanct documents of the US, including the *Federalist Papers*.

In addition to covering the early political theory of US democracy, the *Federalist Papers* also tell us a great deal about how the founding fathers viewed their own political theory and sovereignty, in direct relationship and contrast to Indigenous peoples. The *Federalist Papers* are eighty-five essays written by Alexander Hamilton, John Jay, and James Madison. Speaking of Hamilton, are we done celebrating some slave owners rapping on Broadway? I appreciate the artistic genius of the Lin-Manuel Miranda show *Hamilton*, but as with any artistic form, once it's in the public sphere, it can easily be celebrated outside of the author's intent. Maybe Miranda did not intend the play to be a liberal, uncritical view of history, but that is one consequence of being so widely celebrated. Also, Hamilton was a slave owner. As an alternative to *Hamilton*, I would highly recommend the Ishmael Reed play *The Haunting of Lin-Manuel Miranda*, directed by Rome Neal.[7]

Written to help ratify the Constitution, the *Federalist Papers* can be found on the US Congress website, which makes it easy to perform a targeted text search. Searching for the word "Indian" reveals that it was used thirteen times in the *Federalist Papers*. Hamilton uses the term "savage" only once, in Federalist No. 24, titled, "The Powers Necessary to the Common Defense Further Considered." The words "Indian" and "savage" are used in the contexts of defense and issues of sovereignty. As Hamilton notes, gaining land and maintaining a military to protect that land was essential for the developing nation's security against possible Indigenous attacks. Although concerned with Britain and Spain, he notes, "the savage tribes on our Western frontier ought to be regarded as our natural enemies, their natural allies, because they have the most to fear from us, and most to hope from them."[8]

The use of the terms "Indian" and "savage" in the *Federalist Papers* demonstrates two things. First, it represents the necessity to create a political other to feed into the need for dispossession. Second, it reveals that the dehumanization of Native people was central to the founding political theory of the United States. Indeed, to celebrate documents such as these, without a critical eye, reveals that we fully accept the narrative of Indigenous dispossession as inevitable.

The term "negroes" emerges only three times. Hamilton or Madison use it in Federalist No. 54 to suggest that Black folks had been transformed into property. The other use is to explain that they can help further the representation for electoral voting, which did happen, in the form of the Three-Fifths Compromise. The Three-Fifths Compromise counted enslaved Africans as three-fifths of a person, an agreement that was made so that the southern states could have what they considered an equal amount of representation in the House of Representatives. Central to early US political theory is the idea of sovereignty, especially who would belong and who would not. White men desired to create a democracy based upon racial inferiority, exclusion, and land expropriation, which all form the basis of whiteness today. This, of course, set the stage for the many forms of resistance that Black and Indigenous people used to maintain their land and acquire their freedom.

THOMAS JEFFERSON AND THE FORMATION OF WHITE NATIONALISM

Thomas Jefferson was a wealthy slave owner. He was a white nationalist. Neither of those statements should be controversial. He was also brilliant, the author of the Declaration of Independence, and the third president of the United States (1801–09). Black and Indigenous activists in the US and people from around the world have quoted and paraphrased that damn thing to death! While this document is often read as a key moment of the colonial states' formal breaking away from the British Crown, it is, in fact, deeply anti-Indigenous. The document criticizes the king for not allowing the colonists to populate the area: "He has endeavored to prevent the population of these States;

for that purpose obstructing the Laws of Naturalization of Foreigners; refusing to pass others to encourage their migrations hither, and raising the conditions of new Appropriations of Lands."[9] Jefferson and the co-signers were concerned about their right to be sovereign, but also wanted to make sure that they could fill up the land that they had taken from Native nations. Jefferson then charges the king with creating hostility from within: "He has excited domestic insurrections amongst us, and has endeavoured to bring on the inhabitants of our frontiers, the merciless Indian Savages whose known rule of warfare, is an undistinguished destruction of all ages, sexes and conditions." Many Native people today now refer to the "merciless Indian Savages" quote when explaining how anti-Indigenous colonists were from the beginning. The document was propaganda to ensure that colonization and enslavement would be ratified. Still, there is much to learn from Jefferson as a representative of the early colonists.

Jefferson, in addition to being the third US president, also ushered in the Louisiana Purchase (1803), which would go on to have devastating consequences for Indigenous peoples and further cause controversy around slavery. He believed that Black people were hardly human and deserved to be enslaved, and produced mixed-race children with Sally Hemings, whom he owned as a slave. He argued that enslaved Africans should be returned to Africa. He also believed that the US should expand west—on land that belonged to Native peoples. With the Louisiana Purchase, he authored the Lewis and Clark Exposition of the "west" and the Pacific Northwest. He was deeply invested in antiblackness and Indigenous dispossession. Historian Anthony F.C. Wallace argues that Jefferson held a conflicting stance toward Indigenous peoples. Jefferson, in the words of Wallace, "played a major role in one of the great tragedies of recent world history, a tragedy he so elegantly mourned: the dispossession and decimation of the First Americans."[10] Although that is a generous reading of Jefferson, he did have a certain curiosity, one rooted in the fundamental dispossession of Native people.

Moreover, children in US history classes from high school to universities are taught about Jeffersonian democracy. The story goes something like this: he wanted everyone to be created equal; government should be limited; and civilized people—white male property owners—should be citizens. Yeoman farmers should be independent and be able to work their land. Ideologically, Jeffersonian democracy "saw 'the people' as a culturally homogenous mass of equals, a national community sharing uniform political institutions and internalizing uniform moral values so thoroughly that no coercion would ever be required, all bound together by a republican social contract that required its participants to have achieved the state of civilization."[11] He cemented these ideas in his First Inaugural Address.

On March 4, 1801, Jefferson, during that address, told his fellow citizens about the importance of working for the common good. Jefferson believed that the common good was an essential ideology that connected everyone. It was the "voice of the nation" and designed "according to the rules of the Constitution." He encouraged citizens to "arrange themselves under the will of the law, and unite in common efforts for the common good." He also reminded them of the importance of protecting minority opinions: "All, too, will bear in mind this sacred principle, that though the will of the majority is in all cases to prevail, that will be rightful must be reasonable; that the minority possess their equal rights, which equal law must protect, and to violate would be oppression."[12] It is tempting to think of Jefferson as a complicated man, who internally toiled with his belief in freedom and democracy, and his enslavement of Africans and his policies that dispossessed thousands of Indigenous peoples. Jefferson was no doubt a brilliant thinker, but he was an enslaver and settler, and only believed in the equality of white men.

His belief in enslavement and dispossession was very explicit in his written work, including in *Notes on the State of Virginia*. He first published the book privately in France in 1781, and then published an English version in Britain in 1787.[13] It was the only full-length book Jefferson published in his lifetime and was written in response to questions about Virginia. While its discussion is about one particular place, its ideological underpinnings extend beyond Virginia. For my purposes, the book is important for how he discussed Black people and enslavement and Native peoples.

In a chapter in the book titled "Laws," Jefferson responded to the idea of abolishing slavery. The proposed bill, although never accepted, would have essentially traded the enslaved Africans for whites.[14] He asked, "Why not retain and incorporate the blacks into the state, and thus the expence of supplying, by importation of white settlers, the vacancies they will leave?" The first thing Jefferson seemed to fear in this scenario was conflict:

> Deep rooted prejudices entertained by the whites; ten thousand rec-ollections, by the blacks, of the injuries they have sustained; new provocations; the real distinctions which nature has made; and many other circumstances, will divide us into parties, and produce convulsions which will probably never end but in the extermination of the one or the other race.[15]

It is interesting to note that Jefferson would assume that Black folks might revolt and remember their oppression. The next fear he raised related to miscegenation. Because of Black peoples' skin color, he asked, "Is it not the foundation of a greater or less share of beauty in the two races?" As a comparison, he wrote on the mixing of whites and Native peoples, remarking, "Are not the fine mixtures of red and white, the expressions of every passion by greater or less suffusions of colour in the one, preferable to that eternal monotony, which reign in the countenances, that immovable veil of black which covers all emo-tions of the other race?" He even suggested that Black people prefer whites over their own kind.[16]

Jefferson, while at times seeming to want an end to slavery, sup-ported it when convenient. He believed that Black people required less sleep and only sought fun. "A black, after hard labour through the day," he wrote, "will be induced by the slightest amusements to sit up till midnight, or later, though knowing he must be out with the first dawn of the morning."[17] Jefferson ignored the necessary moments of pleasure that enslaved Africans surely needed beyond the family and social responsibilities they had to attend to. Finally, Jefferson believed Black folks were inferior in intellect to whites.[18]

Blacks lived among and alongside whites but, according to Jef-ferson, didn't learn much from them. Because he apparently learned nothing from Black people, he found it necessary to compare Black and Native people and see if Native people were better in some way. While Black folks "all lived in countries where arts and sciences are cultivated to a considerable degree," Native people, Jefferson argued, "with no advantages of this kind, will often carve figures on their pipes not destitute of design and merit." He also commented on Native peoples' rhetorical ability: "They astonish you with strokes of the most sublime oratory; such as prove their reason and sentiment strong, their imagination glowing and elevated." However, in regard to Black folks, "never yet could I find that a black had uttered a thought above the level of plain narration; never see even an elementary trait of painting or sculpture." He even had time to comment on Phillis Wheatley, noting, "Religion indeed has produced a Phillis Wheatley; but it could not produce a poet. The compositions published under her name are below the dignity of criticism."[19] Wheatley never met Jefferson, and it is not known whether she responded to him. Nonetheless, as Henry Louis Gates Jr. notes, "no encounter with a Founding Father would prove more lasting in its impact than that with Thomas Jefferson."[20] However, people like the Black nationalist David Walker, author of *David Walker's Appeal* (1829), called out Jefferson's *Notes* for the racist beliefs of the author. Walker wrote, "Mr. Jefferson, a much greater philosopher the world never afforded, has in truth injured us more, and has been as great a barrier to our emancipation as any thing that has ever been advanced against us." Walker followed up, writing, "I hope you will not let it pass unnoticed."[21]

TOCQUEVILLE: ETHNOGRAPHER OF WHITE SUPREMACY?

Tocqueville was an astute ethnographer of US democracy. Political theorists and historians typically discuss his conception of democracy and its relationship to the political and cultural politics of a developing nation. However, Tocqueville wrote at the beginning of chapter 18, "The absolute supremacy of democracy is not all that we meet with in America; the inhabitants of the New World may be considered from more than one point of view." He was also concerned with the Black and Indigenous experience. However, he wrote that "he had never been able to stop in order to show what place these two races occupy in the midst of the democratic people whom I was engaged in describing." Tocqueville was very much concerned with the relationship between whiteness and US democracy—something that critical race theorists of the twentieth century were also concerned about.[22]

Tocqueville placed the histories and current realities of African and Indigenous peoples together within the context of US democratic institutions. "These two unhappy races have nothing in common; neither birth, nor features, nor language, nor habits," he wrote.[23] However, their relationship was fortified "in their misfortunes." Three core misfortunes touch both peoples. They both "occupy an inferior rank in the country they inhabit; both suffer from tyranny; and if their wrongs are not the same, they originate, at any rate, with the same authors." The authors of their peculiar predicaments were wealthy white men. Tocqueville's ethnographic reading of the US revealed the deep impact of white supremacy on Black and Indigenous peoples. He articulated the point of enslavement and colonialism: to exploit and destroy. Tocqueville, perhaps a nineteenth-century prophet of American democracy (rooted in dispossession and enslavement), wrote, "[The European] makes them subservient to his use; and when he cannot subdue, he destroys them."[24]

Throughout chapter 18, Tocqueville refers to two tropes: the inherit state of servitude of Africans and the untamed savagery of Indigenous peoples. For Africans, he wrote, "The Negro of the United States has lost all remembrance of his country; the language which his forefathers spoke is never heard around him; he abjured their religion and forgot their customs when he ceased to belong to Africa."[25] Here, Tocqueville engaged in the dual process of erasing the African past, a part of capitalism's justification for further exploiting African peoples, as well as subtly describing the purpose of enslavement: the attempted complete eradication of anything related to Africa. However, that did not happen. While Africans, perhaps, lost their connection to land, even elements of their language, it was not a complete loss. Africans forced to come into contact created a new oral communication, what we would today call African American Vernacular English, or simply, Black English. As sociolinguist Geneva Smitherman, who you'll see again in a later chapter, argues, Black English is "Euro-American speech with an Afro-American tone, nuance, and gesture."[26] This language, in addition to other cultural and spiritual elements, began to emerge during the Middle Passage and once those enslaved had to put aside their cultural differences in order to "make a way outta no way" on the plantation. They produced a new way of talking to not only communicate with one another, but create a counter-language that could at times be wholly unintelligible to white people. The creation and sustained use of Black English is, in spite of the traumatizing nature of enslavement and its ongoing aftermath, one of the most brilliant things to happen in the modern world; just ask the corporations who have been exploiting this Black cultural element for decades. Africans who were enslaved maintained their cultures and produced new elements of it.

Indigenous people, according to Tocqueville, had a sense of unbridled freedom. He wrote, "The savage is his own master as soon as he is able to act; parental authority is scarcely known to him; he has never bent his will to that of any of his kind, nor learned the difference between voluntary obedience and a shameful subjection; and the very name of law is unknown to him."[27] Though Tocqueville also understood the greed of European Americans to exterminate and exploit, he also continued to engage in the trope of Native people being unable to operate in modern, European society. The Native person could not truly enter into democracy because, "as he delights in his barbarous independence, and would rather perish than sacrifice the least part of it, civilization has little power over him."[28] Of course, we should challenge Tocqueville's idea of "civilization," but it was powerful, as Native people from the nineteenth century and even today continue to try and assert their humanity against centuries of Indigenous stereotypes suggesting that Native people can never be modern. Tocqueville was also a prophet of race relations.

While Tocqueville argued that Indigenous people were disappearing, he made it clear that "the most formidable evil threatening the future of the United States is the presence of the blacks on their soil."[29] He further stated, "I do not imagine that the white and black races will ever live in any country upon an equal footing."[30] Tocqueville believed that white Americans' antiblackness would never cease, and thus, they and Black Americans would not be able to live together, at least peacefully. He predicted that "if [Black people] are once raised to the level of freed men, they will soon revolt at being deprived of all their civil rights; and as they cannot become the equals of the whites, they will speedily declare themselves as enemies."[31]

Tocqueville predicted the civil war that would happen less than thirty years from the publication of his book. However, Black people were and continue to be enemies to US democracy because their exploitation for the development of racial capitalism in the US required a constant subjugation—and it was always morphing to meet new labor needs. From enslavement to Jim Crow to the New Jim Crow, Black people have struggled for their humanity, and belonging as citizens. And when they openly declared that the United States' racist, capitalist state was an enemy of Black people—and all people—the state used every tactic to imprison, exile, and murder them.

If the *Federalist Papers* and *Democracy in America* are the roots of ideological white supremacy, then why do we hold them in such reverence? How can we teach them to our youth without sacrificing historical truths that have contemporary consequences? This nation was built on enslavement and dispossession, and the political documents that we hold as sacrosanct, while brilliantly conceptualized in some ways, are also shortsighted, even dehumanizing. If these documents form the United States' modern political thought and our very notion of democracy, then we need to question why we teach them without first highlighting their social implications for Black, Indigenous, and poor people.

CHAPTER THREE

ENSLAVEMENT, DISPOSSESSION, RESISTANCE

*The most magnificent drama in the last thousand years of
human history is the transportation of ten million human
beings out of the dark beauty of their mother continent
into the new-found Eldorado of the West. They descended
into Hell; and in the third century they arose from the dead,
in the finest effort to achieve democracy for the working
millions which this world had ever seen.*

—W. E. B. DU BOIS, *Black Reconstruction in America*[1]

IN NOVEMBER 1976, the *New Yorker* published a profile of Black
American novelist Ralph Ellison. Ellison, mostly known as author
of the novel *Invisible Man*, discussed what it was like growing up
in Oklahoma. He was born on March 1, 1914. Always wanting to
shed light on the invisibility of Black folks, he told the interviewer a
brief history of Black and Indigenous relations in Oklahoma. "Do you
know what a native in Oklahoma is?" he asked. They are "a black
American or Negro American who was part of the five great Indian
nations that were swept into this virgin territory after 1830 under
Andrew Jackson's Treaty of Dancing Rabbit Creek."[2] Ellison's history
is oversimplified; among its issues is its erasure of the Native nations
who were already there. He continued, "Many of the Negroes had
been acquired through horse-trading or had simply run away from
other states to join the Indian tribes." Ellison articulated how Black
folks viewed Indian territory and their relationship to place by constructing a narrative out of a familiar blues lyric:

I'm going to the nation,
Going to the territory.
Going to the nation, baby,
Going to the territory.

This was a common lyric in Indian territory, and it appears that Black, Indigenous, and Afro-Indigenous peoples sang it.[3]

In explaining this history, Ellison establishes for the reader how Black and Indigenous folks came to a particular place. He also sheds light on the contested terrain that defined the nineteenth-century Black and Indigenous experience: removal and belonging.[4]

This chapter's epigraph was taken from W. E. B. Du Bois's magnum opus, *Black Reconstruction in America* (1935). In chapter 17, "The Propaganda of History," he writes about all of the revisionist history and straight-up lies that white historians had written about Reconstruction, especially the negative portrayal of Black Americans. Like most of us who have ever read this book, I agree with Du Bois, and it is still perhaps essential reading for understanding Reconstruction. However, Indigenous dispossession is also a tragic part of this history. And while formerly enslaved Africans became citizens (albeit second-class ones), Indigenous peoples don't necessarily have this narrative. They continued to be dispossessed of their land and were written about as if they disappeared. Historians often focus on all the changes and developments in the nineteenth century and conclude that, taken together, all of them worked to steer the country toward equality and justice, but that is way too rosy of a picture, especially considering the ongoing dispossession of Indigenous peoples and Reconstruction's failures in fostering equality and progress for Black people.

Yet, the persistent belief in the triumph of US democracy during crucial periods in our history, beginning with the end of slavery, remains a part of the country's propaganda—and something that many of us accept as factual. We concede that once slavery ended, and Black folks were granted citizenship with the passing of the Fourteenth Amendment during Reconstruction, all was all right. However, historian Eric Foner notes, "Reconstruction represented less a fulfillment of the Revolution's principles than a radical repudiation of the nation's actual practice of the previous seven decades. Racism, federalism, and belief in limited government and local autonomy—Reconstruction challenged these deeply rooted elements of nineteenth-century politi-cal culture."[5] The story of the nineteenth century was rooted in rapid changes, but the story is not as triumphant as we might picture.

During my undergraduate and graduate school training, I was excited and mortified to read about how the US was constructed sys-tematically through dispossession, enslavement, class warfare, and gender inequality. However, I also enjoyed reading the everyday forms of resistance, or the "weapons of the weak" that Black and Indigenous peoples used.[6] While there were moments of great disruption—includ-ing various forms of Native peoples' armed resistance against settler encroachment as well as a whole civil war—it was often through indi-vidual everyday acts of resistance such as writing, speeches, and other forms of literary production through which Black and Indigenous peoples waged resistance.

This chapter argues that Black and Native people found everyday forms of resistance to challenge their conditions of dispossession and enslavement. They used polemical writing, literature, and protest on the ground. We often don't remember but it is important to recall: Black and Indigenous peoples never stopped believing in freedom, and struggled to attain their liberation. The long nineteenth century was fundamentally about a radical struggle against the abolition of enslavement and dispossession. As historian Manisha Sinha writes, the abolitionist struggle to end enslavement "from its inception was an interracial one and tied to the development of democracy." These abolitionists were "united in their devotion to the slave's cause."[7]

Afro-Indigenous history during the long nineteenth century is characterized, one the one hand, by the simultaneous resistance to slavery and dispossession, and on the other, by the various modes of resistance that Black and Indigenous peoples used to belong within and alongside the rapidly developing nation-state. The ways they vari-ously belonged to democracy and existed alongside it differed depend-ing on their historical circumstance. However, the political ideologies undergirding their freedom dreams were fundamentally rooted in de-fining what liberation would look like in the present circumstance and for the future generations.

What were they resisting? The answer simple: oppression. How-ever, those oppressions varied depending on tribe and the question of being free or unfree. Black and Indigenous people used a variety of modes of resistance to obtain their freedom and to create the steps for liberations. They used nationalism and sovereignty, violence, the breaking of tools and poisoning of masters, the law, writing and forms of solidarity, and even, at times, the adoption of US forms of racism. Led by Black women like Harriet Tubman, along with white allies, enslaved Africans used the Underground Railroad to escape their capture. Even during the Civil War, as Du Bois puts it, as soon as possible, "the slave entered upon a general strike against slavery." And because of their flight, their "withdrawal and bestowal of [their] labor decided the war."[8] The point is, they tried to resist. This chapter documents those examples throughout the nineteenth century.

In general, when people think of Afro-Indigenous history in the United States, a major focus is on the history of the Cherokee Nation and how some of that nation's elites enslaved Africans. In casual conversation with my Black brothas and sisters over the years, when I speak about the possibilities of Black and Indigenous solidarity, many look at me and say, "But Native Americans enslaved Blacks?"

Let me offer two examples. I remember reading *Black Labor, White Wealth* by polemical author Claud Anderson for a Black Politics course. Anderson contends, "All of the five civilized Indian nations were black slave owners and slave traders. Worse, all of these Indian nations supported and fought on the side of the South in the Civil War in fear of losing their black slaves."[9] I remember reading this, shocked, because in my Native American history course I was taking during that same semester, I learned the exact opposite, and therefore understood the nuances of Indigenous enslavement of Africans. I won't spend too much time disputing these historical misinterpretations, but Anderson's commentary is likely more pervasive in the Black community than we might think. As academics, we often tend to easily dismiss errors in interpretation, but we must consider who is reading the work. Go and check out the reviews on Anderson's book on Amazon: it has received 349 reviews, averaging a 4.9 rating out of 5.

When I attended a conference in London at the British Library in 2018, a Black American scholar in the audience responded to my comment about the possibilities of Afro-Indigenous solidarity with, "The Indians enslaved Africans. What solidarity can we even have?!" We have to confront these misconceptions by finding ways to disseminate the true nature of this history. We have to remind people that history is complicated and can be unpleasant, but we must try and come to terms with it for future generations.

Historian Tiya Miles's work has been significant in uprooting some of these misconceptions. In the *Ties That Bind: The Story of an Afro-Cherokee Family in Slavery and Freedom* (2005), she writes that the "liberation of African slaves and self-determination for Cherokee people were often framed in opposition to one another."[10] While Cherokees attempted to defy US encroachment and adopt US forms of modernity, including creating a writing system for their language, some also adopted enslavement as their entrance into modernity. Indeed, race (and antiblackness) became a central component of Cherokee conceptions of sovereignty.[11] People also tend to focus on moments of marronage and solidarity, demonstrated most notable by the Seminole Nation and people of African descent who escaped enslavement.[12] A focus solely on these relationships is the major focus of Afro-Indigenous history. But the Seminole Nation enslaved Africans, too. Again, enslavement is an important topic, but it is also important to capture the moments in history that demonstrate camaraderie and tensions, and what we can learn from them. Before getting into history, I want to briefly reflect on the 2019 movie *Harriet*, about the Underground Railroad freedom dreamer, Harriet Tubman.

HARRIET

I remember when, in the summer of 2019, I learned that screenwriter and producer Gregory Allen Howard and director Kasi Lemmons were going to bring the life of Harriet Tubman to the big screen. I was hella excited. Who didn't want to see the historical person turn into an action figure and engage in some Black feminist rage and shoot a slave owner, as we saw in that Dave Chappelle skit, when Chappelle and the fictionalized "Time Haters" went back into history and shot someone who was whipping a slave? Okay, portraying her as killing slave owners is an exaggeration, and I don't believe in guns, but I did want to see a Black woman on screen. Although my excitement level stayed high, some Black folks were upset when they learned a Black British woman, Cynthia Erivo, was going to portray Tubman on the screen. I thought it was better than say, Julia Roberts, playing Harriet, which producer Howard said was actually something a studio head suggested to him.

Some Black folks was trippin'! Why did they cast a Black British woman? Some argued that it would have been more appropriate to choose a Black American because, I suppose, they would be able to act the part better? Is it because of their post-traumatic slave syndrome? I don't know about Erivo's history, but something tells me her ancestors didn't come on Christopher Columbus's boats.

The other reason Black American folks didn't want her to play the part was because of some tweets she put out in these Twitter streets years ago. In them, she allegedly disrespected Black English. I find any disrespect of Black English offensive. Black Americans have had a strained relationship to Ebonics, too, however. In 1996, when activists and educators from the Oakland Unified School District tried to educate teachers about Ebonics, and make it a part of the curriculum as a way for Black students to more effectively learn so-called standard American English, people—African Americans—across the country were mad. Even civil rights icon Jesse Jackson and the late, literary ancestor-genius Maya Angelou stated publicly that the idea of Black English being a separate language was absurd.[13] My major concern, though, is not actually with Black English.

In *Harriet*, we see Black and Indigenous worlds collide; we see the history of African enslavement and freedom, and a Native person impeding that freedom. The enslaver of Harriet pays a notorious slave catcher money to assemble a team to track and hunt down Tubman. In the scene where the slave catchers receive their orders, there is a Native person who emerges on the screen. In an interview, Focus Features asked Howard, "Are all the characters in *Harriet* written from history?" He responded that most of the characters are either based on real-life people or composites of several people. He further commented, "People don't pay for historical accuracy; they pay for a good story."[14] I wonder how and why Howard, and I assume Lemmons, chose to cast a tribally unidentified Native slave catcher? Where did they find that history, and how does it improve upon a good story about Tubman's role as a conductor on the Underground Railroad to freedom?

Some Native people in tribes enslaved Africans; they were slave owners and slave catchers. Some treaties, like the 1823 treaty between the Florida Native nations and the US government, explicitly mention that tribes that capture Africans who escaped their captivity would be compensated. In 1860, enslaved Africans made up 15 percent of the Cherokee Nation's total population; in the Chickasaw Nation, that number was 18 percent; the Choctaw owned 14 percent and the Creek 10 percent.[15] These are not small numbers, though a large majority were owned by a few elite families. White people also enslaved Native people. The history is clear. A popular myth that Black people perpetuate suggests that a large majority of Native people owned their Black ancestors. That is not true. The movie *Harriet*, in two scenes, falls into the trap of this myth. An unidentified Native male who has no lines of dialogue stands in the background among the Black and white slave catchers trying to capture Harriet Tubman.

It makes me wonder why the producers and scriptwriters included that detail in the first place? Was Harriet Tubman actually followed by Native slave catchers? Did the producers and scriptwriters want a more inclusive history by including a Native person? Did they want to show Native complicity in slavery? The script does not make this clear.[16] In failing to give the person context and a history, we can perpetuate the idea of Native invisibility and erase their own motives for even engaging with enslavement. While it was wrong for the Five Tribes to own Africans, they existed in a time where white settlers were encroaching on their land. They made a difficult and terrible choice to own slaves. And let me be clear: Native slave masters weren't better than white ones.[17] To say that Native people were being benevolent is some sick historical mythology, bordering on reproducing the Noble Savage stereotype. If we could ask some of the enslaved Africans, I'm sure they ain't want to be enslaved at all, whether their treatment was benevolent or not. Owning Africans was an egregious practice, regardless of who the owners were.

I recognize that as a Hollywood production, this film can't cover everything, and that you have to do things for dramatic effect. Nonetheless, Native characters can't exist as some fantasy to serve simply as a foil for Black freedom. If Black and Indigenous solidarity is important, we also have to be fair in our approach to portraying each other on the big screen, in theater, on television, in music. I wouldn't be mad about a Native slave catcher if the character had some dimension to him. Instead, all we see is a Native man, along with Black male slave catchers, trying to capture a Black woman. We can do better than this, and our future visual media must engage in some forms of solidarity.

TECUMSEH AND THE FIGHT FOR INDIGENOUS JUSTICE

In the early part of the nineteenth century, the name Tecumseh represented an important part of British, US, and Indigenous struggles for land and sovereignty. Peter Cozzens, author of *Tecumseh and the Prophet* (2020), argues that Tecumseh "advocated a political and military alliance to oppose U.S. encroachment on Indian land."[18] The majority of these lands were in the Northwest Territory, which consists of the present-day Midwest. He, along with his brother, Tenskwatawa the Prophet, was someone who struggled to bring Native people together and to keep the land that they had intact.

The Treaty of Paris in 1783 formally ended the Revolutionary War between the US colonists and the British. After the thirteen original colonies received their political independence, it created further issues with tribal nations like the Shawnee in the Northwest Territory. But it was the Treaty of Greenville (1795) that created the largest issue. Ninety-nine chiefs signed onto the treaty. They agreed to give up all of their land except for northwestern Ohio. Other parts of the treaty allowed the US to construct forts in the middle of Indigenous land. The tribes were able to continue hunting at will and the US government agreed to protect the tribal land from white settlers trying to take it. However, this treaty sought to fundamentally change Indigenous people's way of life by encouraging them to farm rather than hunt.[19] After the Treaty of Greenville in 1795, increasing numbers of settlers began to populate the region anyway, encroaching on Shawnee land. In addition, the Treaty of Fort Wayne (1809), which gave the US several millions of acres in Illinois and Indiana, flooded the area with whites. But Tecumseh never signed the treaty, as the Shawnee were excluded from it, and the land lost as a result was the tipping point for Tecumseh and others.

In the fall of 1806, Tecumseh sent out invitations to tribes, even ones they had fought, to join him and the Shawnee in Prophetstown, present-day Lafayette, Indiana. Over two summers, in 1807 and 1808, Tecumseh and the Shawnee were joined by Delawares, Ottawas, and Chippewas, Potawatomis, Kickapoos, Miamis, Sacs, and Wyandots.

They were enamored with Tenskwatawa and his message for revitaliz-
ing their cultures in the hopes of forever getting rid of the whites and
reclaiming their land.[20] Tecumseh ultimately sought to form a confederacy of Indigenous nations to challenge US encroachment on Indigenous land. They understood the importance of previous attempts like
that of Pontiac, who forged alliances with tribes seeking to reclaim forts
in the Midwest. However, they surpassed those predecessors by per-
fecting their Pan-Indian alliances.[21] Roxanne Dunbar-Ortiz writes of
Tecumseh, "His program, strategy, and philosophy mark the beginning
of pan-Indigenous movements in Anglo-colonized North America that
established a model for future resistance." While others such as Joseph
Brant and Pontiac "originated the strategy in the 1780s," Tecumseh
and Tenskwatawa "forged a pan-Indigenous framework made all the
more potent by combining Indigenous spirituality and policies while
respecting the particular religions and languages of each nation."[22]

Tecumseh wanted to rally all Indigenous peoples to challenge Indigenous dispossession. In an 1811 speech to the Osages, Tecumseh
consistently spoke of everyone as one people, pitting Native people
against white people. Seeking to gain further allies, he remarked,
"Brothers,—the white men are not friends to the Indians: at first, they
only asked for land sufficient for a wigwam; now, nothing will satisfy
them but the whole of our hunting grounds, from the rising to the
setting sun."[23] He further argued that whites "wish to kill our war-
riors; they would even kill our old men, women and little ones." He
explained that his people, the Shawnee, were "brave and numerous,"
but the white people were too much. However, if all the Native people
united, they would "cause the rivers to stain the great waters with their
blood."[24] Knowing that he needed to help the various nations come
together and set aside their own differences, he implored them to be
united. "We must be united; we must smoke the same pipe; we must
fight each other's battles; and more than all, we must love the Great
Spirit; he is for us; he will destroy our enemies, and make all his red
children happy."[25] It was perhaps a preposterously bold move to try
and unite many tribal nations, but Tecumseh understood that the only
way to struggle against a young US nation was to unite.

In an address to William Henry Harrison, an army officer who
would go on to serve as the ninth president of the United States, Tecumseh spoke of the land that belonged to all Native people. Perhaps

the most important part of that address was the demand to establish a particular territory for Native people—as their own land base. Tecumseh reasoned that the only way for all Native people to stop losing land was to unite: "The way, the only way to stop this evil, is for the red people to unite in claiming a common and equal right in the land, as it was at first, and should be now—for it was never divided, but belongs to all."[26] For the nineteenth century, this was quite a claim: that all of the land belonged to Indigenous people as a whole, ignoring the real tribal differences that existed among them. Still, it was a visionary move, and set the stage for an epic Indigenous resistance during the War of 1812. In the struggle, Indigenous tribes suffered further land loss and Tecumseh lost his life; however, he remains a celebrated figure in Indigenous communities for standing up for justice in his attempt to create a shared, Indigenous homeland.

BAAMEWAAWAAGIZHIGOKWE, JANE JOHNSTON SCHOOLCRAFT

In looking back at the nineteenth century (and other eras), we as a society romanticize Native American violent struggle against US encroachment. In doing so, we risk minimizing other forms of protest. Nonviolent protest, including writing, advocating through the legal realm, and other methods to preserve and produce Indigenous futures for Indigenous nations, has represented one way to challenge the US nation-state.

Jane Johnston Schoolcraft was an exceptional woman. Her Anishinaabe name was Baamewaawaagizhigokwe, which means "a woman who moves, making sound in the heavens."[27] Though her husband, Henry Rowe Schoolcraft, held an important role as Michigan territorial governor, she was known for her own contributions as a writer and poet. Born in Sault Ste. Marie, Michigan territory, in the upper peninsula, Jane Johnston had an Anishinaabe mother and an Irish father. She grew up in a world that was French-Canadian, Anishinaabe, and later, US occupied. She spoke Anishinaabe, English, and French fluently. According to literary scholar Robert Dale Parker, who was the first to publish a collection of Johnston Schoolcraft's poems, the Johnstons were "extraordinary for their political and social influence in Ojibwe, British, American, and métis cultures."[28] They were also well traveled, both across land and in and out of various cultural milieus. In addition, Johnston traveled to England and Ireland as a child. She knew English literature and Anishinaabe folklore, stories, and songs, which she translated. Schoolcraft wrote about fifty poems, translated at least ten Anishinaabe songs, transcribed about eight Anishinaabe oral stories, and contributed other forms of writing. As perhaps the first Indigenous literary writer and the first known Indigenous writer to write poems in an Indigenous language, "her extensive body of writing invites readers to reconsider the role of Indian imagination in American literary history and to consider an achievement on the order of Anne Bradstreet, the first known American poet, or Phillis Wheatley, the first well known African American poet."[29]

She never published her poems and writings during her lifetime, though according to Parker, her friends were fond of her writing.[30] However, her husband, Henry Schoolcraft, published many of them and even plagiarized her ideas, writing them down as his own in the many volumes of books he wrote on Native American history and culture. She left what Anishinaabe literary scholar Scott Richard Lyons calls the "x-mark." She contributed to an idea of Indigenous modernity and culture that, "while not necessarily traditional in origin, can sometimes turn out all right and occasionally even good."[31] She represents the nineteenth-century Indigenous creative genius, and how Native people used a variety of methods to survive. Not everyone was a male warrior and not everyone used violence to resist US colonialism. People like Jane Johnston Schoolcraft used poetry and the transcription of Anishinaabe stories and songs so that her people, and perhaps the rest of the US, would know that Indigenous people produced literature on par with any British or American writer, and did it orally.[32] Through her work, she asserted an Indigenous (Anishinaabe) humanistic sovereignty.[33] Her literary imagination and transcriptions were not outright, defiant protest, which remains at the forefront of the American public's imagination as it pertains to Indigenous people. Her writing was an intellectual and political project rooted in the possibilities of Indigenous freedom.

Johnston Schoolcraft wrote numerous poems and transcribed songs. One well-known and wonderful poem is about her maternal grandfather, Waubojeeg, in which she defends his legacy. Titled "Invocation, to my Maternal Grand-father on hearing his descent from

Chippewa ancestors misrepresented," she speaks in great detail about her grandfather's valor as a warrior. Its first few lines read:

> *Rise bravest chief! of the mark of the noble deer,*
> *With eagle glance,*
> *Resume thy lance,*
> *And wield again they warlike spear!*
> *The foes of thy line,*
> *With coward design,*
> *Have dared with black envy to garble the truth,*
> *And stain with a falsehood they valorous youth.*[34]

Parker notes that "metrically, this is probably JJS's most intricate poem." It is not difficult to see why. She includes in the poem her grandfather's dodem (clan), which was reindeer. She also explains the fearlessness with which her grandfather fought on behalf of his people, and desired that "though thy spirit has fled, / to the hills of the dead / Yet thy name shall be held in my heart's warmest core, / And cherish'd till valour and love be no more."[35]

Johnston Schoolcraft's literary work is important for at least a few reasons. First, as mentioned above, she is likely the first Indigenous female literary writer, akin to Phillis Wheatley. Second, her literary work sought to preserve Anishinaabe stories, songs, and ways of knowing for both white and Indigenous audiences. We should carefully include the work of Schoolcraft's literary brilliance in how we teach nineteenth-century American literature. We also need to continue recovering the literature of other nineteenth-century Indigenous women, in all of its forms, and place them in conversation with African American women of the time. This would offer us an opportunity to understand notions of identity, gender, nationalism, and belonging, but also help us think through how Black and Indigenous women envisioned freedom.

DRED SCOTT AND THE BLACK AND RED DIVIDE

The long nineteenth century is about oppression and how Black and Native people responded to that oppression. But we must not forget that their oppression was deeply embedded in US society, rooted in the rapid development of capitalism and the law. For example, while there were many laws that spoke of the limits of the rights of the enslaved, perhaps nothing more clearly defined that oppression than the case of *Dred Scott v. Sandford.*

John Emerson purchased Dred Scott after Scott's first master died in 1832. Emerson took Scott to Illinois, which was a free state, and later to Wisconsin. There, Scott married his wife, Harriet. In 1837, Emerson moved to Louisiana and married Irene Sandford. Dred Scott joined them, and after a time they moved back to Wisconsin and then back to St. Louis. The Emersons moved once again to Iowa, where John Emerson suddenly died in 1843. Then Irene moved back to St. Louis. In 1846, Dred and Harriet sued their master, Irene, for their freedom. They established their case on the basis of two statutes in Missouri. The first allowed for any person to sue for wrongful enslavement. The second established that a person brought to a free territory was automatically free and could not be re-enslaved. In 1847, the Missouri court ruled against them, but they won their appeal, in 1850. Irene Emerson then appealed the case all the way to the Missouri Supreme Court, which ruled in 1852 in her favor. Emerson's victory assured the Scotts that they would be enslaved once again. Irene transferred the rights of ownership of the Scotts to her brother, John Sanford. In 1853, Scott appealed again to a federal court, which ruled against him, forcing him to once again file an appeal.[36]

Eventually, their case would be taken to the Supreme Court. In 1857, the US Supreme Court ruled against them, 7–2, with Chief Justice Roger Taney opining that enslaved Africans were not citizens. Taney wrote that, dating back to the formation of the US republic, Africans were considered property and not citizens nor human:

> They had for more than a century before been regarded as beings of an inferior order, and altogether unfit to associate with the white race, either in social or political relations; and so far inferior, that they had no rights which the white man was bound to respect; and that the negro might justly and lawfully be reduced to slavery for his benefit. He was bought and sold, and treated as an ordinary article of merchandise and traffic, whenever a profit could be made by it. This opinion was at the time fixed and universal in the civilized portion of the white race.[37]

Chief Justice Taney's Supreme Court opinion was a white nationalist document. What is often missed in reading the Dred Scott decision is how Indigenous "freedom" was used as a foil to determine the "unfreedom" of Black folks. Although Taney, like Chief Justice John Marshall before him, conceded that "the course of events has brought Indian tribes within the limits of the United States under subjection to the white race" and "for their sake as well as our own, to regard them as in a state of pupilage," he allowed that "[Natives] may, without a doubt, be naturalized by the authority of Congress, and become citizens of a State, and of the United States."[38] Taney continued: "If an individual should leave his nation or tribe, and take up his abode among the white population, he would be entitled to all the rights and privileges which would belong to an emigrant from any other foreign people."[39] Taney opined that Native people could become citizens as long as they assimilated and adopted whiteness, and Black people, under no circumstance, could not. Finally, Taney affirmed—within the confines of colonialism—the humanity of Native people, while asserting that Black folks were "articles of merchandise."

We see, again, that in US history, African and Indigenous peoples in the US have been intimately linked. Even more, the creators of the US nation-state and democratic project found ways to connect them in unexpected ways, including via the legal realm.

AMERICAN COLONIZATION SOCIETY

White men in the early part of the nineteenth century understood the connections between creating a white republic, removing Black and Indigenous peoples, and further colonizing the land. It is no surprise that white politicians supported, across party lines, the American Colonization Society (ACS). Founded in 1816, the goal was to remove free African Americans and enslaved Africans and send them to Africa so that they could simultaneously abolish slavery, remove Black people, and create a white republic. White people at that time were scared. They had a reason to be concerned. Enslaved African insurrections were always possible, as demonstrated by Haiti, which through revolution became the first Black nation and the second independent democratic nation in the West. As historian Brandon Byrd argues, "In the antebellum United States, Haiti became synonymous with slave insurrection and black barbarism. It came to mean the specter of abolitionism, and for that it was shunned."[40] For slave owners, Haiti, as a representation of Black revolutionary possibility, "undermined the power of white planters and businessmen who reaped from black labor the greatest profits that the world had ever seen." For those looking for equality, "it encouraged other visions of emancipation and emboldened champions of racial equality."[41] Thus, it is not surprising that white people were interested in removing Black folks from the US because it clearly offered a way for them to form their own white nation-state.

Major supporters included Senator Henry Clay and President James Monroe, author of the "Monroe Doctrine," which sought to expand the borders of the young settler nation. Clergyman and ACS cofounder Robert Finley, who had major fears of a Black planet, did not want a Black republic in the West because he feared it would be a haven for fugitive slaves, Native peoples, and others, which, having lived in South Carolina, he had witnessed happen in neighboring Florida, a state where enslaved Africans had recently found refuge and formed Maroon communities.[42]

The logic of the ACS was rooted in the persistent idea of Indigenous dispossession and enslavement. This again prompts us to ask: What is settler colonization? It is the violent removal of people from land, replacing them, and also *imagining* their replacement, using language, writing, and other forms of displacement narratives. It is both overt and subtle. In general, the imagining happens before the removal or, at times, the two things happen concurrently. However, in the case of the ACS, that process was different. The ancestors of some African people who were stripped of their Indigenous identities would be forced to return to a land of which they knew very little about. In other words, they, after having been colonized, would then participate in the project of colonization. This is not to suggest that they would be without agency in the consequences of colonization. They were stuck between the racism of a white nationalist democratic project and the possibilities of returning to Africa.

When African Americans did leave the US for a place like Liberia, and it appears around fifteen thousand settled there between 1822 and the Civil War, how they "reimagined themselves as Liberians, as free people, and as settlers once they left the United States remained informed by their black American past."[43] Unfortunately, they engaged in forms of colonization that they had seen in the US, often dispossessing Africans and advancing the same Christian civilizing mission as the whites who they had learned it from. Still, Black folks in general did not agree with the ACS. It only reinforced their desire for citizenship and belonging in the US.[44]

DAVID WALKER'S APPEAL

Nothing frightened white America, especially slave owners, more than Black violent resistance to ending slavery. Enslaved Africans learning to read and write was another source of white fear. *David Walker's Appeal*, published in 1828, was an account written by a secondhand-clothing seller, and was, for white America, a terrifying piece of literature. It encouraged enslaved Africans to rise up against their masters and overthrow them. It also offered a fierce critique of American racism. Walker's writings had an impact on the North and the South. Southern legislators passed strict literacy laws further prohibiting enslaved Africans from reading. Even northern white liberals like William Lloyd Garrison, who had been praised for his belief in the abolition of slavery, was taken aback by *Walker's Appeal*.[45] In his attempt to challenge white America to come to terms with its racism and for enslaved Africans to overthrow slavery, Walker also noted that Native people would never suffer under white domination. He appealed to a common trope of nineteenth-century America: the assumption of Indigenous peoples' unbridled violence, which is an offshoot of the European-constructed notion of noble savagery. In his appeal to Black folks, he rhetorically asks, "Why is it, that those few weak, good-for-nothing whites, are able to keep so many able men, one of whom, can put to flight a dozen whites, in wretchedness and misery? . . . Would they fool with any other peoples as they do with us?" He answers his own question: "No, they know too well, that they would get themselves ruined." He then shifts to commenting on how they would not do the same to Native people: "Why do they not get the Aborigines of this country to be slaves to them and their children, to work their farms and dig their mines? They know well that the Aborigines of this country (or Indians) would tear them from the earth.

The Indians would not rest day or night, they would be up all times of night, cutting their cruel throats."[46]

Walker's *Appeal* is a rhetorical text designed to critique white America and to get Black people to think and to end enslavement on their own terms. It is not clear how Walker wanted this to happen, but he suggested it. In using this rhetorical strategy, he underestimated the cruelty of white America toward US Indigenous populations. In his fervor to end the enslavement of his people, he did not consider other forms of oppression. Perhaps Walker, a Boston resident, did not know of the Native people living in that area, which would not be surprising.[47] However, he held firm beliefs that Native people would not sit idly by, so he must have known something of their resistance to white encroachment. Walker represents the prophetic doom of the US and democracy. While he did not live to see it come to fruition in the form of a civil war, he understood that the United States could not go on as it did.

SOJOURNER TRUTH:
THE VOICE OF BLACK FEMINIST ABOLITIONISM

On April 28, 2009, former First Lady Michelle Obama offered remarks at the unveiling of the Sojourner Truth bust at the Capitol. To her audience, she remarked, "I hope that Sojourner Truth would be proud to see me, a descendant of slaves, serving as the First Lady of the United States of America." After a brief applause, she went on to explain how important it was to have a Black woman represented in Emancipation Hall. "Now many young boys and girls, like my own daughters, will come to Emancipation Hall and see the face of a woman who looks like them," she said. Before the unveiling of the bust, Mrs. Obama connected the activism of Truth with the idea of US democracy: "The power of this bust will not just be in the metal that delineates Sojourner Truth's face; it will also be in the message that defines her legacy. Forever more, in the halls of one of our country's greatest monuments of liberty and equality, justice and freedom, Sojourner Truth's story will be told again and again and again and again."[48]

Sojourner Truth, the formerly enslaved woman who became an abolitionist, is best known for her speech "Ain't I a Woman?" High schools and university students throughout the country read this speech, imagining her bravely voicing her thoughts on enslaved Black women and the problems white abolitionists had with race and gender. Truth has become a national symbol, voice of Black feminist freedom of the nineteenth century. In fact, she was perhaps that century's most important Black female abolitionist and rhetorician. Historian Nell Irvin Painter remarks, "We think of Truth as a natural, uncomplicated presence in our national life. Rather than a person in history, she works as a symbol."[49] Yet, as Mrs. Obama's speech demonstrates, Sojourner Truth the person is largely ignored. As Painter further contends, "Because we are apt to assume that the mere experience of enslavement endowed Truth with the power to voice its evils, we may forget a shocking fact: No other woman who had been through the ordeal of slavery managed to survive with sufficient strength, poise, and self-confidence to become a public presence over the long term."[50]

Truth, like other Black feminist icons such as Anna Julia Cooper, challenged the racial and gender order, and centered Black women's voices in an attempt to create liberation not just "from a sexist social order" that white women claimed, but for "racial equality and the women's rights movement."[51] Still, Truth's most iconic achievement remains her "Ain't I a Woman?" speech.

The ironic thing about Truth's speech is that there are two versions, which Nell Irvin Painter discovered in researching her 1996 book on Truth. The original speech was given in 1851, and was summarized by Truth's friend, Reverend Marius Robinson. The "Ain't I a Woman?" speech that has been valorized within US feminist history emerged in 1863 thanks to a white abolitionist, Frances Dana Barker Gage. Gage altered the speech to make it seem more authentically and linguistically Black. However, we now know that Black American language speech patterns differ from one another by region, and the speaking style of Truth in Gage's version is that of a southern Black woman, not a New York State resident, as Truth was. It is important to acknowledge the historical facts. However, I still think it's important to understand both speeches, and to extract as much as we can in order to understand the historical context but also the ways people today might utilize this speech for their own purposes. I will use the one summarized by Reverend Robinson.

Truth walked up to the podium and asked the president if she could say a few words. She then stated:

> I am a woman's rights. I have as much muscle as any man, and can do as much work as any man. I have plowed and reaped and husked and chopped and mowed, and can any man do more than that? I have heard much about the sexes being equal; I can carry as much as any man, and can eat much too, if I can get it. I am as strong as any man that is now. As for intellect, all I can say is, if woman have a pint and a quart—why can't she have her little pint full?[52]

In this version, Truth did not ask, "Ain't I a woman?" but did proclaim, "I am a woman's rights." This phrase is interesting. She asserts herself as a formerly enslaved Black woman at the center of the movement for Black liberation and women's rights. Typical of the Black oral and literary tradition of using the individual story to tell about Black people as a whole, she continues to discuss how her labor was just as good as a man's. She challenges the notions of race, gender, and property. As legal scholar Cheryl Harris contends, slavery was not just a racial structure; it "configured and structured social and legal boundaries of both race and gender." For Harris, "racial patriarchy describes that social, political, economic, legal, and conceptual system that entrenched the ideology of white supremacy and white male control over women's reproduction and sexuality."[53] Truth understood the limitations of white womanhood. White women were seeking the vote and a greater voice within the public sphere, but their labor within the domestic sphere was still a major part of their white woman-ness.[54] By painting the picture of herself toiling in the field, Truth could both challenge white women and men to think beyond the constraints of whiteness (and the white woman) as a category worthy of democracy and liberation. It wasn't just that Black women as laborers deserved their humanity, it was that it sprung forth in their work in the heart of white supremacy and a foundational part of US democracy at the point of production: the fields.

Truth's Black feminist abolition speech was an important critique of white and Black male patriarchy. It was also a moment of a Black women critiquing the capitalist system of labor. Like Indigenous women of the nineteenth century, she sought to create narratives of abolition so that her people's humanity could be respected. She was able to witness it, with the end of enslavement, and her Black feminist abolitionism played a contributing role.

FREDERICK DOUGLASS AND AMERICAN DEMOCRACY

Frederick Douglass, who, in September 1838, at the age of twenty, escaped enslavement, was perhaps the foremost slavery abolitionist in the nineteenth century. A gifted orator, he would go on to be a leading Black voice in advocating for Black freedom and citizenship in the US. In addition to his achievements as an orator, he also wrote one of the most important books advocating for the abolishment of slavery and the possibilities of freedom, one still used today in high school and university classrooms: *Narrative of the Life of Frederick Douglass: An American Slave, Written by Himself* (1845). Douglass wrote in his *Narrative*, "In coming to a fixed determination to run away, we did more than Patrick Henry, when he resolved upon liberty or death." But, for the enslaved, Douglass argued, "with us, it was a doubtful liberty at most, and almost certain death if we failed." For Douglass, "I should prefer death to hopeless bondage."[55]

He was able to witness an end to enslavement and Reconstruction. He is also well known for his advocacy for women's rights as well as a host of other issues, keeping white Americans' feet to the fires of democracy and justice. Douglass was an advocate of Black citizenship and human dignity. He compared the experiences and future prospects of Black Americans and Indigenous peoples in their potential to contribute to American democracy. Douglass was perhaps the greatest "voice of America's terrible transformation from slavery to freedom."[56] Moreover, he was a powerful rhetorician. He knew how to sway an audience and expose them to the horrors of enslavement. In other words, Douglass was a bad dude! Yet, he was not immune to the effects of Indigenous erasure. In September 1866, the National Union Convention was held in Philadelphia, during which Republicans and Democrats met to discuss President Andrew Johnson's policies. Douglass also attended, seeking to create his own political party and advance the cause of Black citizenship.

In April 1866, Congress passed the Civil Rights Act of 1866, which made Black people citizens. However, Black men (along with all women) were still denied the right to vote, and, under President Johnson, southern states created the Black Codes. These were laws created by southern states to restrict the freedoms that Black folks had gained after emancipation, one of which was the right to vote. Douglass believed that if Black folks were to be true citizens, Black men in particular would need the right to vote. It is no surprise then that the "prophet of freedom" would advocate strongly for Black male suffrage. In his quest for Black rights, however, he made disparaging remarks about Indigenous peoples, perpetuating the myth that they were a vanishing race. In many of his speeches and writings, he compared the declining civilization of Native peoples and the emerging possibilities of Black freedom. In his autobiography, he wrote, "The black man (unlike the Indian) loves civilization."[57] Native people were an important foil in his rhetoric.

On May 11, 1869, Douglass gave a speech titled "Let the Negro Alone" in front of the American Anti-Slavery Society in New York City. He covered numerous topics in the speech. He argued that while legal slavery had ended, the vestiges remained in the culture of the South. He spoke on the importance of Haiti as a Black republic. He suggested that one way to leave Black people alone was to look at them as equal and to end employment discrimination so that they could earn a decent wage. Perhaps his biggest demand was that the state allow them to purchase land. He simply wanted Black people to be left alone as they adjusted to the aftermath of enslavement. To make his case, he compared the remarkable progress of Black folks since the end of slavery with the popular belief in the "decline" of Indigenous peoples. The decline, according to the myth, was rooted in their inability to adapt to white civilization. "We are not going to die out [like the Indians]," stated Douglass, and he argued that Black folks were "more like the white man than the Indian." Native people were "too proud," and in their rejection of civilization, they die or retreat. Finally, Douglass remarked that "[The Indian] dislikes your civilization and dislikes and distrusts you."[58] Throughout the nineteenth century, US society believed that Native people would disappear (that is, their cultures and beliefs) and they would be assimilated into broader society. In contrast, society did not imagine that integration into American life was possible for Black people. Although rare, there were some instances of Black people believing in the possibility that Indigenous people could be assimilated and worthy of citizenship, including at Hampton Institute.

Founded in 1868 by white sympathizer General Samuel C. Armstrong, Hampton Institute (now Hampton University) was designed to educate African Americans during Reconstruction. In the late 1870s, the school began to include Native people. Although an imperfect experiment in educating Black and Native people, some Black educators believed that they could teach and *assimilate* Indigenous and Black people.[59] In contrast to Douglass, Booker T. Washington, who would go on to found Tuskegee and become perhaps the most famous Black person in the US during the Progressive Era, shared his positive views about Native people's potential in his autobiography, *Up from Slavery*. While working with Native people at Hampton Institute under the behest of General Armstrong, Washington discovered that Native people were just as capable as Black people in academics and learning trades. He discovered that what they hated most was cutting their hair and giving up things like wearing blankets and smoking tobacco. He concluded that "no white American ever thinks that any other race is wholly civilized until he wears the white man's clothes, eats the white man's food, speaks the white man's language, and professes the white man's religion."[60] Nevertheless, Washington was likely the exception to the rule in that he was able to have direct connections working with Indigenous people in an educational setting.

Humor was a core feature of Douglass's speech acts. He knew how to inflect humor into his speeches, which covered horrific topics yet made the white people he spoke in front of comfortable. To drive a certain point home, Black folks learned how to do this and continue doing this in front of white people. The difficulty in using humor and foils to appease white sensibilities is that some other group can get hurt in the process. In this case, I don't believe that Douglass meant harm to Native people, but the rhetoric fit into the larger narrative of white people's belief in their civilization as the best for all. Liberal whites had accomplished their major goal of ending slavery. Native people's decline was their own doing, and they could not compete with the onward moving civilization of the US. What we can learn from the

Douglass episode is that we should not always cater to white people's comfort; they, too, need to hear the gospel truth.

In Douglass's attempt at obtaining Black freedom, however, he propped up Black possibility while subjugating Indigenous impossibility. He wanted to appease white people for the sake of Black rights, which contributed to the discursive erasure of Native people. Historian David Blight notes that "it is astounding that Douglass would use race this way." He continues, "The marketplace for racism was diverse and terrifying in Reconstruction America. Even its most visible and eloquent homegrown opponent could fall to its seductions in his fierce quest to be accepted by American 'civilization.'"[61] Douglass, like other Black Americans throughout US history, was not immune to Indigenous erasure and producing white-created stereotypes about Native people, particularly when speaking in front of a white audience.

Cora Daniels Tappan, an abolitionist and a member of the American Anti-Slavery Society, immediately followed Douglass's speech to the AASS. She challenged his idea of comparing Black progress and Indigenous decline. She noted that while the southern slave owners subjugated Black people, the US government waged a war of extermination against Indigenous peoples. She believed that Douglass held prejudice against Native people, and though he used Native people as a foil, he "may commit the same sin that the nation has been committing against his own color."[62] She continued by explaining the harm of US government's assaults against Native people, arguing that "we are now in the same danger of extermination of the Indians as we are of the perpetual enslavement of the Black man." She ended her speech by arguing that they should not commit war against any people, for which she received great applause.

I appreciate Tappan criticizing Douglass's comments. Even a man such as Douglass needed a reminder not to engage in discourses of Native erasure. Black men, even today, need to be criticized for Native erasure. Unfortunately, I hear Black men use the same rhetoric as Douglass today, asserting that Native people have disappeared and Black people don't want to "end up like the Indians." It is a discourse that is old and tired, and we need to retire it ASAP. Unfortunately, even for the "prophet of freedom," it was easy to use Indigenous suffering as a prop for Black liberation. However, Douglass, just two years earlier, shared a different message, suggesting a more unbiased view about the racial equality of other people of color.

In 1867, Douglass gave a lecture at the Parker Fraternity Course in Boston, Massachusetts, on the topic of Chinese immigration, which he supported. While that was the main topic, in the lecture, titled "Composite Nation," he also conjoined the situations of Black and Indigenous people in the US. Douglass attempted to imagine a place where all people could live, though not without contradictions. Imagining this open democracy, he also made the case that land was open for all, noting that the continued exclusion of Black and Indigenous people was ensuring this vision could not be realized.

Douglass noted that problem that kept the races unequal was not grounded in the principles of US democracy. It was because of the "peculiar composition of our people; the relations existing between them and the compromising spirit which controlled the ruling power of the country."[63] He took the advocates of US democracy to task, arguing that the problem was that "we have for a long time hesitated to adopt and carry out the only principle which can solve that difficulty and give peace, strength and security to the Republic, and that is the principle of absolute equality."[64]

Douglass continued prophesying about the immigration to Indigenous land that would surely continue. Acknowledging that Europeans and Africans were already here, Douglass remarked, "And the Indian was here before either. He stands today between the two extremes of black and white, too proud to claim fraternity with either, and yet too weak to withstand the power of either." While he did not suggest that Indigenous people would disappear, he did argue for the permanence of European settlement and Black belonging, and admitted that "neither the Indian has been treated as a part of the body politic."[65]

Douglass was able to not only witness but also participate in Reconstruction. He saw Black American men gain citizenship. But he also saw further possibility. He believed in the prospects of US democracy, and rightfully so, though many of the things that Black Americans gained during Reconstruction were retracted with the passing of the *Plessy v. Ferguson* decision of 1896, which ushered in Jim Crow segregation. W. E. B. Du Bois put it best: Reconstruction "was in a certain sense all a failure, but a splendid failure."[66]

While African Americans gained their freedom through a civil war, and Black men later gained citizenship, there continued to be a retreat on Indigenous rights as the United States continued to expand. For instance, during the Civil War, when Black people were fighting for their freedom, the United States participated in wars out west and seized more land. It also further dispossessed Indigenous peoples of their rights guaranteed under treaties, including perhaps the most important one, signed in 1871. That year, the United States formally ended their treaty-making relationship with Indigenous nations. And in 1887, with the passing of the Dawes Act, Indigenous people were further dispossessed of their ability to control land, ultimately altering how they could use, manage, even sell their land. While Native people continued to resist, they also used a variety of legal tactics to lobby white sympathizers and politicians to the best of their abilities, such as those employed by Ely Parker (Seneca).[67] Appointed by President Ulysses Grant, Parker served as commissioner of the Office of Indian Affairs from 1869 to 1871. Grant advocated for a "peace policy" with tribes, a plan designed to remove corrupt agents from reservations and reform the Bureau of Indian Affairs. The peace policy, however, resulted in the US government further dispossessing Native people of their land. Still, people like Parker served an essential role in attempting to provide some resources to tribes and helping them maintain land titles.[68]

After the passing of the Dawes Act, and the murders of Native people at Wounded Knee in December 1890, Native peoples' methods of resistance had to change. They could no longer employ the threat of violence as a strategic option, and thus it became essential to work through the legal system.

CHAPTER FOUR

BLACK AND INDIGENOUS (INTER)NATIONALISMS DURING THE PROGRESSIVE ERA

HISTORIAN RAYFORD LOGAN called the period from the end of Reconstruction to the early part of the twentieth century the "nadir" because that was when Black dehumanization was perhaps at its height after enslavement. As Logan argues, "The plight of the Negro worsened precisely because of the efforts made to improve it."[1] The same can be said of Native Americans. Native people lost their treaty relationship with the US government. The US dispossessed them of large chunks of their land. They could not even govern their own affairs without the United States' say-so. This period is known as the Progressive Era.

Historians describe the Progressive Era as the period from the 1890s until the 1920s. It was a period of middle-class reform, increased urbanization, and the international exchange of ideas across borders. However, the Progressive Era was also a time riddled with contradiction, and thus one's circumstances during it were dramatically varied depending on their race, class, gender, and citizenship. As historian Glenda Gilmore asserts, "One group's progressive reform might become another group's repressive burden. One group's attempts to introduce order into society might depend on controlling another group's behavior."[2] It was also a time when the US nation-state expanded its colonial borders in an attempt to colonize others. The things that the US nation-state learned from colonizing its Indigenous population were applied to other countries around the world, from Cuba to the Philippines.

Still, Native people continued to suffer. Two policies undergirded "the Indian Problem." The first was the passing of the Dawes Act (also known as the General Allotment Act) in 1887. Named after Massachusetts senator Henry Dawes, the act, which began the process of parceling out American Indian lands to whites, produced severe consequences. In 1887, tribal lands occupied approximately 138 million acres; by 1934, they had dwindled to a measly 52 million. In addition, as historian David Chang has argued, by making lands private property, "allotment made it possible for Native individuals to lose them through direct sales, defaulted mortgages, tax forfeiture sales, and other means."[3] The second policy that was damaging to Native people stemmed from the Supreme Court's 1903 decision in *Lone Wolf v. Hitchcock*. The decision effectively gave Congress plenary power over American Indian land rights, meaning that tribal nations would have no control over their land.

As Indigenous peoples were losing their land and political power as sovereign nations, Black Americans were experiencing extreme racial violence. Black folks suffered much under Jim Crow racial terror during the Progressive Era. Convict leasing, a system designed to preserve the enslavement of Black people after their legal emancipation, was perhaps one of the key sites of Black oppression and exploitation. Though slavery was technically illegal, the Thirteenth Amendment allowed for the enslavement of people who had been convicted of a crime. By purchasing the labor of Black people from southern states, private companies would receive free labor and the state would earn revenue. The convict leasing system was an earlier iteration of the current prison industrial complex, which legal scholar Michelle Alexander has aptly called the "new Jim Crow."

Historian Sarah Haley argues that convict leasing was also a gendered experience. Although a minority, Black women suffered under the same system. The state portrayed Black women as deviant in order to exploit them for their labor; their gendered exploitation ushered in what she calls "Jim Crow modernity."[4] She argues that the development of white supremacy during Jim Crow was manufactured through the creation of a carceral state that exploited Black women by using state violence. While all Black folks suffered under the convict leasing system, they also suffered debt peonage and other forms of racial oppression.

Some whites did not want only to exploit Black people but also to remove them. For example, Mississippi senator Theodore Bilbo attempted to advance a Greater Liberia Bill, also referred to as the "Back to Africa bill," which was designed to use federal funds to assist African Americans' relocation to Liberia. Some Black nationalists supported it. As historian Keisha Blain notes, "For Black nationalists . . . the Greater Liberia Bill represented a viable step toward improving the social conditions of black men and women in a world deeply divided by the color line."[5] Black folks forced to come to the United States have always had to deal with whites challenging their claim to citizenship. Still, while some Black folks, especially Black nationalist women, sought to return to the homeland of their ancestors, others wanted to continue in their quest to belong in the US.

Even during their respective nadirs, Black and Indigenous peoples created spaces to struggle against the issues facing them, by forging organizations, such as the Society of American Indians and the Universal Negro Improvement Association, that would respond to their unique conditions. As limited as their visions might be for us today, it was an effort to foster racial pride and nationalism and certainly one worth trying. This chapter also analyzes the intersecting, transnational history of W. E. B. Du Bois and medical doctor Charles Eastman, who attended the Universal Races Congress in 1911. These two are important for several reasons. They were among the most prominent Black and Indigenous voices in the early twentieth century, and their reputation among white sympathizers for their respective causes was almost unmatched. At the time, they believed that by participating in the URC, they could redeem the soul of America. Black and Indigenous people like Du Bois and Eastman began to expand their idea of internationalism when coming into contact with other colonized peoples.[6]

THE SOCIETY OF AMERICAN INDIANS

The Society of American Indians (SAI) was a Progressive Era group of Native peoples interested in the development of their race. They wanted to be treated not as people of the past, but as equal human beings capable of being modern. They were Pan-Indianists. Though the term is now out of date in most circles, it refers to people who "spoke out at celebrations and nationalist commemorations. They criticized the actions of the Indian Office and its authoritarian bureaucrats. The proposed alternatives to the government's boarding schools and its regimented programs for bringing Indians to 'civilization.'"[7] While for their times they might be considered conservative, and even anti-Black at times, they tried to create sovereignty, in micro and macro forms.

The SAI came to fruition in 1911. Fayette McKenzie, a white sociologist and president of the all-Black college Fisk University, had also long been a sympathizer with Black and Indigenous causes. McKenzie invited some of the most prominent Native peoples to meet to discuss the best steps going forward to help Native people advance in US society, including medical doctors Charles Eastman (Dakota) and Carlos Montezuma (Yavapai), activist and writer Laura Cornelius Kellogg (Oneida), and anthropologist Arthur Parker (Seneca).

McKenzie invited Indigenous professionals, especially those who were products of the boarding school era. Boarding schools have been described by some scholars as vehicles of genocide, though others see them as sites of Indigenous agency and as an avenue through which to earn money through programs that allowed students to work outside the schools during the summer and upon graduation.[8] The boarding school era, however, was a moment of great terror. Army officials and missionaries, empowered by the US government, would go into tribal nations and kidnap their children and force them into boarding schools so they would be assimilated into US culture. They wanted to eradicate from the children the meaning of what it meant to be Indigenous so that the US government could fulfill its plans of taking more land.

The leaders met and discussed ideas of how to better organize themselves to protect land and affirm their humanity. After the meeting, they decided to call themselves the American Indian Association. In 1912, at a subsequent meeting, they changed their name to the Society of American Indians. They separated membership in two categories. Recognizing that they had Indigenous sympathizers, they assigned full, active membership to "full" Native people and associate membership to non-Native people. While there were many white sympathizers, perhaps the most important person to become an associate member was the Black intellectual W. E. B. Du Bois.

During its second meeting, the SAI drafted the organization's constitution, which featured a seven-point platform. The rhetoric of the platform contains racial purity language, as was common at the time. However, in its content and general tone, the platform was meant to advance the unique causes of Native people as sovereign nations whose rights had continuously been ignored. The platform read:

1. To promote and co-operate with all efforts looking to the advancement of the Indian in enlightenment which leaves him free as a man to develop according to the natural laws of social evolution.
2. To provide, through our open conference, the means for a free discussion on all subjects bearing on the welfare of the race.
3. To present in a just light a true history of the race, to preserve its records and to emulate its distinguishing virtues.
4. To promote citizenship among Indians and to obtain the rights thereof.
5. To establish a legal department to investigate Indian problems, and suggest and obtain remedies.
6. To exercise the right to oppose any movement which may be detrimental to the race.
7. To direct its energies exclusively to general principles and universal interest, and not allow itself to be used for any personal or private interest.[9]

The seven-point platform was meant to unite all Native people against the Bureau of Indian Affairs, which the SAI believed was an impediment to their progress. A few of the points are worth explaining. Point number three was meant to help alter the negative perception of Indigenous disappearance. As survivors of the boarding school era, SAI members experienced firsthand how the boarding schools tried to "kill the Indian in him and save the man." They desired to challenge the settler idea that all Native people had disappeared. With point number five, they declared their plan to establish a separate legal department that would investigate why all of the treaties had been violated. In other words, the SAI wanted the US government to honor the treaties.

While the SAI as an organization sought some form of assimilation, there were individual members who wanted to transform US society as best as they could. In 1915, Arthur Parker published an essay in the *Quarterly Journal of the Society of American Indians* in which he rebuked American civilization and its so-called virtues. The purpose of the essay was to challenge the idea that there was an "Indian problem." Similar to the question that Du Bois asked in *The Souls of Black Folk* (1903)—"how does it feel to be a problem?"—Parker modifies the question by jumping right into the heart of the issue and arguing that the root of the problem was largely US society.

Parker bemoaned that the US robbed Native people of their inherent right to being human. The US, he wrote, "robbed a race of men— the American Indian—of their intellectual life; Robbed the American Indian of his social organization; Robbed the American Indian of his native freedom; Robbed the American Indian of his economic independence; Robbed the American Indian of his moral standards and of his racial ideals; Robbed the American Indian of his good name among the peoples of the earth; Robbed the American Indian of a definite civic status."[10] The supposed inferiority of Native people wasn't what explained their current predicament, argued Parker; it was the fault of US civilization.

Freedom, according to Parker, was the "first and greatest love of the American Indian. Freedom had been his heritage from time immemorial." "By Nature," Indians, according to Parker, were "independent, proud," and "freedom to the red man is no less sweet, no less the condition of life itself than to other men." While Parker cited well-known US figures such as Patrick Henry, Benjamin Franklin, and Thomas Jefferson, he also cited Native figures who resisted with warfare, including Metacomet (King Philip), Red Jacket, Tecumseh, Pontiac, Black Hawk, Osceola, and Red Cloud.[11]

Laura Cornelius Kellogg (Oneida), like Arthur Parker, believed that Native people had a lot of good to contribute. In her essay "Some Facts and Figures on Indian Education," she argued that Indigenous ideas of education were not inferior than those of white peoples. "To some others anything the Caucasian does is 'educated' and anything 'Indian' is not. To those who have gone the whole way of enlightenment, education has another meaning," she wrote. And that meaning was "a proper appreciation of the real values of truth wherever they may be found whether in an Indian or Paleface."[12]

She then proceeded to voice a critique of the Indian boarding schools and an appreciation of Native ways of education. In addition to breaking down the importance of emotions and feelings in Indigenous ways of knowing, she made sure to explain the virtues of Indigenous education in comparison to white education: "The general tendency in the average Indian schools is to take away the child's set of Indian notions altogether, and to supplant them with the paleface's." She quickly noted that Indigenous education was not better; however, she asks, "why should [the Indian child] not justly know his race's own heroes rather than through false teaching think them wrong? . . . I do say that there are noble qualities and traits and a set of literary traditions he had which are just as fine and finer, and when he has these, or the sake of keeping a fine spirit of self-respect, and pride in himself, let us preserve them."[13] Kellogg was well educated in the white world. She also knew very much about her own Oneida heritage. She knew the virtues of being Indigenous, and the importance of preserving pride in one's idea of culture and history.

THE UNIVERSAL NEGRO IMPROVEMENT ASSOCIATION

It is important to recognize that Marcus Garvey and Amy Garvey both founded the Universal Negro Improvement Association, or UNIA. Although the UNIA was patriarchal, and women didn't hold too many leadership positions, women remained integral to the function of the organization.[14] The UNIA's ideology was not without problems, however. For instance, much of its written literature used the language of the time of "civilizing" Africans on the continent, and referred to Africans as "backward." Still, the UNIA was important for people of African descent throughout the Americas, with chapters forming in New York, Detroit, and as far south as Colombia and Costa Rica. I read the UNIA's work as an attempt to reconnect members with their African Indigenous roots, even if the rhetoric was not always in line with what was necessary for all Africans, on the continent and throughout the diaspora. Indeed, the efforts of groups like the UNIA were meant to reconnect people of African descent with their

Indigenous past, into something that might reconstruct their present and, more importantly, their future.

Founded in 1914 in Kingston, Jamaica, the UNIA recognized a historically rooted problem: that Black folks in the US and Caribbean did not have a homeland. And without a homeland, they could not have racial pride and dignity. Garvey also formed the UNIA in response to the limited function of the National Association for the Advancement of Colored People, formed in 1911.

Garvey was influenced by the self-help message that he read in Booker T. Washington's *Up from Slavery* (1901). Washington was the founder of Tuskegee University. During his time and, depending on how one understands his influence, he was the most important figure in the early twentieth century until his death in 1915. Garvey was so heavily enamored by the story of Washington that he wrote a letter to him, stating, "I have been keeping in touch with your good work in America . . . the fair minded critic cannot fail in admiring your noble efforts."[15] In March 1916, Garvey arrived in New York City, after which he went on a speaking tour extending more than a year, as he ventured through some thirty-eight states. Garvey then returned to New York, and on July 2, 1918, he officially formed a UNIA branch in New York.[16] By 1919, Garvey had established himself as one of Harlem's most important figures.[17]

The UNIA's constitution reveals a lot about how the leaders envisioned their organization would help connect Africans in the diaspora and Africans on the continent. Article 1, section 3 offers eleven suggestions that describe the core ideological tenets of the UNIA: "to establish a Universal Confraternity among the race; to promote the spirit of pride and love; to reclaim the fallen; to administer and assist the needy; to assist in civilizing the backward tribes of Africa; to assist in the development of Independent Negro Nations and Communities."[18] There is a lot to unpack in this section. However, we should first focus on the larger goal of the association. First, it is clear that the UNIA wanted to connect and empower all people of African descent, as demonstrated by phrases such as "to establish a Universal Confraternity among the race" and "to work for better conditions in all Negro Communities." Second, the UNIA sought to liberate Black people everywhere from the European-created notion of nationhood. Instead, it sought to create a new human, a new African, free from European domination. It wanted to create "Independent Negro Nations and Communities." These independent ideas of nationhood were important, for they set the imaginary possibilities of African liberation. The UNIA was also not consumed with the idea of nations and borders. Again, while the idea of civilizing "the backward tribes of Africa" was indeed problematic, the core idea of African nationhood throughout the diaspora was profound.

Similar to other Progressive Era organizations, the UNIA held large conventions in order to showcase its brand for the purpose of attracting new members. On August 13, 1920, at Liberty Hall in New York City, the UNIA members met to discuss how they might move forward in getting the rest of the world to respect African peoples, wherever they may be. At this meeting, the UNIA revealed the "Declaration of the Rights of Negro Peoples of the World," which served as "the Principles of the Universal Negro Improvement Association."

The declaration consisted of twelve complaints against European racism, followed by fifty-four declarations of rights. The preamble read, "Be It Resolved, that the Negro people of the world, through their chosen representatives assembled in Liberty Hall . . . protest against the wrongs and injustices they are suffering at the hands of their white brethren, and state what they deem their fair and just rights, as well as the treatment they propose to demand of all men in the future."[19] The preamble shares similarities with the discourses of other colonized and oppressed peoples—during a period that historian Erez Manela calls the "Wilsonian moment." In *The Wilsonian Moment: Self-Determination and the International Origins of Anticolonial Nationalism* (2007), Manela argues that colonized people in China, Egypt, India, and Korea used the rhetoric propagated by US president Woodrow Wilson during his Fourteen Point Plan, to create their own ideas of self-determination that undergirded their anticolonial struggle.[20] Manela further argues that the Wilsonian Moment "launched the transformation of norms and standards of international relations that established the self-determining nation-state as the only legitimate political form throughout the globe, as colonized and marginalized peoples demanded and eventually attained recognition as sovereign, independent actors."[21]

While it is not known whether or not the Garveys and the UNIA were directly influenced by the words of Wilson—though number

forty-five of their declaration claimed that African peoples should declare the "League of Nations null and void"—it is no doubt that their
fundamental idea of nationhood and self-determination developed as a
part of a broader network of Black and Indigenous peoples imagining
themselves free of oppression, both now and forever. Appearing at the
top of their complaint was that antiblackness was prescient for African
peoples everywhere in the world: "Nowhere in the world, with few exceptions, are black men accorded equal treatment with white men, . . .
[they are] discriminated against and denied the common rights due to
human beings for no other reason than their race and color."[22]

Land was central to their indictment of global antiblackness.
Number three in the list of complaints reads, "European nations have
parceled out among them and taken possession of nearly all of the continent of Africa, and the natives are compelled to surrender their lands
to aliens and are treated in most instances like slaves."[23] The UNIA
made sure to acknowledge that African land—from which all Africans and their descendants derive their roots—was under European
colonial occupation, and that the Africans were treated like slaves on
their land. As historian Robin D. G. Kelley observes, in a statement
referring specifically to the Dutch colonization of South Africa but
that could apply to colonization in general, "Yes, the expropriation
of the native from the land was a fundamental objective, but so was
proletarianization. They wanted the land *and* the labor, but not the
people—that is to say, they sought to eliminate stable communities
and their cultures of resistance."[24]

In the declarations, the first four assert that African peoples were
human and should be treated as such. Africa's freedom remained key
in the declaration's idea of freedom. "We believe in the freedom of Africa for the Negro people of the world, and by the principle of Europe
for the Europeans and Asia for the Asiatics, we also demand Africa for
the Africans at home and abroad," reads the thirteenth declaration.
They believed that each race—albeit limited—should have its own
land. Number fourteen reads, "We believe in the inherent right of the
Negro to possess himself of Africa and that his possession of same
shall not be regarded as an infringement of any claim or purchase
made by any race or nation." And finally, number fifteen reads, "We
strongly condemn the cupidity of those nations of the world who,
by open aggression or secret schemes, have seized the territories and

inexhaustible natural wealth of Africa, and we place on record our most solemn determination to reclaim the treasures and possession of the vast continent of our forefathers."[25]

The reclamation of land is a contested thing, given the historical precedents of US Blacks trying to return to their ancestors' homeland and settling on land in order to colonize those already there. Nevertheless, returning home, and creating place, both the idea and desire for it, have always been among the many core tenets of Africans, diasporic social and political philosophy. The UNIA, understanding that Africa's wealth could lead to a future for Black folks, attempted in its declaration to make sure that Africans could hold fast to a tangible idea of making place. Finally, in a demonstration of solidarity with other oppressed groups, number twenty-seven declared, "We believe in the self-determination of all peoples."[26]

In an article written by Garvey in 1923, titled "An Appeal to the Soul of White America," whose wording is close to the title of Du Bois's essay "The Souls of White Folk," Garvey makes his case for the necessity of Black people to avoid integrating with whites. His audience in this case, though, is white people, especially white liberals, who he believed had a part in trying to control Black people from realizing the necessity of leaving the US.

Garvey begins the appeal, writing, "Surely, the soul of liberal, philanthropic, liberty-loving, white America is not dead."[27] He continues, "There is no real white man in America, who does not desire a solution of the Negro problem." After laying out the brutality that Black people had faced in the United States, the problems with miscegenation, he encourages "foolish Negro agitators" and "so-called reformers" to "stop preaching and advocating the doctrine of 'social equality,' meaning thereby the social intermingling of both races, intermarriages, and general social co-relationship." He concludes the essay by reminding white Americans not to cater to Black folks and suggest that they could become equals: "Let the Negroes have a government of their own. Don't encourage them to believe that they will become social equals and leaders of the whites in America, without first on their own account proving to the world that they are capable of evolving a civilization of their own."[28] Garvey did not believe in the mixing of the races, but he perhaps had a point in raising a key question about white liberals and liberal Blacks at the time: Would Black folks ever belong in the US, and could they ever have a home elsewhere? Could Africa be their home? Garvey thought so, even though his idea was basically an extension of settler-colonial discourse and Christian chauvinism. During his life, Garvey was not without critics. Several Black radicals believed that Garvey was an imperialist trying to conquer Africa.[29] Still, the goals of the UNIA and the SAI—the former seeking freedom and the latter seeking sovereignty—bound them together. They had different priorities, but each pursued a basic vision for how Black people and Indigenous people could live.

In the post-Garvey era, after the US deported him back to Jamaica in 1927, Black women continued the work of Black nationalism. Black and Native people continued the work of internationalizing their particular plights. It is important to remember that, although I hear hoteps refer to Garvey's work, the man never set foot on the African continent. Furthermore, he proclaimed himself to be the provincial president of Africa. Bruh, Africa is a place with thousands of languages and different tribes, histories, and customs. He also described Africans as backward. And let's not forget that Garvey tried to collaborate with the Ku Klux Klan at one point. I don't mean to slander him, but we can't uncritically accept his efforts at African colonization. Although he helped instill racial pride, and he and the UNIA deserve props for that, if Black folks are ever going to obtain freedom, we can't do so by replicating the colonization efforts of the colonizers.

THE UNIVERSAL RACES CONGRESS

As I mentioned in the introduction, we should not restrict Afro-Indigenous histories to the relationship between the Five Tribes and African-descendant people. Black American and Indigenous histories have intersected outside the United States. Amid the growing concern of social progress within the United States, Black and Indigenous actors also sought to transform the US through appeals to the international community. W. E. B. Du Bois and Charles Eastman serve as a prominent example of this, making their international appeal at the Universal Races Congress (URC), held in London, England, in July 1911.

Du Bois and Eastman illustrate the nature of transnational blackness and indigeneity. Du Bois, a Pan-Africanist, transcended the US nation-state color line. As the late historian Manning Marable notes,

"Du Bois's color line included not just the racially segregated Jim Crow South" but also "colonial domination in Asia, the Middle East, Latin America, and the Caribbean among indigenous populations."[30] Nevertheless, Du Bois did demonstrate some form of US colonial domination, especially since he became an associate member of the Society of American Indians, perhaps the only Black American to do so. Although associate members had no authority in the SAI, Du Bois, ever the calculating advocate for social justice, was an important accomplice.

Eastman was influenced by the US nation-state and the Dakota world, as well as his interactions with other tribal nations. He attempted to navigate a world during a time when Indigenous peoples were searching for allies among white sympathizers within the broader context of the United States' thrust to become a global empire. Neither Du Bois nor Eastman considered himself bound to the US nation-state.

In part, they shared ideas of belonging in the US on the basis of their citizenship status. Black people were second-class citizens and Indigenous peoples were not afforded citizenship until 1924, and were being dispossessed in their own homelands. Both defined themselves through their community and connections beyond blackness and indigeneity, allowing them to insert themselves into a larger transnational world. Their positions were sites of struggle that gave Du Bois and Eastman, as representatives in the global struggle against Indigenous dispossession and antiblackness, the tools to critique settler colonialism and neocolonialism throughout the African diaspora and Indigenous communities.

Charles Eastman and W. E. B. Du Bois attended the URC for at least two reasons. First, to expose the deep-seated racism and colonialism within the United States. Second, and in keeping with the theme of the Congress, they wanted to affirm the humanity of Black and Indigenous peoples. They wanted to assert that they were human and deserved to be treated as equals. They believed that a central component to fighting injustice was to advocate for full citizenship. However, it is important to step back and remind ourselves how different their relationships to the US nation-state were. In addition, though Eastman did not necessarily have extensive relationships with people outside the US, Du Bois was well versed in keeping European relationships. With a graduate fellowship, he had traveled to Germany in 1892, where he also traveled extensively throughout Europe. Still, for conceptual reasons Du Bois and Eastman are bound together.

Historian Frederick Hoxie argues that both the NAACP and the Society of American Indians believed that "securing U.S. citizenship . . . would empower their members to become forceful actors in the nation's democracy."[31] He argues further that Native people believed "this new legal status could enable them to live outside the control of the Indian office and battle against hostile assaults from white neighbors."[32] As second-class citizens, Black Americans suffered all sorts of degradation. For instance, through the work of Black activists such as Ida B. Wells-Barnett, people learned about the prolific and violent nature of terror lynchings of Black folks.[33] Recent research conducted by the Equal Justice Initiative has found that between 1877 and 1950, there were over four thousand racial terror lynchings in twelve southern states, which is eight hundred more than previously reported. EJI also documented over three hundred lynchings in other states during the same period.[34] In addition to racial terrorism, Blacks suffered a general type of racism and violence, embedded in the general population's indifference toward Black suffering. Native people suffered too, losing land and generally believed to be disappearing. However, both peoples found creative ways during the Progressive Era to resist their unique oppression, such as holding formal meetings like the URC.

The Congress was rooted in the international movements for peace and specifically the International Union of Ethical Societies. Grounded in Christian and Judaic principles, these societies were meant to provide avenues for spiritual satisfaction and to promote the education of children, as well as moral and social reform. In July 1906, the leaders of the International Union of Ethical Societies Conference met in Eisenach, Germany. The most significant day of the meeting was July 3, when Felix Adler, professor of political and social ethics at Columbia University and president of the Ethical Culture Society of New York, proposed an international races conference. However, it was not until 1908 when the Union took active steps to make the conference a reality, and not until 1909 that it formally began to gather the resources for the meeting of races from all around the world.[35]

A major aim of Progressive Era reform was to bring about understanding through international meetings and education. Du Bois found the Congress to be one of those international opportunities. Du Bois, who at the time believed that a lack of education was at the heart of the conflict between races, was ecstatic for the meeting. To be clear, even the homie Du Bois had to learn a lesson about the pitfalls of believing that simply more education will change the heart and minds of white liberals! He had to come back with some more fire and write *Black Reconstruction in America* and other essays critiquing white folks! Near the end of his life, Du Bois got up and left the US, officially joined the Communist Party, and moved to Ghana. Even this man, who dedicated his life to educating white folks, couldn't take the limits of US democracy.

At the time of the URC, though, Du Bois was a liberal, "talented tenth type" Black man, who believed that "the chief outcome of the Congress will be human contact." It was "not simply the physical meeting," he reasoned, but "the resultant spiritual contact which will run round the world."[36] In this meeting between the global North and South, with discussions of the problems created by Western imperialism and exploitation, Du Bois felt that this meeting would achieve what others hadn't. It wouldn't be northern whites discussing the "Indian problem" or the "Negro problem," without the voices and representation of Black and Indigenous peoples. As Du Bois remarked, "The voice of the oppressed alone can tell the real meaning of oppression, and though the voice be tremulous, excited and even incoherent, it must be listened to if the world would learn and know."[37]

Felix Adler invited Du Bois to serve as co-secretary of the US branch of the URC. This is hardly surprising. Du Bois was the first Black American to graduate with a PhD from Harvard University. He also participated in the 1899 Paris World Exposition. His exhibit, showcasing the progress of Black Americans since slavery, won a gold medal. By 1910, after the publication of the *Philadelphia Negro* (1899) and the *Souls of Black Folk*, as well as his participation in the first Pan-African Congress (1900), Du Bois was one of the most internationally recognized Black Americans. In a 1911 issue of the NAACP's magazine, *The Crisis*, for which Du Bois served as editor, he quoted an article published in the *Gazette Times*, which commented on the then-upcoming URC, "The United States will be represented . . . by Charles A. Eastman and W. E. B. Du Bois."[38] In light of historical and contemporary discourses of Black people erasing Indigenous people,

Du Bois including this information about Eastman along with his photo in *The Crisis* is quite profound.

The secretary and organizer of the URC, Gustav Spiller, wrote to Eastman, thanking him for sending a paper on Native Americans. On January 27, 1911, Eastman wrote a letter to General Richard Henry Pratt, the founder of the Carlisle Indian School in 1879, and infamous for the statement, "Kill the Indian in him, and save the man."[39] Eastman asked Pratt for money to write a book on the Dakotas, but he also promoted the Congress. "The Secretary of the Universal Races Congress has just written thanking me for my 'very able paper' also asking my co-operation in several ways," he wrote. "He asks for a list of the best books on the Indian and especially on Indian Education."[40]

Eastman likely participated in the URC for at least two reasons. First, he needed steady income to support his growing family. By 1910, he earned the majority of his income from lectures and book sales. Second, Eastman certainly wanted to mingle with some of the world's elite, hoping to demonstrate that Indigenous peoples were human and could operate in modernity. Finally, he had secured himself as a national figure within the white imagination. Because of his writings, he also had recognition in Europe.[41] Eastman noted, "Like everyone else who is more or less in the public eye, I have a large correspondence from unknown friends" and "among the most inspiring letters received have been from foreign countries."[42] In other words, Eastman was most certainly feeling himself, and it was well deserved.

Eastman saw his attendance as a political project. In a January 27, 1911, letter to Yavapai Apache doctor Carlos Montezuma, Eastman discussed both his forthcoming book, *The Soul of the Indian*—a title resonant with Du Bois's *The Souls of Black Folk*—and his upcoming attendance at the URC. Eastman stated that all his efforts up to that point in his life were "to show that the Indian is capable of receiving a higher civilization much easier . . . if properly dealt with."[43]

The objective of the Congress was to bring together like-minded people to discuss the problems of race and colonialism. Although rooted in liberal discourses, the organizers believed that what lay at the heart of forms of dispossession, racism, and exploitation was ignorance. If they could get together in one of the seats of empire in London and discuss how they were all similar, race relations would change. Doesn't that sound familiar today? If we educate people—white people—about anti-racism, things will get better? Nevertheless, Du Bois and Eastman, among other oppressed and oppressors, believed that something had to be done. Secretariats, representing at least thirty countries, advertised the URC. In addition, some twenty governments were officially represented there, along with some fifty-three nationalities.

Both Du Bois and Eastman actively promoted the Congress. Du Bois, as co-secretary, did so in *The Crisis*, the official news and popular culture organ of the NAACP. "We doubt," he wrote, "if the Twentieth Century will bring forth a better idea than the First Universal Races Congress held in London, in the summer of 1911."[44]

Although Eastman held no formal positions within the Congress's organizational structure, Gustav Spiller asked him to provide a few photographs of prominent American Indian intellectuals. Eastman sent a photo request to Yavapi Carlos Montezuma, a founding member of the Society of American Indians (SAI). He also asked Montezuma to send him the address of Reverend Sherman Coolidge, an Arapaho Episcopal minister, who would be elected the first president of the SAI.

The URC solicited papers a month in advance so that members could contribute to a large volume that would be pre-circulated. The papers were to be translated into several languages. Eastman likely submitted his essay as early as January 1911. Pre-circulation appears to have had two purposes, beyond letting the attendees read them. First, the organizational staff wanted to use the papers as propaganda to spread the word about the Congress to interested parties.[45] The second purpose seemed to be to help build momentum for the second Congress, which they planned to hold in Hawai'i.[46]

The Congress was well attended. While there were no specific requirements for papers, authors were urged to "make practical suggestions in their contributions."[47] The conference was divided into eight sessions. Du Bois and Eastman participated in the sixth session, "The Modern Conscience (the Negro, the American Indian, etc.)," which was held Friday afternoon, July 28, 1911. At this session, the papers ranged in subject and objective, but they shared many commonalties, including discussions of interracial marriage, characteristics of the Black and American Indian "races," social law and custom, and brief histories of how Black and Indigenous peoples came into poverty.

Du Bois's paper, "The Negro Race in the United States of America," and Eastman's paper, "The North American Indian," read as broad—perhaps even unexciting—histories of Blacks and Native Americans. Yet beneath the surface of these works lie subtle critiques of US colonialism. As scientific racism was a part of public and intellectual discourses, the two men found it imperative to explain how Black Americans and American Indians were products of transnational white supremacy and not simply "less able" races. The papers sought to critique the logic of white civilization and to assert how Black Americans and American Indians could help usher in a truly democratic, anticolonial future.

Du Bois's paper offered a broad social history of Black Americans. Beginning with the movement of Africans to the Americas, he plainly stated, "The African slave trade to America arose from the desire of the Spanish and other nations to exploit rapidly the resources of the New World." In opening the discussion this way, Du Bois placed blame for the current condition of Black Americans squarely on the shoulders of European nation-states. Perhaps uncritically, he reasoned that Europeans were unable to exploit American Indian labor because of "the weaknesses and comparative scarcity of the Indians."[48] After explaining the population growth of enslaved Blacks, Du Bois attempted to show the resilient spirit within the African diaspora through a brief discussion of slave rebellions. "Only two of these [revolts] were large and successful," he wrote, "[that] of the Maroons in Jamaica in the seventeenth century, and of Touissant L'Ouverture in Hayti [sic] in the eighteenth century."[49]

Du Bois's writing on slave rebellions in the African diaspora was likely influenced by his meeting other Africans in the diaspora from the late nineteenth century until around 1900. Before coming to London for the URC in 1911, he had attended the First Pan-African Conference, held in July 1900.

After identifying the social discourses that justified slavery, Du Bois illustrated the agency of Black Americans during Reconstruction. Once they learned of the US political system, "the Negroes secured a better class of white and Negro leaders." With these new leaders, reasoned Du Bois, came "a more democratic form of government," "free public schools," and "the beginnings of a new social legislation."[50] These relative successes were short-lived. Beginning in 1890, the neocolonialism against Black Americans took full hold. Virtually all Blacks were excluded from voting, as well as from other political and social opportunities afforded to first-class citizens. "With this legislation have gone various restrictive laws to curtail the social, civil, and economic freedom of all persons of Negro descent," wrote Du Bois. The legitimacy of Black exclusion from social, economic, and political arenas, he reasoned, constituted "the Negro problem." Of course, Du Bois reminded his audience that the "Negro problem" was actually an American, white supremacist problem.

Eastman's paper offered a similarly broad history of American Indians. His intention, however, like his life's focus, was to bridge the white and American Indian worlds, to show the former the virtues of a "simple" life and what a civilization that purported to promote democracy could learn from Indians. Eastman began with a general geographic and physical description of the American Indian. He then described the virtues of American Indian political philosophy and institutions. After explaining the structure of tribes and clans and the roles of chiefs, he switched gears, telling the world that "American historians have constantly fallen into error by reason of their ignorance of our democratic system." Because of their belief in a superior white civilization, Eastman reasoned, historians failed to learn from a true "government of the people, one of personal liberty," one that gave "equal rights to all its members."[51] For Eastman, a true democracy did not exist only in political terms, but also in terms of economics. He began the "Economic" section of his paper by pointing out the contradictions of the settler nation-state: "It appears that not freedom or democracy or spiritual development, but material progress alone, is the evidence of 'civilization.'" However, the "American Indian failed to meet this test," Eastman wrote, "being convinced that accumulation of property breeds dishonesty and greed." The American Indian "was unwilling to pay the price of civilization."[52]

As with the life paths of Du Bois and Eastman, at first glance their essays appear to have little in common. Du Bois's subject experienced slavery and exclusion through social and political law. Eastman's subject suffered dispossession of resources and culture because of warfare and white greed for land. Beneath the explicit content of their essays, however, lies an important, previously unnoted link: their similar belief in the virtues of "the souls of Black folk" and "the soul of the Indian." As Kiara Vigil notes, "Eastman's argument centered on an American contradiction, the same dilemma that drove Du Bois: How could Indian people participate in a democracy that was itself so undemocratic with particular regards to them?"[53] In spite of slavery and colonialism, they believed their people could usher in a new, democratic society, one based upon social, political, and economic inclusion, not white supremacy.

Du Bois located the roots of Black disenfranchisement not with the passing of *Plessy v. Ferguson* in 1896. Rather, he began in 1890—the year of the US cavalry's slaughter of Dakotas, mostly women and children, at Wounded Knee. If 1890 marked the beginning processes of Jim Crow segregation, for American Indians it marked an end to using war as a means for securing sovereignty. It also required a new generation of Native women and men to assert their right to citizenship claims and sovereignty within a new US political domain that claimed social and political reform, but continued to subjugate people of color all over the world. Du Bois and Eastman understood these changing times, as well as the connection between the exploitation of land and labor, both at home and abroad. Eastman called the reservation system a "miserable prison existence."[54] Du Bois argued that, after slavery, those former masters who wanted cheap labor turned to criminalizing Blacks: "Crime and long sentences for petty offences have long been used as methods of securing cheap negro labor."[55]

Eastman believed that a future free of colonialism would begin not only with education but also as soon as the "huge, unwieldy system that has grown up both at Washington and [on reservations]" ended.[56] He referred, of course, to the Office of Indian Affairs. Du Bois believed that only through the equal treatment of Black Americans could a truly democratic US society emerge. White society would not be able to bring in civilization. Instead, Du Bois argued, "the destinies of this world will rest ultimately in the hands of darker nations."[57]

For Du Bois, the URC was significant because "it marked the first time in the history of mankind when a world congress dared openly and explicitly to take its stand on the platform of human equality." "What impressed me most," said Eastman, "was the perfect equality of the races." He also said that it was a great privilege to see three nationalities "come together to mutually acquaint themselves with one another's progress and racial ideals."[58] Their attendance was meant not simply to crack the door to full US citizenship, which was still closed. Rather, it was their attempt to assert a human rights agenda on a global stage, so that one could be both an American and a Black American or Native American. This they did on behalf of all Black and Native Americans.

I have always wondered if Du Bois and Eastman talked at all during their time in London. Did they give each other the 1911 version of a dap/pound after their talks (what non-Black people commonly refer to as a "fist bump")? Did they think to themselves, "Damn, are we really going to be able to change these white folks' mind?" Did they share a smoke? Maybe enjoyed a Pimm's? The historical record does not reveal if they were able to chop it up, and they likely had their own bougie adventures with friends while in London. However, I do think they both had a great deal of respect for one another. For these transnational progressives, the URC had even greater implications. It showed that the histories of Blacks and Natives in the United States, while distinct, were also intimately related. We can use Du Bois's and Eastman's participation in the URC as a foundation for better understanding subsequent twentieth-century Black and Indigenous social movements.

In my view, what their sharing of a platform in 1911 means for this contemporary moment is that we need to continue to share platforms. We don't always have to speak in terms of solidarity, but being in the same room, listening to our respective oppressions, and then finding common ground is as important as ever. Another lesson we could learn from this moment is that it ain't always Black and Indigenous peoples' job to educate liberal white people. I don't knock any Black or Indigenous person taking the time to explain to liberal whites what anti-racism and white fragility are; though history says they don't listen well enough. I wonder what that 1911 conversation might have looked like without liberal whites? They may have discussed their plights, no doubt, but they might also have been on some Nat Turner and Tecumseh type shit, trying to in fact gain true liberation. This is all hypothetical, but it does make you wonder, damn, what if?

CHAPTER FIVE

BLACK AMERICANS AND NATIVE AMERICANS IN THE CIVIL RIGHTS IMAGINATION

AMONG THE MOST frustrating things I encounter are certain people's reactions to my work. The reactions have seemed to be stuck between two different responses. One is Indigenous antiblackness—expressed as, "See, Black people can be racist, too!" They also assert that Black Americans are settlers. ("Let's not forget that there was this thing called slavery!") The second response, by Black folks, is to simplify the history of Black and Indigenous relations. They easily fall into the old line of, "See, those Indians are racist too! They owned slaves!" I think some Native people have used my work to suggest that Black people are no better than white settlers. And some Black people have called me out for minimizing the history of Native-enslaved Africans. As a Black and Indigenous person, I suppose I'm just Mr. In-Between, a brotha without a home.

This particular comparative discourse has existed for a while. For example, on December 10, 1949, Charles Eagle Plume, a Blackfeet Indian, was quoted in the *Chicago Defender* comparing the plight of Native people to Black Americans. "The Southern Negro is better off than the average American Indian," he remarked. Eagle Plume, an army veteran and graduate of the University of Colorado, stated, "The Georgia Negro eats better than the American Indian." Finally, he remarked, "Negroes can own property, but a majority of Indians cannot unless they are under the jurisdiction of the government."[1] Eagle Plume's statement, in a Black newspaper, demonstrates perhaps a general Native American point of view regarding African Americans. On the one hand, they acknowledged the problems that Black people faced. On the other hand, in the observations, we can see a trend that continues today: the need to compare two forms of oppression and ignore the complexities of the conditions that another oppressed group faces.

During the 1930s and through the 1940s, New Deal policies offered new protections for white Americans. This was a period of great reform that also further embedded racism. For Indigenous people, they experienced significant changes as a result of the Indian Reorganization Act of 1934 (IRA), albeit with mixed results. Signed into law by President Franklin Roosevelt as the Wheeler-Howard Act, the IRA was designed to compel tribal nations to implement constitutions that would be legible to the US government; however, it often created other problems, including undermining traditional leadership styles for particular nations and effectively forcing them to reform their structures of governance, in order to receive federal funds. It seems eerily similar to the logic of postwar structural adjustment policies forced upon countries on the African continent and in South America! Above all, the IRA created an unclear notion of tribal sovereignty in regard to the exercise of power and the ability to govern tribal members and implement justice.[2]

Throughout the 1940s, Black Americans also continued to experience different forms of oppression. They moved from southern states to northern cities to escape Jim Crow racism in the South. What they thought was a promised land of integration ended up being one of segregation. In northern cities like Detroit, a combination of white homeowners, homeownership organizations, local government officials, and federal housing policies was created to keep Black people from integrating into all-white neighborhoods.[3] At the same time, the US carved an easy path to middle class stability through the creation of suburbs, Social Security, and housing policies that fostered homeownership. As political scientist Ira Katznelson contends, this was a period when "affirmative action," which we typically think is for African Americans and other people of color, benefited white people. To be clear, affirmative action as an official policy did not emerge until the late 1960s, but, as Katznelson asserts, contemporary conservative arguments that the federal government "gives" people of color handouts via affirmative action ignores the longer history of the federal government actually creating policies that supported white people largely. These policies, such as the homeownership subsidies that created the racial wealth gap we have today, are rooted in earlier policies from the 1930s and 1940s. Sanctioned by the government, these policies did not on the whole benefit Black and Latinx peoples.[4]

In postwar America, in the aftermath of a world war in which Native Americans played a major role, including being the population that served the most per capita in the armed services, they, as they had always done, were fighting for their place as sovereign people on their land, living in the US and being forced to integrate in greater ways. Yet, the 1950s consisted of a series of changes. For example, several thousand Indigenous peoples moved to cities as part of the urban relocation program in the 1950s and ended up in cities such as Chicago and Los Angeles.[5] African Americans also migrated from the South, traveling to urban centers like Detroit and Oakland. The great migration did not safeguard them from white supremacy, however, and Africans Americans still held a diverse set of views of Indigenous peoples. Perhaps no event held more sway than the Lumbee resistance to the Ku Klux Klan in January 1958.

In early January 1958, the Klan placed a burning cross in the front yard of a Lumbee family's home in North Carolina. They, along with other Lumbees, were infuriated. One man named Sanford Locklear, who became a leader of the resistance, sought to meet them head on because, as Lumbee historian Malinda Maynor Lowery puts it, "the Klan not only was insulting Indian people but was infringing on Indian land."[6] On January 18, 1958, Catfish Cole, a local Klan member, decided to hold a rally at Hayes Pond. In attendance were about fifty Klan members, including women and children. They were soon surrounded by some five hundred Native people, mostly military veterans and some women, all armed with guns and knives. The Native people started firing guns in the air, and the Klan members ran into the swamps and ditches.[7]

The moment was remembered fondly by Black activists, including Robert F. Williams, author of *Negroes with Guns,* who fled the US in 1959 to Cuba and later China to avoid trumped-up charges of kidnapping. Writing for the *Chicago Defender,* Langston Hughes, perhaps our greatest Black American poet, wrote about how the Lumbee Indians fought off the Klan in North Carolina. In a short, satirical story, Hughes narrates a fictitious conversation between himself and a person named Jesse B. Semple (often spelled "Simple"). The story is essentially a discussion of the relative merits of violence and nonviolence, and the approaches used in working within the system versus creating change by other means, including separation or the use of force. In the story, Simple says,

> I say, I love them Indians! And it is stone time they went on the warpath again. Indians has been too quiet in this country too long. Outside of the movies, I have not hear tell of them scalping any white folks in a hundred years.
>
> And I can think of no better scalp to scalp than the scalp of a Ku Klux Klanner. I wish them Indians had snatched each and everyone of them Klansmen baldheaded, and left them nothing but their empty hoods.[8]

Hughes responds to this sensational comment, "How bloodthirsty you are!" "Besides," he continues, "rioting in a cornfield solves no problems. Anyhow, nobody went on a warpath." He further corrects Simple by explaining that the Natives just "shot guns in the air—nothing more and surely didn't carry any tomahawks."

Hughes then asks Simple, "You are such a race man, and the Negro race has suffered so much at the hands of the Klan, so tell me why no Negroes have ever broken up a Klan rally? Huh? Why did we leave it to the Indians?"

Simple responds, "Negroes ain't united enough. . . . To attack the Ku Klux Klan in person you need a tribe. But all us Negroes has is the NAACP."

Hughes then cites all of the benefits of the NAACP, including civil rights, education, voting, and peaceful protest through the legal system. Simple replies that these are not as fun as "scalpings," to which Hughes retorts, "Think how vital it is to preserve the right to vote. Would you rather vote than scalp?"

"It's all according to who I am voting for. To scalp a Klansman and remove his wig would be more fun than voting for Eisenhower.

"Besides, you only votes for president once every four years. But Klansmen down South burns a cross somewhere almost every day. A scalped Klansmen would not burn a fiery cross again.

I am 100 percent behind my Indian brothers in North Carolina. In fact, I move that the NAACP give all of them life membership in the National Association for the Advancement of Colored People."

Black Americans remembered this Indigenous triumph against the Klan as a significant movement against white supremacy in the South, though Robert F. Williams, who then was head of the Monroe, North Carolina, NAACP chapter, wrote that the resistance they led two weeks earlier did not get the same attention, "We had driven the Klan out of our country into Indian territory. The national press played up the Indian-Klan fight because they didn't consider this a great threat—the Indians are a tiny minority and people could laugh at the incident as a sentimental joke—but no one wanted Negroes to get the impression that this was an accepted way to deal with the Klan."[9] Williams's comment suggests that he didn't respect the Indigenous resistance. On the contrary, he did. He pointed out a longer history of how white society viewed Indigenous peoples as a disappearing culture. They would not garner that level of attention until nearly fifteen years later with the emergence of the American Indian Movement.

Even though some were advocates of nonviolence, even supporting the NAACP, Hughes captured the core issues greatly: using the legal system for gaining more rights was important, even foundational, but forms of forceful resistance had their place in the pantheon of Black struggle. And Black Americans, for a moment, were able to look to Indigenous peoples as a sign of what justice could look like.

The beginning of the 1960s was a tumultuous time for Black and Native people. Indigenous people were fighting for fishing rights in the Pacific Northwest. Native American organizations such as the National Congress of American Indians, founded in 1944, sought to protest the termination of tribal nations.[10] Throughout the 1950s, and then significantly, in 1961, the year of the landmark Chicago American Indian Conference, Native individuals wanted to use the "language of the larger world," including that from nations on the African continent and throughout Latin America, to challenge the US colonial order.[11]

Black Americans were struggling for the basic right to sit down at a lunch counter and order food. They, too, were resisting their oppressive conditions. However, they didn't always see themselves in struggle together with Native people, with a few exceptions. For instance, as noted author James Baldwin wrote in *The Fire Next Time*, "And today, a hundred years later after his technical emancipation, he remains—with the possible exception of the American Indian—the most despised creature in this country."[12] While Baldwin was not intentionally stating that Black folks had it worse than Native folks, it is clear that he, if not knowing their present condition, did understand that anti-Indigenous sentiments were just as bad for Native people. Three additional civil rights icons who also engaged in this rhetoric were Fannie Lou Hamer, Martin Luther King Jr., and Malcolm X. It is important to comment on how these Black civil rights icons understood the Indigenous condition, for through their example we can learn how to think and, perhaps, even talk about solidarity with other oppressed groups, especially the original people of this land.

James Baldwin, Fannie Lou Hamer, Malcolm X, and Martin Luther King Jr. all analyzed and criticized the Black American condition within US democracy. They also hoped to imagine a Black future where they lived outside of white supremacy. It is important to discuss why I'm using these civil rights icons as examples. In some ways, these people represent two competing notions of Black belonging in US history, nationalism and integration. The late Black liberation theologian James Cone argued that these competing ideas were a response to enslavement and segregation. He also argued that no Black person or organization was purely nationalist or integrationist. Rather, each existed on a continuum, and desired different means on a path to Black liberation.[13]

Furthermore, these Black intellectual strands were based upon what one believed the potential of the US could be. Today, when people tell Black, Latinx, or Indigenous protesters to "go back home" or to "leave the country" it is an insult. They are suggesting that we all can't do better and live with each other in peace. Black people have desired to largely reform the US. And when they could not because of white racism, they sought other means, including separation. Baldwin, Hamer, Malcolm, and Martin exude what historian Peniel Joseph calls "radical black dignity."[14] They challenged white supremacy and injustice and believed in the possibility of racial and economic justice for Black Americans.

It seems today that Dr. King is popular among a wide array of people. From right-wing pundits, to college football coaches who want to silence the protests of Black athletes, to socialists who want to highlight Dr. King's critiques of capitalism, he remains as popular as ever. Dr. King belongs to everyone. According to a study released in 2008, Dr. King is the most well-known figure in US history.[15] In the preface to *A More Beautiful and Terrible History: The Uses and Misuses of Civil Rights History* (2018), historian Jeanne Theoharis notes that Dr. King and other civil rights figures' legacies have been tainted. People forget that it took fifteen years for the government to put into law Dr. King's birthday as a national holiday. Thereafter, his "I Have a Dream" speech and ideas became popular. As Theoharis notes, "By 1987, 76 percent of Americans held a favorable opinion of the civil rights leader, almost the reverse of his popularity at the end of his life (only 28 percent of Americans had a favorable opinion of him in 1966)."[16]

I also focus on Malcolm X because his legacy is timeless. The hip-hop generation created renewed interest in Malcolm X as a part of its culture, perhaps most notably in masculine framings posited by KRS-One on the cover of his album *By All Means Necessary*, and also Public Enemy's use of Malcolm's image in various videos and references in their lyrics. Spike Lee followed suit with his 1992 movie *X*, superbly played by my favorite actor, Denzel Washington. In 1998, *Time* magazine named *The Autobiography of Malcolm X* one of the ten most influential books of the twentieth century.[17] Regardless of the mixed reaction to the late historian Manning Marable's biography of Malcolm, *Malcolm X: A Life of Reinvention*, it was an epic undertaking, and brought, once again, renewed interest in the meaning and legacy of El Hajj Malik El Shabazz (Malcolm X's Muslim name). More recently, writer Ta-Nehisi Coates, author of *Between the World and Me*, winner of the 2015 National Book Award, described the meaning of Malcolm X in his own life: "I loved Malcolm because Malcolm never lied, unlike the schools and their façade of morality, unlike the streets and their bravado, unlike the world of dreamers. I loved him because he made it plain."[18] Malcolm's influence is enduring, always arriving just in time for new political moments. To deconstruct his words within the context of indigeneity is essential to understanding, in part, Black-Indigenous relations.

I highlight Fannie Lou Hamer because she held a radical vision of what democracy could look like. Hamer, in the Delta South, represented the importance of Black women to the civil rights movement, and helped usher into the movement a more egalitarian structure that allowed local people to lead in their own liberation.[19] James Baldwin is also an important contributor to understanding Black views of Native people and histories. He not only believed in the possibilities of US democracy but that white people could not be free without Black liberation. Indeed, these four individuals highlighted the importance of freedom. Collectively, though, they often reinforced Indigenous erasure, which I will emphasize below.

MARTIN LUTHER KING JR. AND THE NATIVE QUESTION

It seems as if everyone has a version of Dr. King. Old civil rights activists criticize younger generations by pointing to Dr. King's nonviolent approach and arguing that is how protest is done. Black and white conservatives pull one quote from Dr. King's speech and say that poor Black folks need to focus on the "content of our character" or some other nonsense. If they did that, they would be free to live in this "free," capitalist society. Others point to the Dr. King who argued that three evils shaped US society: militarism, capitalism, and racism; this is my favorite Dr. King.

However, what most people don't know is that, in Dr. King's understanding, the foundations of racism, as a theory and practice, began with the violent dispossession of Indigenous peoples and its aftermath. In *Why We Can't Wait* (1964), King observed that in order to understand the complexities of racism, one had to also understand the root causes of social, political, and economic racism. He reasoned, "For too long the depth of racism in American life has been underestimated," and the "surgery to extract is necessarily complex and detailed."[20] Understanding racism's root causes is important for going forward. King further reasoned, "The strands of prejudice toward Negroes are tightly wound around the American character." And yet, he also realized that you cannot have a good clue about the foundational understanding of racist ideas without focusing on Indigenous people: "Yet to focus upon the Negro alone as the 'inferior race' of American myth is to miss the broader dimensions of evil."[21] The broader evil, of course, was racism. But it was also about colonialism. Dr. King understood the importance of employing a dual analysis of anti-Black racism and settler colonialism that affected both Black and Indigenous peoples:

> Our nation was born in genocide when it embraced the doctrine that the original American, the Indians, was an inferior race. Even before there were large numbers of Negroes on our shores, the scar of racial hatred had already disfigured colonial society. From the sixteenth century forward, blood flowed in battles over racial supremacy.[22]

Here, King describes the root of racist ideas and thinking that shape this society: settler colonialism. More importantly, he articulates a crucial understanding of the function of racism: that it bled into the realm of American popular culture.

US popular culture is one of the key ways that ideas about Black and Indigenous people circulate. Indeed, land dispossession and erasure in the realm of popular culture go hand in hand in further dispossessing Native people, and erroneously educate the general populace, including Black folks, that Native people no longer exist. Again, I cannot reiterate enough how important it is to understand the relationship between literal dispossession and symbolic dispossession through representations of Native people within popular culture. For example, although the Washington Football Team has decided to get rid of its racist symbol and nickname, two Major League Baseball teams, Atlanta and Cleveland, have yet to drop the "Braves" and "Indians," respectively, in their team names. Neither has the Kansas City "Chiefs." I love me some Patrick Mahomes and the rest of the brothas on that team, but it ain't a good look to be asserting Black Lives Matter while not also critiquing the nickname of the team. I hope they at least get rid of the tomahawk chop and chant. King correctly noted that "our literature, our films, our drama . . . all exalt" the erasure of Native people. Finally, King was also correct in asserting that "it was upon this massive base of racism that the prejudice toward the nonwhite was readily built, and found rapid growth."[23]

It should not be surprising, then, that King understood the connections between race and class. Indeed, in May 1967, at a Southern Christian Leadership Conference retreat at the Penn Center in Frogmore, South Carolina, he told his staff, "We must see now that the evils of racism, economic exploitation, and militarism are all tied together, and you really can't get rid of one without getting rid of the others."[24] He essentially understood these three things are key facets of colonialism.[25] Up until the end, just months before his assassination, Dr. King did not forget the plight of Indigenous peoples. He also seemed to warn his primarily Black audience about the limits of trusting white liberals.

In Dr. King's last book, *Where Do We Go from Here: Chaos or Community?* (1968), he reminded his readers that there was a reason why white folks did not embrace equality with Black folks and eliminate their antiblackness: "In dealing with the ambivalence of white America, we must not overlook another form of racism that was relentlessly pursued on American shores: the physical extermination of the American Indian."[26] Once more, Dr. King reminded his audience that it was not simply the actual killing of Native peoples; it was also how that genocide circulated in popular culture. He wrote, "The poisoning of the American mind was accomplished not only by acts of discrimination and exploitation but by the exaltation of murder as an expression of the courage and initiative of the pioneer." Through the massacre of Native people, white settlers were able to affirm their status as the rightful owners of the land. They fought for it, and won. King carefully entangled Black and Indigenous histories: "Just as southern culture was made to appear noble by ignoring the cruelty of slavery, the conquest of the Indian was depicted as an example of bravery and progress."

It is crucial that we expand our view of Dr. King's activist and intellectual agenda so we recognize the lens through which he saw the world did not only include anti-Black racism, economic exploitation, and US military aggression; his lens was wider than that. He also understood that the way the United States treated the Indigenous people and Black Americans within its own borders was easily replicated around the world.[27] This reevaluation of Dr. King helps us rethink how racism developed the United States and what we know about the Black freedom struggles of the 1960s. It should also remind us that racism is not rooted only in anti-Black racism; it is also rooted in Native colonization.

Finally, we may question the need to lump together the struggles of Black and Indigenous peoples, and we can quibble with the fact of Dr. King perhaps naively believing in the ideals of US democracy, liberty, and justice—maybe. But we cannot question his belief that US society needed to change, both in its values and its economic order. He made that focus clear in his final book, "As we work to get rid of the economic strangulation that we face as a result of poverty, we must not overlook the fact that millions of Puerto Ricans, Mexican Americans, Indians and Appalachian whites are also poverty stricken. Any serious war against poverty must of necessity include them."[28] For Native people, King might have challenged anti-Native racism more. Whatever his shortcomings, it is now up to our generation (and the one after) to continue to dismantle not only anti-Black racism but also anti-Native racism and colonialism as well as the racist treatment of the Latinx communities. It is our duty, and will require all of us working as a collective to achieve the radical transformation people like King had fought for, for so long.

FANNIE LOU HAMER

Fannie Lou Hamer should be considered the Queen of Democracy in the South. Working with Black and white organizers, she helped them understand that "Power to the People" meant exactly that. She believed that to organize a mass movement, the people—not the vanguard—should be instrumental in their own change.

Fannie Lou Hamer was born on October 6, 1917, in Montgomery County, Mississippi. Born to James Lee and Ella Townsend, share-croppers in Mississippi, she was the youngest of twenty children. She was the last born, and because plantation owners at that time would compensate families for providing a future field hand, her parents received fifty dollars after her birth, which assisted the family in buying supplies for the winter.[29] Her parents could not escape the racism and exploitation of sharecropping. Hamer had to work hard as a child, and she remembered a particular song that her mother would sing in search of better opportunities for her family:

I'm going to land on the shore.
I'm going to land on the shore.
"I'm going to land on the shore,
Where I'll rest for evermore.

The preacher in the pulpit,
With the Bible in his hands—
He preaching to the sinners
But they just won't understand.

I'm going to land on the shore.
I'm going to land on the shore.
I'm going to land on the shore,
Where I'll rest for evermore.

I would not be a white man,
White as the dropping of snow.
They ain't got God in their heart.
To hell they sho' must go.[30]

The song is more than simply a Christian hymn mixed in with some criticisms of white people. It is a longing for home, which if we listen to many songs in the Black gospel tradition, the singers aren't just referring to returning to heaven. They are also imagining a return to the home of their ancestors, as Aretha Franklin suggests in "Going Down Slow," recorded during her Atlantic Records days. Hamer's mother refers to "land on the shore." What exactly did she mean? It was not simply heaven. It was an imaginary notion of returning home, to exist as Black people—to be free and sovereign, away from white people. The depths of anti-Black racism in the US, coupled with the capitalist system's exploitation, tells us all we need to know about how much whiteness has negatively impacted Black folks, including

Hamer. In this regard, it is no wonder that Hamer became so politicized at an early age. She desired to know why she could not simply
be, and also wanted more for herself, family, and community.

Politicized from an early age, she ascended as a key figure in the
civil rights movement after being fired for trying to register to vote.
She turned that experience into working with the young Black and
white students from the North who wanted to help Black people get
the right to vote. More than being a matter of simply getting the vote,
their actions were a direct challenge to white supremacist rule in the
South. In this way, they were doing a radical act—one that got many
people murdered.

Fannie Lou Hamer is considered a foundational figure in understanding participatory democracy in the US South during the 1960s.
Participatory democracy is different from representative democracy,
which is what we have in the US. In theory, it is the idea that everyone
can participate in the democratic functions of society, and on this
basis, everyone is equal. It is expressed in a term they used to say in
the 1960s: "people power." While the Athenians and Romans im-
plemented participatory democracy in some capacity (they excluded
women and slaves), Black activists like Hamer tried to use it as a
means for Black people to rid themselves of white terror and exclusion
from basic rights such as voting. She understood everyday people,
how to organize and work with them, and helped train and educate
Northern whites and Blacks who came down to help get Black people
registered in Mississippi. She helped people understand that "power
to the people" meant just that—everyday people realizing that real
democratic change and power began and ended with them. She believed that in order to organize a mass movement, the people—not the
vanguard—should be instrumental in their own change. Although not
formally educated, she understood the problems of racial capitalism,
and served as a bridge leader between the local people with whom she
worked and the larger, male-dominated civil rights leadership.[31]

In August 1964, she, as part of a mix of Black and white delegates
that made up the Mississippi Freedom Democratic Party, traveled to
Atlantic City, New Jersey, to unseat the staunch white supremacists
who ran the Democratic Party. They sought a seat at the table so that
they would be able to vote the racists out. In Atlantic City, Hamer gave
a powerful speech, highlighting the abuse she experienced for simply

trying to register to vote. About a month after returning from Atlantic City, Hamer gave a speech at the Negro Baptist School in Indianola, Mississippi.

In that speech, titled "We're on Our Way," she begins by stating where she was from, Ruleville, Mississippi. And she then recounts the time when, in 1962, she and other activists tried to register to vote. By the time she got back to Ruleville, she had already been fired. The white man for whom she worked told her, "You will have to go down and withdraw or you will have to leave." "I didn't register for you," she responded. "I was trying to register myself."[32]

That night, white people shot into three houses she knew of. After recounting this violence, she asks, rhetorically, "Is this America, the land of the free and the home of the brave? Where people are being murdered, lynched, and killed, because we want to register to vote?" She also details the problems associated with not earning a decent wage in Mississippi, her mother working for "one measly dollar and a quarter a day." She then says, "I first wished I was white." Her reason was that white people were "the only people that wasn't doing nothing, but still had money and clothes. We was working year in and year out and wouldn't get to go to school but four months out of the year because we didn't have nothing." Hamer wanted to acquire the class benefits of being white. She articulates what racial capitalism tells us: that class distinctions are borne through race, and race is reflected through class. As W. E. B. Du Bois argues in *Black Reconstruction in America* (1935), whites received a public and psychological wage for being white, even though their actual wages did not increase. Poor whites were accepted by the white elite simply for being white and were given deference over Black people. Their whiteness allowed them the opportunity to say, "Hey, at least I'm not Black." During the 2020 protests in the wake of the murders of Breonna Taylor and George Floyd, President Donald Trump continued to stoke the fires of racial division, arguing that the words "Black Lives Matter" are a symbol of hate. His rhetoric created further division by tapping into a longer history of white elites telling poor and working-class whites that they are losing out on jobs because of the Latinx community coming into the country. Hamer pointed out that the capitalist system of the South exploited Black workers, which created different outcomes for Black and white workers under the Jim Crow system.

Later in the speech, Hamer recounts the severe beating she experienced in a jail in Mississippi, a horrific and vile event, after returning from a voting educational workshop in Charleston, South Carolina, on June 9, 1963. She asks, "How can they say, 'In ten years' time, we will have forced every Negro out of the state of Mississippi?'" Her response to this challenge illustrates another aspect of her radicalism—that of staying put. That is, she and other Black Mississippians were not going anywhere. This was their home. "But I want these people to take a good look at themselves," she says, "and after they've sent the Chinese back to China, the Jews back to Jerusalem, and give the Indians their land back, and they take the Mayflower from which they came, the Negro will still be in Mississippi." Hamer here articulates a point of Black belonging that has been a powerful form of resistance: the steadfastness of blackness. In spite of the trauma of enslavement and white supremacy, Black people will remain. However, she also articulates a point about Black futures on Indigenous land. Although being sent back would be the outcome for the other immigrant groups, this would not be the case for Native people or Black people, who would stay put. Hamer understood that Mississippi and the rest of the US was Indigenous land, and she envisioned a shared future with Indigenous people.

These micro moments are important since they indicate a clear understanding of the violent nature of land being stolen from Native people and the importance of having solidarity with them. It is not clear if Hamer knew people from the Choctaw Band of Mississippi, but it would not be surprising if she did. The Choctaw of Mississippi had formed into their modern iteration in the 1930s under the Indian Reorganization Act. They benefited from the civil rights activities as well. Hamer also likely understood the challenges that Native Americans had faced in Mississippi, especially that of removal and erasure.

MALCOLM X

I have read *The Autobiography of Malcolm X* every summer since I was sixteen; it is my favorite book. During a particularly difficult time in my life, my Advanced Placement US history teacher, Mr. K., gave me a copy of the book after trying to get me to talk to him about my situation. For reasons I don't remember, I did not want to hear from this white man! He pulled out of his bag an original copy of *The Au-tobiography*. As he handed it to me, he said, "I'm white, and I know you've completely tuned me out. But I'm going to give you this old copy of *The Autobiography of Malcolm X*. I hope it helps." I went home that day and read it all within a few days. I could not put the book down. How Malcolm, without apology, described racism and its source helped me see clearly for the first time in my life why I was often very angry. Racism had impacted my life in ways I had never really thought about, and Malcolm gave me the language to understand it. The book changed my life.

During this past summer, while doing my annual re-reading, I was struck by how Malcolm discussed Indigenous people and histories. Malcolm described to Alex Haley how he would go "fishing" for potential new converts, tell them about the history of the "white man's crimes" and why Islam was the religion for the Black man. He made a brief reference to Manhattan: "Go right on down to the tip of Manhattan Island that this devilish white man stole from the trusting Indians for twenty-four dollars!"[33] There are two points here. First, where did Malcolm learn this? Second, it suggests he *was* at least vaguely familiar with Indigenous histories of New York City, though he mistakenly framed Native people as trusting, docile, and without agency.

In another part of the book, the local hustlers taught him how to live a life of crime; they also explained to him histories of Harlem's demographic change over time. Hustlers explained that Harlem was first a Dutch settlement; then came the Germans, then the Irish and Italians, and then Jews. "Today, all these immigrants' descendants are running as hard as they can to escape the descendants of Negroes who helped to unload the immigrant ships."[34] Malcolm continued, "I was staggered when old-timer Harlemites told me that while this immigrant musical chairs game had been going on, Negroes had been in New York City since 1683, before any of them came."[35]

In Malcolm's framing, these European immigrants came to the US, importantly, as settlers who *displaced* Black Americans who, in his estimation, have a more legitimate, even indigenous connection to New York. By mentioning that Black folks were there *first*, he was, in essence, asserting Black claims to New York's origins. This historical rendition tells us about Black relationship to land, but it also suggests a form of ownership, or that Black people were the original people.

Malcolm said nothing of the Indigenous inhabitants, who would have been the Munsee Delaware. "Manhattan" is an Indigenous word that means, "the place where timber is procured for bows and arrows." It is one of the few names found on early colonial maps in New York that has never been removed.

Malcolm used a variety of discourses concerning Black peoples' relationship to the United States, which seemed revolutionary and contradictory. At times, they centered on Black peoples' relationship to place. At other times, he connected to the diaspora. And then at others, he offered direct critiques of US colonization and empire. Ultimately, he was concerned with the condition of blackness and belonging in the US.

Malcolm's idea of liberation was based upon control and domination of land, and though he articulated a vision going forward, it was based upon white masculine logics of land ownership. Malcolm's conception of land is diametrically opposed to Indigenous people's conception of land. And Indigenous feminists' conceptions of land provides important analytical tools in offering alternative visions of human and non-human relationships to land. For example, the artist and activist Michi Saagiig Anishinaabe and the public intellectual Leanne Betasamosake Simpson argue that our conception of land should be based upon consent, and include a deeper meaning of the word "place," which should be a "part of us and our sovereignty rather than an abstract natural resource for unlimited use."[36] For Native people, land is more than a physical space. It is where they construct ideas about themselves. In many Indigenous languages, their tribal identities and stories are rooted in specific places. How they understand history, how they practice culture, and the way they live their lives is based upon their conception of land. Land is not just owning a title to it, but it is also a tribal nation's shared sense of belonging.[37]

MALCOLM X'S BLACK BELONGING

In *Autobiography of Malcolm X*, Malcolm frames Indigenous histories and realities to justify why Black Americans should be granted their rights, based upon their exploited labor: "Twenty-two million black men! They have given America four hundred years of toil."[38] He continues, "They have bled and died in every battle since the Revolution."

He underscores that Blacks have been here before the pilgrims and the massive influx of Eastern European immigrants. And "they are still today at the bottom of everything."[39] Black belonging for Malcolm centered on Black peoples' exploited labor and their rights to land because that labor was central in founding the US nation-state. And yet, in the 1960s they were still not given human dignity and due rights that they clearly deserved.

Early in his political development, he placed a great deal of belief in the power of political lobbies. Malcolm believed that US politics was based on being organized in political blocs, especially lobby and special interest groups. In the *Autobiography*, he asks, "What group has a more urgent special interest, what group needs a bloc, a lobby, more than the black man?"[40] A student of the US political system, he was fully aware of how the government functioned. Itemizing a few of the federal departments and their functions, he mentioned that there is a Department of the Interior for Native people, which for him raises the question, "Is the farmer, the doctor, the Indian, the greatest problem in America today? No—it is the black man!"[41] Malcolm has a particular constituent to whom he is talking to, based upon the black-white binary. But he dismisses the complicated relationship between Indigenous people and the Department of the Interior, which Indigenous people staunchly opposed.[42]

Land was key in Malcolm's understanding of Black liberation and freedom. Black studies scholar Abdul Alkalimat explains, "Our reading [of Malcolm's meaning of land] can be full and accurate only when we understand that he uses the word 'land' to represent political economy, the basis for a people's survival."[43] Alkalimat describes Malcolm's analytic use and construal of land in four ways: (1) land as agriculture for domestic consumption, to grow the domestic market, (2) land as production resource for export to the world markets for hard exchange, (3) land as space for national unity, (4) land as a place for a state, either a national state or multinational state.[44]

If land is central, how does Alkalimat also forget that we live in a settler state? If land is a space for national unity or a multinational state, as Alkalimat argues, where are Indigenous people supposed to go? We do not know because Malcolm X never went on record about what he might do with the "Indigenous question," likely because he believed that the "white man" had exterminated the "Indian."

Malcolm's style, frankness, and ability to "make it plain" for his audience made him one of the more well-known, if not beloved, Black activists of the 1960s. As a result, he remains, among a wide range of activists, from Black nationalists to communists, an icon long after his death. Although he did not invent the Nation of Islam or its rhetoric of Black supremacy, his efforts made that discourse open to both the Black and white public spheres, with mixed results. Yet, as powerful a rhetorician as he was, Malcolm X was, on the one hand, a powerful voice of the Black oppressed, and, on the other hand, an uncritical participant in settler-colonial discourse, at least early on in his political development. In other words, he accepted the European American belief that Native people had disappeared. Malcolm based his belief that the US government owed Black people land on two conclusions: one, because Native people were "invisible" as a result of being duped out of their land, the US government had land that it could entrust to Black people; and two, Black folks had earned a right to land through their labor during slavery.

Malcolm believed that Black separation from whites was essential for Black freedom. That is, white Americans were not going to truly accept Black people into their society; therefore, they should have land of their own. While civil rights activists sought to reform US society so that it would become integrated, Malcolm reminded Black people that they weren't anything more than second-class citizens, and would never be full citizens because, unlike white people, Black people "didn't come here on the *Mayflower*."[45] Instead, he reminded them, they were brought here by the architects of US democracy.

He also argued that Black people were owed land because of their exploited labor and the blood they had shed in wars. Black people had indeed fought in every war since the American Revolution, for the ability to be a citizen of the US. Black people had made a "greater sacrifice than anybody" and had "collected less" than any other group. For this reason, Malcolm believed no one deserved land more than Black people. Malcolm's argument exists in certain Black nationalist discourses today, including that of the American Descendants of Slavery, or ADOS. Let's sit back and think about the implications of Malcolm's argument. If Black people deserve land, what about the Native people who were forcibly removed from those southern states? It is a question that Black nationalists have rarely, if ever, truly engaged with. In other words, we can't uncritically assert Black land ownership without understanding the possibilities of continuing the ongoing genocide and land theft against Native people.

Malcolm's belief in a separate land for Black people made a lot of sense. If a nation-state that purports to uphold democracy, equality, and freedom does not actually do so in practice, and if Black folks are barred from voting and participating in civic life, why wouldn't you advocate for separation? However, Malcolm's erasure of Indigenous histories and rights would have benefited his case greatly.

Since the writing of the US Constitution, the US government understood Native peoples to be sovereign nations, although unequal in status to the US. In the *Cherokee v. Georgia* decision of 1831, Chief Justice John Marshall wrote that Native Americans were a "domestic dependent nation." They were separate from other US citizens, and to be governed by different laws but dependent upon the higher authority of the US government. This idea of the domestic dependent nation is the basis for contemporary legal relations between the US government and tribal nations. It raises tough questions, such as, are tribal nations truly sovereign under this arrangement? Has the ideology of the domestic dependent nation hampered our ability to be visionary about what a future would look like outside of this arrangement? Finally, how sacred are treaties if one party—the US government— doesn't keep its end of the bargain?

Perhaps Malcolm best articulated the importance of Black land as an integral part of Black liberation in a speech delivered in Detroit. That speech, titled "Message to the Grassroots" and given on November 10, 1963, remains perhaps one of his most eloquent public speeches on the necessity of a Black revolution. In this speech, he spends significant time outlining his historical understanding of revolution, including the American, French, and Russian Revolutions. While many read this speech as an outline of Malcolm's belief in the need for revolutionary violence—juxtaposing it against the use of nonviolence—I understand this speech to be a call for Black land ownership in the US, different from the vision of Elijah Muhammad. While Muhammad wanted a separate land in order to build a Black nation, it was solely so it could be left alone. Through his reading of historical revolutions, Malcolm, on the other hand, believed the only way to get land was through revolution. For Malcolm, land was a necessary condition of Black liberation in the United States.

Malcolm began "Message to the Grassroots" by stating, "I would like to make a few comments about the difference between the Black Revolution and the Negro Revolution." To make this argument, he defined the term "revolution" by offering historical examples. Malcolm explained, "When you study the historic nature of revolutions, and the methods used in a revolution, you may change your goal and you may change your mind." He continued, and here I quote at length:

> Look at the American Revolution, in 1776. That revolution was for what? For land. Why did they want land? Independence. How was it carried out? Bloodshed. Number one it was based on land—the basis of independence. And the only way they could get it, was bloodshed. The French Revolution, what was it based on? The landless against the landlord. What was it for? Land. How did they get it? Bloodshed. Was no love lost, was no compromise, was no negotiation. I'm telling you, you don't know what a revolution is, cause when you find out what it is, you'll get back in the alley, you'll get out of the way. The Russian Revolution, what was it based on? Land. The landless against the landlord. How did they bring it about? Bloodshed. You haven't got a revolution that doesn't involve bloodshed.[46]

While he is simplifying the goals of these revolutions for his particular audience, his point should not be understated. Malcolm was very adept at discussing political revolutions on the African continent and throughout the underdeveloped world. His discussion of land poses a difficult question that he, and those that tried to follow his logical conclusion after his assassination struggled with: How can you compare the decolonization efforts occurring on the African continent with what *should* happen in the US, given that the US was not Black land? Decolonization efforts on the African continent happened on Africans' land, marking a fundamentally different situation than what Black people faced. Indigenous people in the US settler society did not even register in these analyses except as they related to the white-constructed idea that white people had simply wiped out all of the Indians. While attempting to place the Black American struggle

within worldwide efforts for liberation, Malcolm and others participated in discourses of omission.

Malcolm's discourse of Black belonging as it related to land unfortunately perpetuated racial projects in the US—one that was based
upon a Black and white racial binary, as well as a very masculine,
settler idea of how land should be utilized. Though going global in
his analyses and pointing toward a connection with the Global South
and peoples' attempts to rid themselves of colonialism, he failed to
clearly understand the *actual* social and political conditions in a land
they called home. Malcolm's reference to the American Revolution
presents another point of contention. In one sense, yes, that revolution
was about land. But once the revolution was won, they needed to remove Native people to secure that land. Furthermore, Native peoples
participated in that fight with their own agendas of maintaining land,
on both the American and British sides. Though unable to develop
fully his ideas for Black liberation, Malcolm did develop an elementary rubric for placing Black Americans within the global struggle for
human rights.

In the last two years of his life, especially after his split from the
Nation of Islam and Elijah Muhammad, Malcolm X exemplified a
greater analysis of the Black American condition within the larger
international struggle against colonialism. He discussed the North
Vietnamese's fight for freedom and traveled extensively throughout
the African continent. Speaking with dignitaries like Jomo Kenyatta
and Kwame Nkrumah, he saw firsthand how they challenged European colonialism. As a result, he framed his own thinking about the
Black American condition within colonial terms. Yet, this framing and
analysis begs the question: How can you discuss Black Americans as
primary settler-colonial subjects when the US is (1) a settler-colonial
state and (2) Indigenous people still lived on this land? Yes, everyone
is impacted by settler colonialism, but the experiences of people vary,
especially if this is not one's land. While we cannot have expected
Malcolm to be all-encompassing in his understanding of colonialism,
his thinking was responsible for a generation after him who continued
to frame the Black American condition in colonial terms, even while
they acknowledged that those terms were imperfect.[47]

In one of his final speeches, given in February 1965 at the Ford
Auditorium in Detroit, Malcolm made clear his attempt to globalize

the US Black freedom struggle. He articulated a particular version of colonialism: "I might point out right here that colonialism or imperialism, as the slave system of the West is called, is not something that's just confined to England or France or the United States."[48] Malcolm continued, "It's one huge complex or combine, and it creates what's known not as the American power structure or the French power structure, but it's an international power structure."[49] He understood the nature of imperialism, and how it connected in unique ways. This international power structure that Malcolm articulated was "used to suppress the masses of dark-skinned people all over the world and exploit them of their natural resources."[50] Although the labor of Black Americans was being exploited, the question of whose land was being exploited and, more importantly, who belonged on that land was still in question.

Again, this discourse ignores Native histories and claims of exploitation in difficult ways. Unfortunately, because of the assassination of Malcolm X, we cannot know for sure his thoughts on Black liberation as it related to Indigenous people. There were moments, however, where Malcolm understood the preciousness of Black belonging in the United States was based not only on how the state treated Black people but also how it treated its Indigenous population.

BLACK BELONGING AND THE AMERICAN NIGHTMARE?

To be clear, Malcolm did not believe that Black people could integrate into the burning house that was US democracy. He crafted a perspective on Black belonging in the US that erased Indigenous peoples and histories. For example, in the now resurrected "three chapters" that were recently purchased by the Schomburg Center for Research in Black Culture, not included in the published version of *The Autobiography of Malcolm X*, he made many remarks about Indigenous genocide as a foil through which to understand the possibilities of Black liberation in the US.

Malcolm understood well the connections between the image and history of people and how it played out in the cultural domain. He understood that the Black image was used for exploitation: "When I say that the Negro is an invention of the white man, think of what an 'invention' is for. When anyone invents something, it is something he needs to make his life easier, to make him richer, and meanwhile something that he can control."[51] Here, Malcolm offers a deep reading of racial capitalism, and the connections between imagery and Black exploitation. To see Black people as nothing much more than workers helps to continue that exploitation.

Malcolm did not believe in US democracy. He sharply criticized the belief that Blacks could be integrated into US society. In one of his more well-known quotes, taken from a speech he made in Cleveland in 1964, he discusses the American nightmare:

> No, I'm not an American. I'm one of the 22 million black people who are the victims of Americanism. One of the 22 million black people who are victims of democracy, nothing but disguised hypocrisy. So, I'm not standing here speaking to you as an American, or a patriot, or a flag-saluter, or a flag-waver—no, not I. I am speaking through the eyes of the victim. I don't see any American dream; I see an American nightmare.[52]

He urged Black people to understand that if white Americans didn't include the Indigenous people, then why would they treat their formerly enslaved population with human dignity? Malcolm wrote, "This American white man even here doesn't extend 'democracy' and 'brotherhood' to the native, American born, non-white."[53] It is not clear as to what Malcolm understood about the Indigenous condition during his time. However, he also wanted Black folks to understand their outsider status in the US. "And the 'Negro,' for years has been physically in America, but functionally outside, looking in."[54] This is ironic given the centrality that Black folks played in the development of the US economy. Still, Malcolm warned Black folks that they "must realize for all practical purposes that [the Black person in the US] is not an American, in the Constitutional sense, nor in the other ways that white people are Americans."[55]

Finally, Malcolm had hope for the future of radical transformation in society. Though he did not mention any specifics of who was doing what, he wrote, "The black and brown and red and yellow peoples have begun rebelling today, and are sick and tired of it."[56] It is clear that as Malcolm traveled more, encountered more people, he began to understand the interconnectedness between colonialism and racism, and how this worked globally. However, he was murdered in 1965, and we don't know how he might have developed different viewpoints at the height of Indigenous radicalism in the early 1970s. I'm sure he would have been more than supportive.

After Malcolm was assassinated, his half-sister, Ella L. Collins, took over the leadership of the Organization of Afro-American Unity (OAAU). Malcolm had formed the group in 1964 after the Nation of Islam forced him out of his leadership position as national spokesman. It was a secular organization that allowed him to engage in the larger Black movement for liberation. According to an April 1967 article in the *Chicago Defender*, Collins said that the OAAU was close to purchasing a thousand acres of land in an unknown site in New York. Called a "back-to-farm effort," she believed that the "colonies" that would settle on the land would not only end the oppression of Black people but also end the need to protest. She argued that they would create their own laws based upon their "original culture and moral foundations." And if white people tried to stop them, they would "fight back," in the words of her late brother, "by any means necessary."[57] It is not known if they were successful in securing land, but the question remains: even if they got land, what about the Indigenous peoples of New York? Where would they have fit into those Black "colonies"? If Malcolm X sought to secure land, James Baldwin sought to liberate the US from itself, through critique and love.

JAMES BALDWIN

Most of us who have read the novels and nonfiction writing of James Baldwin have our own version of him. Some see him as a brilliant, Black queer novelist. Others see him as a voice that dared hold a mirror up to white America so it might see itself. In yet another version, he's like close family—my close friends refer to him as "Uncle James or Uncle JB." I loved his work from the time I was introduced to him in a civil rights course in James Madison College. He helped me think beyond Malcolm X and then circle back and gain greater appreciation for him. If Malcolm X helped me think in terms of American's inability to reform and include Black Americans on an equal basis, Baldwin helped me imagine that maybe, just maybe, if we all critique and struggle for the soul of the US, if white people really understood how oppressed people feel, things can change. Although I'm pessimistic about the reformation of American democracy, Baldwin remains a reminder of possibility—that freedom is just around the corner.

In 2017, Raoul Peck's documentary *I Am Not Your Negro* was released, and I was excited to see it and think with it. After watching it twice, I eventually wrote a reflection called "Indigenous Genocide and Black Liberation," which was originally published on the *Indian Country Today* website and was received well by many Native people. I share parts of it here as a way to offer a critical reflection of Baldwin and his understanding of Black belonging.

In February 2017, during a warm Sunday afternoon in North Carolina, I went to watch *I Am Not Your Negro*. I felt all of the emotions. Anger. Sadness. Joy. Deep reflection. I appreciated the genius of Baldwin combined with the narrative and visual storytelling of Peck. I felt the despair of racism and idealism of liberation. I suppose I experienced all of the emotions that James Baldwin would want someone to feel when they engage with his work.

The documentary is a discussion of race in the United States. It is, like much of Baldwin's work, a mirror for white America to see its problems. In his writing, he encouraged Black people not to accept the visuals of blackness that white people propagated. As he wrote in *The Fire Next Time*, "There is no need for you to try and become like white people" for "they are, in effect, trapped in a history which they do not understand; and until they understand it, they cannot be released from it."[58]

The documentary is based on thirty pages of a book Baldwin was going to write on the meaning of the deaths of his three personal friends: Medgar Evers, Malcolm X, and Martin Luther King Jr. The film blends historical interviews featuring Baldwin and other notable figures, as well as recent video of the rebellion in Ferguson. The images make it powerful and disturbing, reminding one of the long history and all-encompassing nature of antiblackness in this country. We must recognize antiblackness (and anti-Indianness, too!) as a core part of this country's material and psychological development, and Baldwin reminds us of that. As English literature and Black studies scholar Christina Sharpe argues in *In the Wake: On Blackness and Being* (2016), "At stake is not recognizing antiblackness as total climate."[59] In other words, anti-Black racism is foundational to the US;

culture, it is everywhere, and we are all products of it. Through the words of Baldwin, narrated by Samuel L. Jackson, the documentary is powerful.

But I couldn't help but notice how Baldwin's rhetoric and Peck's use of images at various points in the documentary relied on the history of Indigenous genocide. For instance, Baldwin, at a debate with the conservative personality William Buckley, held at Cambridge University, stated:

> In the case of the American Negro, born in that glittering republic, and the moment you are born, since you don't know any better, every stick and stone, and every face is white. And since you have not yet seen a mirror, you suppose that you are too. It comes as a great shock, around the age of five, or six, or seven, to discover that the flag to which you have pledged allegiance, along with everybody else, has not pledged allegiance to you. It comes as a great shock to discover that Gary Cooper killing off the Indians, when you were rooting for Gary Cooper, the Indians were you. It comes as a great shock to discover that the country which is your birthplace and to which you owe your life and your identity, has not, in its whole system of reality, evolved any place for you.[60]

Here Baldwin uses the history of Indigenous genocide to describe how race was constructed, and how Black Americans should be cautious about what could ultimately be their own demise: genocide. The issue here is that Baldwin, like other activists during the time, described Indigenous genocide as an afterthought, ignoring Native resistance. Baldwin used the history of settler colonialism as a prophetic tool, a prop to Black Americans to say this: if you don't resist white supremacy and racism, if you don't fight oppression, you will be treated just like the "Indians," and killed off.

Peck blended Baldwin's words with images of Native genocide, including old westerns where white men were shooting Native people. Perhaps the most egregious example was a scene from *Soldier Blue* (1970), directed by Ralph Nelson, which was a rendition of the Sand Creek Massacre in 1864. In this scene, four soldiers, holding a Native woman at gunpoint, ripped off her clothing, leaving her naked for the audience's gaze. In the following scene in the documentary, you see pictures from the Wounded Knee Massacre, which occurred in December 1890, and remains one of the largest massacres in US history. As you see dead Indigenous bodies, you can hear Samuel L. Jackson narrate, "It reveals the weakness, even the panic, of the adversary."

This sequence of scenes is both disturbing and illuminating. It reveals the erasure of Native people in the contemporary sense, as well as the fear that Black people have of their demise—they know what white people have done and can do. Imagining Black death is cruel indeed, but seeing Indigenous death with no illustration of people who fought against settler encroachment is bone-chilling. It perpetuates the settler nation-states' myth constructed as a fact, of Indigenous disappearance.

Native people did not disappear. The Native disappearance myth is as old as the founding of the country. Just as racism is embedded into the fabric of society, so, too, is Indigenous disappearance.[61] Native people have fought and continue to fight. Whether it is the Shawnee warrior trying to carve out land for Indigenous peoples, or the water protectors at Standing Rock trying to halt the building of the Dakota Access Pipeline, or Indigenous rappers producing rhymes to assert their presence, Native people are not disappearing, and will exist in the aftermath of settler colonialism and white supremacy.

These scenes demonstrate a tension between Black liberation and Indigenous dispossession. They elucidate how the settler state constructed the parallel but different treatment of Black and Indigenous peoples and continues to construct it today, and also how Blacks construct an idea of liberation.

REMIX AND REFLECTION ON BALDWIN

As you can see, I was critical not just of Baldwin but also of Peck and the imagery he used. However, I want to explain my new reluctance to be so critical. First, I think that there are some Native people that used my own work to readily engage in antiblackness. It's a hard thing to prove, but the fact that some were so easily in agreement (even excited?) about my criticism of a Black civil rights legend and literary giant made me pause. Is it because Native people want some clout? It's hard to tell. However, I want to give Baldwin more context and engage in some of his work as it relates to how he viewed Black Americans in the formation of US democracy, and where he viewed them going forward. I also want to give fuller context to his debate at Cambridge University with the 1960s conservative darling Buckley.

The debate between the two men was held on October 26, 1965. Baldwin was surely still in shock over the assassination of Malcolm X earlier that year. They debated the question "Has the American Dream been achieved at the expense of the American Negro?" Baldwin won the debate by a wide margin, but I don't want to spend too much time analyzing the debate.[62] What is important for me is his discussion of the American Dream, and how Black people did not fit into it.

In his opening remarks, Baldwin expressed his thoughts on what exactly the American Dream meant. He shifted the rhetorical meaning, and argued that the way one engages such a topic depends on their reality. He connected the white South Africans and the French in Algeria—both settler colonies—and the Mississippi sharecropper as people who brutally enact oppression. He told his British audience that white supremacy came from Europe. It is in this context in which he discussed the longer history of violence toward Black people. Baldwin then goes on to explain all the ways a white supremacist nation-state impacts Black people, arguing,

> By the time you are thirty, you have been through a certain kind of mill. And the most serious effect of the mill you've been through is, again, not the catalog of disaster, the policemen, the taxi drivers, the waiters, the landlady, the landlord, the banks, the insurance companies, the millions of details, twenty-four hours of every day, which spell out to you that you are a worthless human being. It is not that. It's by the time you've begun to see it happening, in your daughter or your son, or your niece or your nephew.

Baldwin gave an entire context to his problem with racism and Black belonging. White supremacy—and all of the structural barriers that Black people face in trying to belong to a place they were forced to come to in the first place—is a cyclical phenomenon. Eventually, a family's children suffer the same effect.

Baldwin also made a claim to land. As I've emphasized, land has always been a major part of Black belonging. "If one has got to prove one's title to the land, isn't four hundred years enough? At least three wars? The American soil is full of the corpses of my ancestors. Why is my freedom or my citizenship, or my right to live there, how is it conceivably a question now?" Baldwin asked. While he can be critiqued for erasing, or not including, Native claims to land, what do we do with his comment about American soil having the corpses of his ancestors? We should sit with this question, and reflect deeply on it. It is not just a claim to land because one's ancestors worked it, and therefore they should own a piece of the American Dream. I would argue that Baldwin, and others as well, engaged in something deeper. If the history and effects of enslavement are real, then those bones could never really rest. Their spirits may continue to wander because this was not their home, even as they attempted to make home as best as they could. Having to engage in this sense of loss is important.

In addition, Baldwin also commented on the lack of history that Black children came to understand as their own. "When I was growing up, I was taught in American history books, that Africa had no history, and neither did I. That I was a savage about whom the less said, the better, who had been saved by Europe and brought to America. And, of course, I believed it. I didn't have much choice." Baldwin was not the first person to make such an observation, but his point remains: it's difficult to construct a sense of place outside of antiblackness when you don't know your own history. Finally, Baldwin commented on the deep significance African Americans drew from decolonization during the postwar era: "This gave an American Negro for the first time a sense of himself beyond the savage or a clown." For Baldwin, focusing on Black belonging and Native genocide was a way to analyze the importance of coming to terms with the problems of white supremacy—the root cause of the Black situation and why they could not obtain the American Dream, a dream premised on Black inequality.

Baldwin had a particular way of writing about Black people that served as a mirror for white Americans, illustrating how they think about themselves. One of Baldwin's most important nonfiction works was *Notes of a Native Son* (1955), his first collection of essays, the majority of which he wrote living in Paris. Let's first unpack his title. The use of "native" in the title is not to suggest that he is an Indigenous person in the United States. However, within the white-constructed image of Black people in US society, it suggests that he and other Black people are a creation of white America. That is, their ancestors did not desire to come to the US, but within the context of the travesty of enslavement, they were forced to come to deal with the reality of white racism.

For instance, in the essay "Many Thousands Gone," which is a critical reflection and discussion of the meaning of Richard Wright's acclaimed novel *Native Son*, Baldwin offers his thoughts on Black people in the white imagination. In the second paragraph, he writes, "The story of the Negro in America is the story of America—or, more precisely, it is the story of Americans."[63] He directs his focus not on the forced creation of Black people of their own accord but on what it reveals about American society. Baldwin continues, "What it means to be a Negro in America can perhaps be suggested by an examination of the myths we perpetuate about him."[64] Here, Baldwin points to the visibility of Black people (or lack thereof) in the white imagination, what he identifies as a set of myths that simply exist to perpetuate the invisibility of black humanity in the eyes of whites, non-Blacks, and even Black people—even as Black people have fought over and over again to imaginatively assert their humanity throughout US history. In this way, Black humanity's invisibility is not much different from the invisibility that Indigenous peoples experience, albeit their existence is ignored altogether. What binds the Black and Indigenous experiences together, and what we might extrapolate from Baldwin, is that to have your humanity invisible renders you inhuman to white people, and thus, they can construct you in any way they desire.

Baldwin also challenged white Americans to think about what it means to be a Black person on this continent: "Negroes are Americans and their destiny is the country's destiny." In search for a respect and recognition from white Americans, Baldwin wrote, "They have no other experience on this continent and it is an experience which cannot be rejected, which yet remains embraced."[65] For Baldwin, in order for any recognition of Black humanity to occur, white people had to understand that Black folks were their kin. I disagree with Baldwin. For one, there are white allies who have recognized that the US was a fundamentally flawed project, including one of my favorite nineteenth-century abolitionists, John Brown, who attempted to take over Harpers Ferry in 1859, for which he was hanged. And white women like Viola Liuzzo, who left her home in Detroit to travel to Selma, Alabama, to march for Black rights during the historic March in Selma on March 25, 1965. A mother of five and the wife of a union leader, she was murdered by the Ku Klux Klan that same night.

For the majority of white Americans, it is debatable whether or not they even believe in Black and Indigenous equality, let alone seeing all three of their destinies going in the same direction. However, for Black and Indigenous peoples, Native people in the US might consider seriously that their destinies have been tied together since European settlement. If Indigenous dispossession and genocide and African enslavement and atmospheric antiblackness have remained parallel yet intertwined social, political, and economic processes, then we should continue to find common ground in our pursuit for liberation. To put it simply, Black people are Indigenous North America's destiny, and Native people are Black America's destiny. And for those non-Black and non-Indigenous people of color and white allies who want to hop onto the Black and Indigenous freedom train, just check your anti-blackness and anti-Indianness before you board. Collective liberation is possible, and we will need everyone.

If this chapter has illustrated anything, it reveals that even Black folks, who truly want freedom, can erase Native peoples. It can be difficult for non-Indigenous people of color to really remember and include Indigenous peoples in their idea of liberation. But we must do so. If we end anti-Black racism today, will that also end Indigenous erasure and ongoing settler colonialism? To be honest, I'm uncertain; I'm not confident it will. That is why we have to end all forms of oppression at the same time. While we are focused on making sure that black lives matter, we need to do some behind-the-scenes work on other fronts so that, when the time comes, we all get our freedom.

CHAPTER SIX

BLACK POWER AND RED POWER, FREEDOM AND SOVEREIGNTY

IN JUNE 1976, the *Black Scholar* published a special issue titled "The Third World." While the discourse of third world struggles focused on liberation efforts in Africa, Asia, and Latin America, the folks at the *Black Scholar* also considered how third world oppression also operated within the United States. "For the Third World peoples have a common history of dehumanization and oppression based on race," wrote the editors. "This is what binds Afro-Americans, Mexican-Americans, Asian-Americans and Native Americans to their ancestors and relatives in distant lands." They went on to describe the specific histories of what connected these seemingly disparate socio-historical relationships:

> This common history of oppression began with the advent of European colonialism and its brutal accomplice, the slave system. Native-Americans found their lands ruthlessly stolen and themselves decimated by enslavement and European diseases. Millions upon millions of Africans were torn from their villages, tossed into slave vessels and transported thousands of miles to be forced to labor in mines and on plantations in the "New World."[1]

They believed that unity and liberation were possible because of their shared oppression, their colonial situation. They wrote, "Thus the common struggle—the struggle of Third World people inside and

outside the U.S. for freedom and independence—is far from completed. No doubt there are many uphill battles yet to be waged. But
a history of unity in oppression has laid the basis for a new unity in
struggle among Third World peoples—and this growing unity is the
best assurance that a world free of racism, oppression and exploitation—a truly new world—can be born."[2] It is interesting that Black
radical intellectuals and activists held this belief; however, the settler
state has erased our collective memories and our imagination about
what might be possible for our collective freedom.

This chapter seeks to analyze the contested relationship between
Black and Indigenous intellectuals and activists during the freedom
struggles of the 1960s and 1970s. During this era of what historian
Jeffrey O. G. Ogbar has called "radical ethnic nationalism," Black and
Indigenous activists sought to radically transform their predicaments
in a white supremacist settler society.[3] They forged coalitions. They
viewed their movements separately, but what brought them together
in protest and ideological struggle was a complete overturning of the
capitalist, settler-colonial, and white supremacist system that had kept
them oppressed for centuries.

During the Black freedom struggle, which, for analytical purposes,
lasted from the late 1950s until the late 1970s, there was also a parallel
movement for Indigenous treaty rights. Native Americans, just like
Black Americans, struggled for power. They wanted a return of land
and a restoration of sovereignty. Like Black folks, they held sit-ins,
they held fish-ins.[4] While Black folks were creating rebellions in the
North and South, Indigenous peoples were traveling to cities from
reservations in great numbers. They were also fomenting rebellions
of their own; from taking government buildings to taking over Alcatraz Island, Indigenous people showed that they were alive and well.
These groups also overlapped ideologically. As Robert Warrior and
Paul Chaat Smith note in their book *Like a Hurricane* (1995), radical
Indigenous groups like the American Indian Movement, led by Dennis Banks, Clyde Bellecourt, and, later, Russell Means, "forged key
alliances with progressive lawyers, civil rights activists, and journalists. They also understood that good news coverage was an involved
and two-way process."[5] Smith and Warrior also note that AIM members also "borrowed from the Black Panthers or other groups when

necessary."[6] Not only did Indigenous activists and intellectuals borrow from Black Power groups, but they also diligently studied them and worked with them.

DISCOURSES OF BLACK AND RED POWER

The discourse of Black Power and Red Power existed side by side. The phrase "Black Power" emerged as a rallying cry in Greenwood, Mississippi, in June 1966, in a speech by Stokely Carmichael during the March Against Fear, which was organized after the shooting of James Meredith.[7] While there were earlier iterations of "Black Power," Carmichael popularized it.[8] In *Black Power: The Politics of Liberation*, Carmichael and Charles Hamilton wrote, "The adoption of the concept of Black Power is one of the most legitimate and healthy developments in American politics and race relations in our time. . . . It is a call for black people in this country to unite, to recognize their heritage, to build a sense of community. It is a call for black people to begin to define their own goals, to lead their own organizations and to support those organizations. It is a call to reject the racist institutions and values of this society."[9] Though Carmichael would later think beyond nation-state borders, he did understand that one had to have a clear sense of self before demanding rights and protections from a state that was predicated on your exploitation.

Native people also participated in the rhetorical power games, raising a fist and utilizing the phrase "Red Power." Though the etymology of the phrase is not entirely clear, it was most definitely an assertion of Indigenous sovereignty, a declaration that Native people were there to stress to the white settlers that they were reclaiming their right to sovereignty—guaranteed by their treaties. Indigenous intellectuals like Vine Deloria Jr. agreed.

Deloria Jr., a Standing Rock Sioux intellectual, was long a prominent voice for Indigenous rights, including in his role as the executive director of the National Congress of American Indians from 1964 to 1967. In perhaps his most provocative book, *Custer Died for Your Sins: An Indian Manifesto* (1969), Deloria shared his belief that the rhetorical assertion of Black Power was an important step toward Black nationalism. For him, white Americans did their best to segregate Black people from entering their neighborhoods, their schools, and their political system. They wanted Black labor but not their full participation in society. In contrast, white people attempted to assimilate Native people in order to take their land.[10] Deloria beckoned Black people to understand that mainstream society had no desire to include them.[11] After reading Deloria, I was like damn, was he trying to do his best Malcolm impersonation? Regardless, Deloria's assertion generally remains true. Instead of keeping Black people out, corporations with hardly any people of color will ask an activist or scholar of color to teach them how to be antiracist. They might pay you, but they don't want the truth. Anti-racism is not something that can be taught once; it requires a sustained relationship and a dedication to systematically ending racism.

For Deloria, the discourse of civil rights was a road to nowhere, and designed to make white liberals feel good. He realized that the state did not want Black self-determination, writing:

> Civil rights as a movement for legal equality ended when the blacks dug beneath the equality of fictions which white liberals had used to justify their great crusade. Black power, as a communications phenomenon, was a godsend to other groups. It clarified the intellectual concepts which had kept Indians and Mexicans confused and allowed the concept of self-determination suddenly to become valid.[12]

Deloria understood the power of Black rhetoric for others. He believed that Stokely Carmichael's declaration of Black Power made more sense to Indigenous peoples because it was based upon the language of power and sovereignty. Deloria advocated for Black folks to find a home. "To survive, blacks must have a homeland where they can withdraw, drop the façade of integration, and be themselves," he wrote.[13] Finally, Deloria left open the possibility of Black and Indigenous solidarity and, perhaps, even a shared space: "Hopefully black militancy will return to nationalist philosophies which relate to the ongoing conception of the tribe as a nation extending in time and occupying space. If such is possible within the black community, it may be possible to bring the problems of minority groups into a more realistic focus and possible solution in the years ahead."[14] I understand Deloria to being open to forming a new society, where Black and Indigenous peoples share a common space, where we all live and work together—imagining the aftermath of ongoing dispossession.[15]

Black and Indigenous people also participated in each other's struggles for liberation. They showed up to each other's protests, including the takeover of the Bureau of Indian Affairs in 1972 and the occupation of Wounded Knee in 1973. In 1972, while in Washington, DC, Pan-Africanist Stokely Carmichael showed up during the third day of the takeover of the Bureau of Indian Affairs, in which Native activists stormed the office, took it over, and retrieved thousands of documents related to tribal issues. Carmichael, speaking as head of the All-African People's Revolutionary Party (AAPRP), offered to "support this movement 100 percent. The question of native Americans is not just a question of civil rights," he said. "This land is their land . . . we have agreed to do whatever we can to provide help . . . there can be no settlement until their land is returned to them."[16] Carmichael understood what it meant to be in solidarity with Indigenous peoples on their land. Vernon Bellecourt, a founding member of the American Indian Movement who became one of its key spokesmen, fondly remembered Carmichael's sustained support of Native causes in the US. At a memorial service in 1998 celebrating the life of Carmichael at City College, Bellecourt remarked, "Brother Kwame Ture was the first to come in and show his solidarity with the indigenous struggles of the Americas. One year later, at Wounded Knee, the AAPRP and Kwame Ture were there standing with us."[17] Another example of solidarity was that of Angela Davis. Davis, a radical Black intellectual who had at the time been recently forced to go on the run, attempted to show up and support the resistance at Wounded Knee, though the FBI denied her from joining the occupation.[18]

On February 24, 1974, in Detroit, Michigan, Davis participated in a rally to end political repression. Sponsored by the Michigan Alliance Against Repression and attended by more than one thousand people, Davis gave a speech covering a variety of topics, including the recent election of Detroit's first Black mayor, Coleman A. Young. Regarding this historic event, she remarked, "The fires of revolutionary struggle are raging in Detroit."[19] Also there was Clyde Bellecourt, a member of the American Indian Movement, demonstrating the forging of a Black and Indigenous radicalism that had been vibrant since the 1960s. There to raise funds for those under political repression who occupied Wounded Knee, Bellecourt shared with the Detroit audience that he hoped the US would live up to its treaty obligations toward tribal nations. He also commented on the limitations of being an Indigenous person born in a settler colony, remarking that they become "political prisoners of the United States at birth."

They also showed some historical and ideological connections in public discourse. While this discourse is not always cordial, it demonstrates to me that Black and Indigenous people were aware of each other's struggles, and did their best to understand how this relationship might look going forward. Though some in the Black media did not believe that Wounded Knee was a Black issue, others disagreed. Writing for the Black newspaper the *Los Angeles Sentinel*, Emily Gibson asserted, "Black-controlled media has a special role to play informing us and laying the foundation for a unity which is broader than race."[20] Nevertheless, people like Bellecourt and Davis understood that to achieve radical change, they needed to support one another. Although their political goals might be different, they both wanted a complete uprooting of the capitalist colonial order.

Others believed that issues like those raised at Wounded Knee offered Afro-Indigenous peoples the opportunity to rightfully claim their heritage. In the *Chicago Defender*, Reverend Curtis E. Burrell Jr., a longtime Chicago activist and reverend who identified as a Choctaw Freeman from Mississippi, wrote that it was time for Black Indians to reclaim their history. He called upon Black people to "look at their Indian heritage which goes beyond civil rights consciousness." He desired that Black folks "deal with a consciousness of sovereignty." In the context of the struggle at Wounded Knee, he believed that "we must . . . not confuse civil rights with sovereign rights." He challenged civil rights activists, such as Ralph Abernathy, who went to Wounded Knee, to think critically about what possibilities civil rights offered:

> The black protest represented by Martin Luther King was a call for equal treatment under the Constitution for all citizens. But the Indian heritage says—we have never nullified our sovereign rights as a nation and we see the white man setting up a sovereignty within our sovereign boundaries. He, therefore, does not seek equal rights under the Constitution—he rejects the Constitution as having authority over him, for he has his own laws and customs and values,

and is non-conformist to the white man's ways. He charges the government which represents this Constitution with violating 371 treaties of agreement.

Therefore, civil rights and sovereign rights have a vast difference between them. The civil rights leaders who rushed off to Wounded Knee, ought to think before they speak. They must ask themselves if they are prepared to relate to their total history as black Indians. They must therefore, ask themselves if they are ready to deal with this.[21]

It is difficult to know how much this opinion affected the Black readers of the *Chicago Defender*. But as one of the premier Black newspapers, it hopefully had some impact on readers and prompted them to think carefully about the meaning and possibilities of Indigenous sovereignty, and also reclaim and assert Afro-Indigenous heritage. While some in the Black media were engaged in the work of solidarity, groups like the Republic of New Afrika were making their own claims to freedom.

IN SEARCH OF A PLACE CALLED HOME:
THE REPUBLIC OF NEW AFRIKA

The assassination of Malcolm X, on February 21, 1965, remains a sore spot for Black folks and human rights activists around the world. Scholars still speculate about the trajectory of Malcolm's political and social thought and, although I won't recount that here, I do want to trace his intellectual trajectory through those who followed him. It is here that we can see some of the rhetorical consequences of his rhetoric, in how his self-proclaimed disciples took up his mantle. The Republic of New Afrika was, perhaps most notably, the group that took up his masculinist idea of land, and used Indigenous histories to construct it.

In late March 1968, nearly five hundred Black nationalists convened in Detroit to discuss Black Power and how they might achieve Black liberation. Out of this historic meeting emerged one of the more important groups, which would later be called the Republic of New Afrika (RNA). The RNA's mission was straightforward. The wanted to create a government for Black folks. Beyond ending a common oppression, it would build a nation within a nation, funded by the hundreds of billions of dollars that the United States owed them for their exploited slave labor. The RNA based its argument on the belief that, upon the ending of enslavement, Black folks were not asked what they would like to do, given the fact that they were brought to this land as exploited labor.

More importantly, though, the members of the RNA were the ideological descendants of Malcolm X. Imari Obadele (formerly Richard Henry) stated in his autobiography that when the RNA was founded, it carried out what it believed to be the "Malcolm X Doctrine," which was basically realized through its program for setting up a nation within a nation in the Deep South.[22] Obadele stated that this idea for a separation hadn't existed before: "It was not until Malcolm X came to repeat what Messenger Muhammad had taught him and to enlarge upon those ideas—namely, that we are an African people, in the wilderness of North America."[23] It was these experiences that undergirded the idea of a separate Black nation.

On March 4, 1970, Gaidi Abiodun Obadele (formerly Milton Henry, brother of Imari), a Yale-trained lawyer from Detroit and also a leader and founder of the RNA, gave a speech at a Black Power conference in Guelph, Ontario, Canada. It is here he outlines the necessity and historical logic of Blacks deserving land in the Black Belt South, using the Cherokee example of removal.[24] He begins his speech with stereotypes about Native people and their connection to the land: "The Indian saw the earth, the land, as a sustainer and reviver of the internal spirit of man." He continues, "The Indian would see in today's concrete buildings and paving the glaring evidence of a people who, having no life spirit whatever or love of nature . . . were doing everything . . . to . . . insulate themselves from life and life's dynamic spiritual processes."[25] He paints a picture in which Native people and cities are in fact, not incompatible, and in which Native people cannot operate in modern times by enjoying city life. He also explains that in the postwar era, Native Americans began coming in droves to cities, both at their own choosing and because of federal termination and relocation policies.[26] While this is a problematic statement, because it perpetuates the idea that Native people cannot adapt to modern life, including living in cities, what is worse is how Obadele uses Native histories as a proxy to construct an ideal living situation for Black Americans.

First, he outlines his definition of sovereignty, observing that animals of all kinds "know that sovereignty and power over land are essential for any kind of life." He defines sovereignty as "simply the right to exercise dominion over a place of land, coupled with the power to preserve that right against all outside intrusion and assault."[27] Contrary to how Indigenous people understand land, his conception is that it is there to be occupied and exploited. As I mention in the previous chapter, land is not just a physical space to be occupied but represents the culture and identity of a people.

Obadele further uses a negative tone to describe Native people. Referring, in stereotypical fashion, to how the European came to this land, he states that "when he came ashore, he came with his smile and a willingness to smoke the Indian's peace pipe." He places Native people as stoic, unknowing, innocent people who knew very little about European peoples. Native people were very much aware about the necessities of diplomacy for survival, even if, in retrospect, it did not work well for them. Obadele continues, "[Indians] would have been suspicious of their ingratiating manner, but they could not have had any basis for suspicions since in all their experience they had never met any men like those in basic dishonesty." This scenario paints Indigenous people as victims, and ignores actual history of Native agency in responding to the colonial demands of Europeans. He then moves into a specific analysis of the Cherokee Nation's relationship with the US government, which I will quote at length:

> Almost contemporaneous with the smiling and the smoking of the peace pipes, came elaborate, wordy documents for the Indians to sign, drafted by the whites to define the conditions under which the two peoples would occupy the Cherokee land. That such documents were sought by the whites and made necessary for the joint occupation of the land by the whites should have alerted the Indians to the inherent dishonesty of the newcomers. But only after the signing of 18 such documents, more properly, "treaties," that the Cherokee began to understand the nature of the trouble they were in for.[28]

This ignores the political astuteness of Cherokee people (and other southeastern tribal nations) in terms of negotiating land rights.[29] While they found themselves in a position of swiftly changing power

Civil rights activist Kwame Ture (formerly Stokely Carmichael) came to St. Paul, Minnesota, to support Dennis Banks and Russell Means during the Wounded Knee Trials, 1974.

North and South American activists demonstrate solidarity as they prepare to go to the United Nations. Left to right: Raul Salinas; Nilo Cayuqueo, South America Indian Council; Vernon Bellecourt, White Earth Ojibwe Council; Bob Brown, All-African People's Revolutionary Party; and Pat Scott, Navajo/Hopi Joint Use Area Representative. White Earth Reservation, Minnesota, June 1981.

Kwame Ture speaking at a rally in support of Dennis Banks and Russell Means during the Wounded Knee Trials. St. Paul, Minnesota, 1974.

Dennis Banks and Harry Belafonte at a rally during the Wounded Knee Trials. St. Paul, Minnesota, 1974.

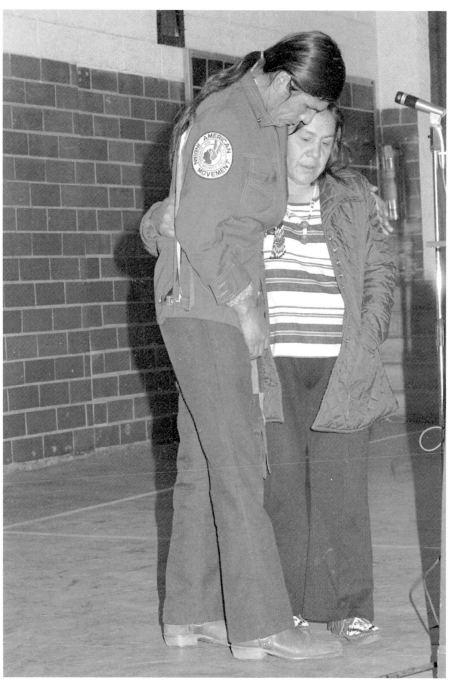

Dennis Banks and unknown woman at a rally during the Wounded Knee Trials. St. Paul, Minnesota, 1974.

Russell Means and Dennis Banks during the Wounded Knee Trials. St. Paul, Minnesota, 1974.

Audience at a rally in support of Dennis Banks and Russell Means at the Wounded Knee Trials. St. Paul, Minnesota, 1974.

Angela Davis, right, walks with Oren Lyons, an Onondaga chief from Nedrow, New York, after he left Wounded Knee, South Dakota, March 23, 1973. Lyons was escorted to near the government lines by armed members of the American Indian Movement. Lyons had been in Wounded Knee for several days to learn about the AIM takeover and report to the Six Nations Iroquois Federation.

Former South African president Nelson Mandela with Clyde Bellecourt.

American Indian Movement member and Indian rights activist Clyde Bellecourt speaks into microphone at Cobo Hall in Detroit, February 24, 1974.

dynamics, they were not completely without agency. In fact, the Cherokee were arguably one of the most astute tribal groups. Native people knew what were in those documents, and did their best to thwart Euro-American expansion; some community members were divided about the negotiation. Regardless, this rhetoric presents Native people as without agency, the implication being that if Blacks did not organize and demand that the United States give them land in the South, the same thing could happen to them.

Obadele demanded that the US pay Black Americans $400 billion, what he considered "chump change." In addition to the financial settlement, he also demanded "the transfer of five states to our sovereignty": Alabama, Georgia, Louisiana, Mississippi, and South Carolina.[30] While this never happened, it is important to engage in the historical art of speculation so that we can determine who they might have bumped up against. Surely, the Catawba, Creek, Cherokee, Chickasaw, Chicora, Choctaw, and other tribes lived there. What about their claims to land? While white settlement surely forced many to live elsewhere or die, many remained. How could these competing histories and ideas of sovereignty have co-existed?

Unfortunately, we do not know because it never happened. However, it does illustrate that, in a clear moment of liberation and attempts at coalition, some Black activists omitted the original people of this land for the development of their own political ideals. In fact, Obadele stated that he expected land in those states through "both diplomatic and political means, but we also are keeping full in mind the case of the Cherokee Nation and the State of Georgia."[31] These omissions were unfortunate. It reveals, though, the limits of Black nationalism. They understood that Indigenous histories existed, and that whites dispossessed Native people, but they did not acknowledge Native agency in the process. There were Black activists during the Black freedom struggle, though, who aligned themselves with Indigenous people on Indigenous issues, and worked toward a world free of both white supremacy and settler colonialism.

"ECONOMIC SECURITY FOR ALL AMERICANS"

Black activists showed up for Indigenous issues in real and symbolic ways. In the months preceding the Poor People's Campaign, Martin

Luther King Jr. and others began to organize a collection of poor and working-class people to meet together in order to think radically about changing the economic order that had kept Black and other people of color economically exploited. Dr. King traveled throughout the country to organize people to be a part of the Poor People's Campaign. In Atlanta on March 14, 1968, three weeks before he was assassinated, Dr. King, along with other members from the Southern Christian Leadership Conference, met with seventy-eight leaders from fifty-three organizations, hailing from seventeen states, to discuss organizing strategies for a demonstration in Washington, DC.

Dr. King met with Indigenous organizations, Mexican American and Puerto Rican organizations, and poor whites from Appalachia to figure out what actions they would take to end the economic oppression. The demonstration was set to begin on April 22. In what they hoped would be a "stay-in," Dr. King told reporters that they sought "economic security for all Americans."[32] He continued traveling for nineteen days, to California, Mississippi, and Boston, to further understand the unique conditions facing poor people in each place. At the invitation of King and the Southern Christian Leadership Conference, a variety of activists met in Atlanta on March 14 for a Minority Group Conference. Among the Native attendees were Hank Adams (Assiniboine), Mel Thom (Walker River Paiute), and Tillie Walker (Mandan-Hidatsa). They had long been involved in activism, including participating in the National Indian Youth Council, fish-ins, and the 1961 American Indian Chicago Conference. It is not clear that King and Abernathy fully understood everyone's positions, but they listened, and their comrades appreciated that.[33] Because of his tragic assassination, he was unable to see the impact of his efforts. However, Ralph Abernathy took over the leadership reins. Native people played a central role in the Poor People's Campaign as well.[34]

It should not be surprising that Indigenous peoples participated in civil rights issues. As historian Daniel Cobb notes, "The fact is that Native people have always engaged in political activism—whether or not it captured the imagination of the dominant society."[35] While they always fundamentally sought Indigenous sovereignty, they also understood that Native people had immediate needs and, in some ways, found comradery with Black Americans who also suffered under the boot of exploitation and subjugation. For some, fighting for the basic needs of Native people, especially the poor, did not stand in contradiction to their goals of tribal sovereignty.[36] They coalesced with a broad range of people. On May 1, 1968, Hank Adams, speaking on behalf of the Natives who traveled with him to DC, explained to Stewart Udall, the secretary of the interior, and Robert L. Bennett, commissioner of the Bureau of Indian Affairs, why he and other Native people were joining the Poor People's Campaign:

> We have joined the Poor People's Campaign because most of us know that our families, tribes and communities number among those suffering most in this country. We are not begging, we are demanding what is rightfully ours. This is no more the right to have a decent life in our communities. We need guaranteed jobs, guaranteed income, housing, schools, economic development, but most important, we want these things on our own terms.
>
> Our chief spokesman in the Federal Government, the Department of the Interior, has failed us. In fact, it began failing us from its very beginning. The Interior Department began failing because it was built and operates under a racist and immortal and paternalistic and colonialistic system. There is no way to improve racism, immorality, and colonialism. It can only be done away with.[37]

Adams explained how Native people were treated, and he also demanded that it be rectified. But his statement in some ways differed from even those who advocated tribal sovereignty. He argued that the entire system needed to be "done away with." It seems that Adams suggested, at least in this moment, that US democracy needed to be abolished, and, perhaps in some ways, so did the limited idea of tribal sovereignty.[38]

To be clear, not every Native person or tribe was enthusiastic about the Poor People's Campaign. The criticisms were either anti-Black in that they adopted racist beliefs about Black people from the media, or they believed that their issues—the fight for tribal sovereignty— were different from Black issues.[39] Solidarity did not always work in their favor. However, for those who attended, it was an opportunity to coalesce with their comrades and demand justice, economic and otherwise.

We don't have room to delve into the details of the Poor People's Campaign, but it's clear that while both Black and Native people fought to end their economic subjugation, Native folks often felt that their issues were not always central, which is a challenge for any coalition. Even Ralph Abernathy couldn't cease the constant marginalization of Indigenous activists during the event. Many felt that they were disrespected by Black militants, and weren't truly shown the solidarity that Dr. King had promised when he was organizing. Fred Connors, Mad Bear, and Beeman Logan, as well as Clifton Hill, were upset how they were treated as organizers. Connors, echoing the ninety-five supporters who agreed with him, remarked, "We have yet to have a say in what is planned or in our place in the Poor People's campaign and they voted unanimously to support" the chiefs.[40] Though Indigenous leaders weren't meaningfully included in the campaign's activities— another reason is perhaps that they were organizing on two different planes, one for civil rights and belonging in the US nation-state and the other for the guarantee of a simple respect for treaties—people like Ralph Abernathy did demonstrate some good faith, even if they misunderstood the problem.

On May 27, 1968, Native activists, including Adams and Tillie Walker, went to Washington, DC, to show support for Puyallup and Nisquallies as they awaited a decision on whether their treaty rights would be affirmed and they would be able to fish freely without interference from the State of Washington. The Puyallup and the Nisqually had been protesting since at least the 1950s so that they would be able to fish.[41] They were ready to protest the court's decision if they did not grant the tribes fishing rights off-reservation, which Adams and Walker believed was the inherent right of the tribes.

In front of the Supreme Court Building, Abernathy and Indigenous activists were waiting outside for the Supreme Court decision to determine whether or not the fishing rights of Indigenous nations in the Pacific Northwest were protected in their treaties. Interviewed about the position he and the Southern Christian Leadership would take, and likely understanding the criticisms of Indigenous delegates to the Poor People's Campaign, Abernathy decided to explicitly state that he was there to support and not lead. Importantly, he made a key remark that acknowledged the particular differences in how Black people and Native people lived but also the relationship to being poor:

> We are not insisting on anything other than support be given to our Indian brothers and we are insisting that they have the right to live as brown, black and white men have the right to live. And when we don't have food stamps down in Mississippi and Alabama, and Indians do not have the right to fish in Washington, it is all a process of genocide in this country, and we are against that. And we are going to do everything we can to put an end to it because we feel that everybody has the right to live, and in fact, we're guaranteed that by the Declaration of Independence, the Bill of Rights, and the Constitution of the United States.[42]

Abernathy surely learned a lot about Indigenous rights and treaties through conversations with Indigenous leaders. Nevertheless, he framed Indigenous rights within the realm of US democratic possibilities, ignoring the key differences between Black civil rights advocates and Indigenous peoples: the United States' treaty obligations to Native peoples. He at least understood the term "genocide."

Black entertainers also participated in symbolic gestures for Indigenous causes. On June 20, 1970, actor Ossie Davis and comedian Dick Gregory, both deeply invested in Black civil rights activities, showed solidarity with their Indigenous comrades. Gregory had already participated and was arrested for participating in fish-ins with Native tribes in the northwest in 1966.[43] Both men participated in the signing of a petition seeking the United Nations to condemn the US of genocide.[44] It is not surprising that Black folks supported Indigenous peoples in their quest for international recognition through the United Nations. Black Americans had appealed to the United Nations in their fight for human rights during the postwar period, though that was largely quelled by the Cold War, anti-communist sentiment, Southern Democrats, and white liberals.[45] The gesture further demonstrates the possibilities for Black and Indigenous solidarity in the groups' struggle against the US nation-state.[46]

The aftermath of the Poor People's Campaign showed how fleeting Black and Indigenous solidarity could be. Native folks and those who aligned with struggles like the Poor People's Campaign wanted to challenge the foundations of American capitalism. They also wanted the US nation-state to respect tribal sovereignty. More established groups, like the National Congress of American Indians, did not want to involve themselves with "Black issues." Native peoples' radical vision of coalescing with other groups—while demanding a "new America" and asserting tribal sovereignty—was not the business-as-usual approach to things. The important lesson we can take from their organizing efforts is that they tried, and we must too.

DENNIS BANKS AND THE BLACK SCHOLAR

In 1976, Dennis Banks (Turtle Mountain Chippewa), a cofounder of the American Indian Movement, was on the run. He was fighting his extradition to South Dakota, where he was being called to stand trial on trumped-up charges. In his fight for justice and freedom, he also sought allies, and it's not surprising that he connected with Black folks in solidarity—and that Black radicals, especially the Black Panthers, showed up for him.

In June 1976, for the *Black Scholar*'s special issue on "The Third World," Dennis Banks conducted an interview in which he gave an overview of the history, goals, and philosophy of the American Indian Movement. He spoke of the racism that Native peoples faced. He also expressed the impact that Black activists had on Native people.

The interviewer asked Banks, "What do you see as some of the more significant factors that have influenced the AIM organization?" Banks responded, "I think first of all, what has and it is unfortunate that what inspired AIM to get moving was the many deaths in this country of Native Americans—inspired us to get off what we were doing, which might have been nothing for many of us, and to get up and stand with the people who were standing already in the country."[47] He then shifted into a treatise on the importance and meaning of Malcolm X. "Malcolm X was standing, and god damn it we should have been standing right along with him, no matter his beliefs," he said, "because this man was fighting for social change in this country."[48] The meaning of Malcolm X transcends generations and geographies; his story has influenced revolutionaries around the world, during his life and even more after his assassination. But Banks didn't end there.

He also paid homage to Martin Luther King Jr. as well as struggles facing Asian Americans, Chicanx communities, and even poor whites:

> I think we are going to win this, we are going to win a major victory pretty soon, and we should after so many hundreds of years. We have been divided. Indian people are being killed and we are the only ones fighting for Indian people. Blacks are being killed and only blacks are fighting for blacks. Poor whites are fighting for change in the poor white section. Asians and Chicanos are the same way. I think that inspired AIM to stand up finally and say look, we have got to pull it together, and that is where we are at right now, trying to bring non-Indians and the Indians together and bring about massive change in this country.[49]

Banks understood the importance of solidarity with all oppressed peoples. Only through solidarity and unity can change occur. He believed that unless we are all free, none of us is truly free. I hope that, going forward, we can resurrect this idea of coalitions across races, across borders, especially as global capitalist exploitation, neocolonialism, and imperialism continue to impact us all, albeit at times in different ways.

THE BLACK PANTHER PARTY

Whenever I teach about the Black Panther Party, my Black students usually love it. They are enamored with young Black people brandishing guns to challenge the assumed authority of the police, who continue to terrorize Black, Brown, and Indigenous communities. As a young college student, I loved the Black Panthers too. I, too, admired their use of guns and that they directly challenged the police state. I also admired their commitment to class struggle and their critique of racial capitalism. Shit, I still admire them! They continue to be one of the most studied radical groups during the era of Black Power.[50] What I didn't initially notice was their engagement with Indigenous peoples' movements.

In spite of their many faults, including male chauvinism and patriarchy, they demonstrated solidarity with a variety of groups in fantastic fashion. They showed solidarity with poor and working-class whites, the Brown Berets, the gay and lesbian movement, and Palestine. They also showed this solidarity with Indigenous peoples. Their many acts of solidarity were rooted in their Black internationalist and Marxist-Leninist philosophy of global class struggle and the fight for racial justice. Their solidarity in covering Indigenous struggles in their newspapers should not be taken lightly, especially when we consider how difficult it was for Native people to receive coverage in most non-Indigenous newspapers.

The Black Panthers' media organ, the Intercommunal News Service, covered a number of struggles in the US and around the world, from the murder of young Black men to the happenings in Vietnam. And the news was enhanced by the artwork of the revolutionary artist Emory Douglas.

By the mid-1970s, the Black Panthers were in decline. Having suffered assassinations, imprisonment, and exile, they began to rebrand and focused more on their community efforts, as well as on issues close to home. As they were declining in relevancy, the Native struggle continued, and the Black Panthers supported those struggles.

For example, in 1974, Elaine Brown, who became the chairperson of the Panthers after Huey Newton fled to Cuba after facing a murder charge, attended a rally in Custer, South Dakota, to protest the extradition of American Indian Movement member Dennis Banks. Standing in front of the crowd, Brown stated, "The Black community of Oakland, I am certain, will become more involved in the issue of Dennis Banks." She also noted the connections between Black and Indigenous struggles. "Not only did they come here and rip off this country from the Indian people," she said, "they also ripped off our territory and brought us here to work for them." By acknowledging that Africans forced to come to the Americas originally had a home, she was also highlighting a major point we tend to forget: that those Africans were from a variety of Indigenous groups with particular customs, beliefs, and political structures.

Brown continued expounding on the connections between these groups. "The Indian people taught them what to do because they were too stupid to know how to work the land and then they broke our back to do the work." She suggested that the crowd think of fighting for Dennis Banks as an act of solidarity, and that it was "an issue of human beings who are beginning to struggle together, who believe in Power to the People."[51] The Intercommunal News Service also documented other events, including the Longest Walk in 1978. In this action, various Native people organized a caravan of people from all across the country in what became the "Longest Walk" to protest the US government's continued violation and complete disrespect of its treaties with Indigenous nations.

Black organizations continued to show support and make ideological connections with Indigenous peoples. There were offshoot organizations such as the Black Liberation Army (BLA), that believed in armed revolution. While the Black Panther Party believed in armed self-defense, the BLA believed that the time for revolution was now, and that it had to use a variety of tactics against the US government to further its idea of revolution. While there are at least a few well-known members of the BLA, including Mutulu Shakur, the stepfather of the late rapper Tupac Shakur, perhaps no one garners more emotional responses than Tupac's godmother, Assata Shakur, who today is still in Cuba. In 2013, the FBI declared that it had added Shakur to the "Top Ten Most Wanted Terrorists" list—the first time they had placed a woman on that list.[52] She remains a cultural icon for Black people throughout the diaspora.

Shakur, a Black revolutionary, is best known for fleeing to Cuba after being rescued from prison in New Jersey. She was originally arrested and convicted because of her alleged involvement in the killing of New Jersey state trooper Werner Foerster, after he stopped and pulled over two of her BLA comrades, Sundiata Acoli and Zayd Malik Shakur. In 1979, she was liberated from prison, and later escaped to Cuba, which granted her asylum in 1984. Shakur also wrote for the news organ of the Third World Women Alliance (TWWA), *Triple Jeopardy: Racism, Imperialism, Sexism.*

Founded in the summer of 1970, TWWA first emerged out of the Black Women's Liberation Caucus of the Student Nonviolent Coordinating Committee. BWLC, with Frances Beal playing a leadership role, had formed in response to patriarchy within SNCC. It then turned into the Black Women's Alliance and, upon ideologically identifying with the third world liberation struggles, changed its name again to the Third World's Women Alliance.[53]

"To My People," an essay Shakur published in 1973, discusses the long history of Black struggle and clearly explains who the true criminals were. She opens her essay, "My name is Assata Shakur (slave name JoAnne Chesimard), and I am a revolutionary. A black revolutionary. By that I mean I am a field nigga who is determined to be free by any means necessary." After detailing how the press characterized the Black Liberation Army, she then shifts the discourse, identifying the real criminals and thieves: "But it was not us who stole millions of black people from the continent of Africa." She describes the processes of dispossession, stating that Black people were "robbed of our language, of our Gods, of our culture, of our human dignity, of our labor and our lives." Black revolutionaries like Shakur were more than only concerned about Black dispossession. "They call us thieves," she wrote, "but we did not rob and murder millions of Indians by ripping off their homeland, then call ourselves pioneers."[54]

It is important to note, however, that Black women did not just discover global white supremacy and colonialism during the 1960s and 1970s. As Black international feminist historian Keisha Blain argues in her book *Set the World on Fire: Black Nationalist Women and the Global Struggle for Freedom*, Black nationalist women laid the intellectual and political foundations for later struggles for Black freedom.[55]

Black revolutionaries understood that the problems of dispossession that they faced were similar to those of their ancestors who were taken from the African continent. It is here, in the larger connection to Africa, where revolutionaries forged common ideological struggle. No one did this better than Stokely Carmichael.

STOKELY CARMICHAEL AND PAN-AFRICANISM

One of the most important voices of Black internationalism from the United States was Stokely Carmichael, who would later change his name to Kwame Ture. Carmichael was a strong advocate for Black Power, first proclaiming it in June 1966, in Greenwood, Mississippi. He later evolved his message into one that centered African diasporic connections and Africa as Black people's homeland. Unlike Garvey, he would go on to live on the continent. According to Carmichael biographer Peniel Joseph, "Ture's journey from civil rights militant and Black Power icon to the revolutionary socialist who unfurled the Pan-African banner high enough for much of the world to see indelibly changed the black freedom struggle."[56]

For Carmichael, land was a central component. In the 1969 inaugural issue of the *Black Scholar*, he wrote, "We need a land base." Echoing Malcolm X's famous 1964 speech, "Message to the Grassroots," Carmichael remarked, "In the final analysis, all revolutions are based on land." While he believed that "the best place" and "quickest place that we can obtain land is Africa," he also left open the possibility that they might find land in the US. More importantly, he noted, "but I do not see it clearly in my mind at this time. We need land immediately."[57] The hesitancy likely stems from his opposition to the United States' ongoing occupation of Indigenous land. He was perhaps a unique individual, understanding that it would be wrong to impose oneself upon other people's land without their consent, even if their blood, sweat, tears, and pain are deeply rooted in the soil.

In addition to his own organizing and education in the United States, Carmichael learned a great deal about Pan-Africanism and its broadening approach from his mentor, Kwame Nkrumah. In 1969, Carmichael moved to Guinea, whose head of state at that time was Sékou Touré. There, he became a mentee of Nkrumah. Nkrumah was in exile following the US-backed coup that led to his removal from power in 1966. While in Guinea, he wrote political primers on behalf of Nkrumah, even traveling and speaking on his behalf. Carmichael considered him a father figure and a revolutionary leader.[58]

Nkrumah became the first president and prime minister of Ghana in 1957, helping lead the colony to independence. He attended Lincoln College in Pennsylvania in the 1930s. Nkrumah wrote many books on Pan-Africanist philosophy and scientific socialism. He was invested in totally liberating Africa and then unifying it. He wrote extensively on neocolonialism and the transnational financial institutions that attempted to maintain control over the resources of African nations. In *Class Struggle in Africa* (1970), Nkrumah wrote, "The neocolonialist period begins when international monopoly finance capital, working through the indigenous bourgeoisie, attempts to secure an even tighter stranglehold over the economic life of the continent than was exercised during the colonial period."[59]

Nkrumah argued that revolution required unity across the African diaspora. For him, African revolution was a part of the global movements for decolonization. Wherever Black people lived, their resistance was a move toward the end of colonialism.[60] Only through revolution and unity across the African continent could true liberation occur.[61] Although he often ignored religious and political differences among ethnic groups and tribes, he deeply influenced the Pan-Africanist thought of Carmichael.

Carmichael's idea of Pan-Africanism was a critique of settler colonialism as well as a reclamation of Black people's indigenous connection to Africa. He understood that settler colonialism was a global phenomenon, existing in the US, South Africa and Zimbabwe, and Israel. He wrote, "Africans today, irrespective of geographical location, have a common enemy and face common problems. We are the victims of imperialism, racism, and we are a landless people."[62] In regard to the landless, he described two groups: "One group was taken from the land (slavery), the second group had the land taken from them (colonialism)." He continued, "We are Africans. Africa is our home. Even if a man cannot return home it is his dying wish."[63] Carmichael's vision of returning home was not just some blind, idealistic return to ancient Africa, or one that erases the differences between Africans in the United States and those on the continent. It identified a common ground between the two groups in the global sphere of enslavement and dispossession, with the land issue being the central thread.

Nkrumah believed that African unity rested on a common language and land base. But those were not the only things that would hold together a sustained revolution.[64] Nkrumah, like Carmichael, understood that the African diaspora required new ideas of how people belonged to Africa, and if Africa were to have total unity, they would have to include those on the continent and those throughout the diaspora.[65] Nkrumah did not delve into the major regional, cultural, and ethnic differences among tribal groups; however, the economic component affected African peoples throughout the diaspora in different ways.

Settler colonialism functions to impact African peoples throughout the diaspora, albeit differently. In light of Carmichael's ideas for revolution and his articulation of Pan-Africanism, it is not surprising that he and others from the All-African People's Revolutionary Party would align themselves with Indigenous peoples under US colonial occupation.

THE ALL-AFRICAN PEOPLE'S REVOLUTIONARY PARTY

In 1972, Carmichael helped form the All-African People's Revolutionary Party (AAPRP). Basing its vision on Kwame Nkrumah's ideas of scientific socialism and the larger unity of Africans both on the continent and throughout the diaspora, this group was also dedicated to the end of capitalism, colonialism, and imperialism.[66] It also attempted to connect with other oppressed peoples, including Native Americans. For example, from June 4 to June 11, 1981, the AAPRP was an active participant in the International Indian Treaty Council (ITTC) and held the Seventh International Indian Treaty Council Conference on the White Earth Reservation. In an invitation to potential attendees, Bill Means, then executive director of the ITTC, wrote, "All Indian Organizations, Tribal Governments and concerned people are invited to participate together in a spirit of friendship and cooperation." The conference would cover a number of themes, including, "Land Rights of Indigenous Peoples, International Treaties and Agreements, Indigenous Philosophy and The Land, Trans-National Corporations and the Land, Land Rights of Indigenous Peoples and Nuclear Disarmament Hunting and Fishing Rights and International Indian Prisoners' Rights." Years later, reflecting on the importance of the conference, Bill Means stated:

> It brought a lot of people from Latin America so that they could see how Indian people lived other than South Dakota. . . . It was a very important conference in terms of non-Indian support. We had a concert there at which Bonnie Raitt and Jackson Browne played. This added great visibility for the Treaty Council in terms of non-Indian anti-nuclear and peace movements.[67]

The attendees were asked to bring proposals for actions to the rest of the group, and those chosen would then be presented at the International NGO Conference on Indigenous Peoples and Their Land in Geneva, Switzerland, in September 1981. At this meeting was also a Black American named Bob Brown, who can be seen in a photograph with others, raising their hands in solidarity.[68] He was a member of the Congress of Racial Equality, a director of the Midwest office of the Student Nonviolent Coordinating Committee, and a cofounder of the Illinois chapter of the Black Panther Party. Brown has remained active in Pan-African and other struggles worldwide.

So, what would a person who so strongly identified with a Pan-Africanist group, founded by Kwame Ture, be doing at a meeting among "Indigenous" peoples? Given his longtime activism for oppressed people, his affiliations with Kwame Ture and coalition-building with Fred Hampton in Chicago, it is not surprising. It was not just that he wanted to show solidarity with Native peoples, though that was part of it. He considered himself an Indigenous African, and Africa as his true homeland, not the US. Although the AAPRP's platform was intended for people of African descent, it actively created solidarity with other groups, including Indigenous peoples in the United States. People like Vernon Bellecourt returned the favor.

In May 1986, Vernon Bellecourt and Larry Anderson (Diné) were touring the Midwest and eastern United States, appealing to Black Americans to show support for the US government's repeal of the Navajo and Hopi Relocation Act. Designed to clear land for companies to mine Big Mountain in Arizona, the act had been passed in 1974. Bellecourt and Anderson were also seeking support of the bill so that Ronald Reagan would not be able to veto Senate Bill S1396, the White Earth Reservation Land Settlement Act of 1985, which sought both compensation and the return of illegally taken land to the White Earth Anishinaabe.[69] Bellecourt, committed to Black and Indigenous solidarity, remarked, "American-Indians were being cheated, robbed and removed from their lands as African-Americans were cheated and robbed of their 40-acres-and-a-mule agreement with the government after the civil war." He also demonstrated his knowledge of ongoing injustices in South Africa, remarking that the plan to remove Native people from Big Mountain "is every bit as treacherous as the forced removal of the Black majority population in South Africa from the best lands into the Bantustans."[70]

In response to his rhetorical act of solidarity, Oliver Reginald Kaizana Tambo—then president of the African National Congress, operating in exile in Lusaka, Zambia—sent a "pledge of firmest solidarity with the people of Big Mountain." The ANC statement also proclaimed "that what is happening to you is exactly the lot of our people in South Africa." What connected the two groups was their common experience as Indigenous people whose lands had been taken for capital. Under apartheid, Indigenous Africans "are time and again forcibly removed and resettled against their will, in the interest of capital." Finally, the pledge remarked, "The struggle against capitalist exploitation and total disregard of human beings is an international struggle."[71] It was already known that Bellecourt and Kwame Ture had a relationship. However, this act of solidarity demonstrates that Indigenous people on the African continent and in North America had a common struggle, and perhaps had more engagement with one another than we have previously realized.[72]

BLACK AND RED POWER MEET IN LIBYA

In September 1991, Stokely Carmichael, now Kwame Ture, and Vernon Bellecourt reconvened, this time in Libya. Bellecourt was there to receive, on behalf of the Indigenous peoples in the Americas, the Gaddafi Prize for Human Rights. The occasion represented a new era of activism for both men. To be sure, they were still actively involved in creating a new way of life for Africans and Indigenous peoples. But this occasion was different. No longer was Stokely showing up to lend his support to Indigenous struggles in the US, and no longer were they filled with the energy of youth. They still maintained their fire, but now their hair was gray, and you could see on their faces that the years of study and struggle had taken its toll.

Bellecourt and Ture were on a panel discussing the "rights of Indigenous peoples." They were joined by two professors, Hans Köchler, president of the International Progress Organization in Vienna and professor at the University of Austria, and Silas Cerqueira, a political scientist from the University of Portugal. The panel was moderated by Harold Hudson Channer, a television personality based in New York City. While the panel was on the struggle of Indigenous peoples in the Americas, it was also an opportunity to discuss why the Gaddafi Prize existed, and who the previous awardees were.

Nelson Mandela won the inaugural award, in 1989, followed by Palestinians, and then Native people in the Americas. The prize was awarded until 2011, and discontinued after the murder of its namesake,

Libyan leader Muammar Gaddafi. It is not clear why Bellecourt was chosen; though, given his connections to Ture, as well as his continued activism with the United Indian Liberation Front, which included Indigenous peoples throughout the Americas, it is not surprising.

Ture began the panel discussion by explaining the logic of how award recipients were chosen. The award was first given to Nelson Mandela because of his struggle against a "racist, settler regime" in South Africa. "This year the prize is being awarded to the Indigenous people of the Western Hemisphere, commonly called American Indians, for their continuing struggle against 500 years of aggression, occupation, and genocide."[73] The panelists included lawyers, academics, and revolutionaries who advanced humanity and celebrated those whom the West might not recognize as humanitarians because they do not fit into the Western definition of a humanitarian.

Bellecourt began by introducing himself in the Anishinaabe language. He then stated that although he was accepting the award, that Native people throughout the Americas, from the Dené in the Northwest territories to the tip of Argentina, continued to struggle against ongoing occupation.

Professor Cerqueira then spoke, explaining that the prize existed as a direct criticism of the United Nations and other prizes awarded to those who many activists deemed war criminals. "Our purpose here is to recognize just struggles, human struggles for human rights, which have been abandoned, neglected, ignored by the media and establishment," he said.

Bellecourt began to speak again. After describing the American Indian Movement occupation of Wounded Knee in 1973, he made a point to offer comments about his dear comrade, Ture: "He came out of the struggles of the Africans in America. And he came to our people, and he offered his friendship, his love, his respect and his solidarity." Bellecourt continued, "One time I remember a speech he was giving. And here's what he said, 'The Indians have a history. The Indians have a glorious history. It's not to be found in America's history books. But it will be when the Indians have their proper nationalism and there is no power on earth that can stop it.'" Bellecourt loved Ture so much because of his revolutionary passion and his unflinching support for Indigenous peoples in the US. Ture did not speak much during this segment. He spent only a few minutes critiquing the logic of racial capitalism and the proliferation of multinational corporations, and arguing that the current system is unsustainable. Still, even though Ture was an elder statesman, there was no match for his onscreen presence and bursts of energy.

In November 2000, Nelson Mandela traveled to Minneapolis to accept an award for his struggle for human rights.[74] Clyde Bellecourt was there, and perhaps believing that he could also seek solidarity from South Africans, he went up to Mandela and shook his hand. He asked him to support the pardon of Leonard Peltier (Turtle Mountain Chippewa), who had been imprisoned since 1977, convicted of murdering two FBI agents, though the trial and sentence are deemed unjust by activists around the world who have been seeking his pardon.[75] It was a symbolically powerful moment, the sight of these two people shake hands, but nothing came of it.

The Black and Red Power generation did not eradicate oppression and implement the revolution as they had hoped. They did not seize the power they wanted. However, at the award ceremony in Libya, some twenty years after the rise of Black Power and Red Power, these leaders demonstrated a revolutionary love and commitment to international struggle that must continue today.

CHAPTER SEVEN

BLACK AND INDIGENOUS POPULAR CULTURES IN THE PUBLIC SPHERE

In the history of problematic appropriation in America,
we could start with the land and crops and cuisine
commandeered from Native peoples along with the
mass expropriation of the labor of the enslaved.

—LAUREN MICHELE JACKSON, *White Negroes*[1]

ONE OF THE most difficult discussions to have between two oppressed groups is that of cultural appropriation. If a white person commits this racist act, it is almost as if we expect it—we have a brief sense of outrage and then move on. In other words, we expect white people to be who they be. On the other hand, when it comes to say, a Black person "playing Indian" or an Indigenous person performing minstrelsy, we become even more outraged, and expect them to *know* better—as if we all grew up to be Malcolm X's daughters, who had the fortune of not only having revolutionary parents but also got to hang around James Baldwin and Nina Simone.

We should pause and question why we expect another oppressed group to automatically understand how oppression impacts other people—although that might be difficult given how quick we are to "cancel" someone over social media. First off, we need to stop canceling people or we all are going to be canceled, because all of us have much learning and evolving to do. By "cancel," I don't mean holding people accountable; to varying degrees, we all require accountability, we all need to engage ourselves in a process of constant reflection and change. But canceling is not created equal. Depending on someone's race, gender, sexuality, class status, and influence, it is possible they might not ever be "canceled." Although on an uneven plane of power, we are all capable of doing something we should not. As Ibram Kendi notes in his award-winning book *Stamped from the Beginning: The Definitive History of Racist Ideas in America* (2016), "Racist ideas are ideas. Anyone can produce them or consume them."[2] It is a simple but profound statement. I would add to this that anyone can reproduce a settler-colonial idea as well. Further, the reproduction of racism and settler colonialism is about power, that is, who can create some negative outcome for those most vulnerable. We can all perpetuate stereotypes about Indigenous peoples, and, of course, Indigenous peoples can engage in stereotypes about themselves. I recall hearing older members of my family, Black and Indigenous, recount that when they went to see those racist John Wayne cowboy movies, they rooted for his ass! If I take anything from this lesson, we can all uncritically accept narratives rooted in popular culture. It should not be surprising, then, within a settler-colonial society, that even Black folks can slip up and reproduce harmful imagery of distorted Indigenous cultures or straight-up culturally appropriate them.

Still, there seems to be some basic disagreements over what cultural appropriation is, who can do it, and what the impacts are. Again, *anyone* can reproduce racist or colonial ideas. However, there is also a thin line between cultural appropriation and appreciation. In this chapter, I will analyze cultural appropriation, the discourses of solidarity, and how this all plays out within the realm of Black and Indigenous public cultural spheres. I want to do this by analyzing particular examples within the Black and Indigenous popular cultural realms.

CULTURAL APPROPRIATION VS. CULTURAL APPRECIATION

It is becoming almost cliché to use the term "cultural appropriation." Everyone uses it. White people appropriate hip-hop culture, understood as Black culture. White people wear headdresses at Coachella. Actually, everyone wears headdresses—Black, white, green—just hang around a college campus on Halloween. (Those same people will also wear costumes that are disrespectful to my Latinx and Asian homies.)

Europeans go to places like Oaxaca, Mexico, learn how to make mezcal, and then bring it to California and act like it is brand new.

They take artistic practices and incorporate them into their own art but say they are "inspired" by other cultures because they are "well traveled"—whatever that means. White people have had a monopoly on appropriating cultures and cornrows for centuries; that's just what they do. I'm not even all that mad anymore. They really like Black culture, and I understand—who would be proud of bland food and hardly any culture that is theirs? I guess they have the Leaning Tower of Pisa, and the dopeness of Picasso, and Marxism, but that's about it. And to be clear, young people should learn about European art and culture. The history is incredible. But, again, people really like Black culture? I guess they have Elvis and all of those artists who appropriated Black culture and now a "woke" Taylor Swift, but that's about it. Shit, now that I think of it, what important thing have they given to the world that was indigenous to, umm, Europe? Capitalism? Exploitation? Racism? Pumpkin pie (I love vegan pumpkin pie)? But I digress. Let me get back to the topic of cultural appropriation.

I ask in this section, is our discourse about cultural appropriation the final word? Is our constant reactionary stand to it finished? In Black cultural studies theorist Stuart Hall's essay "What Is This Black in Popular Culture?," he remarked, "The question is whether we are any longer in that moment, whether that is still a sufficient basis for the strategies of new interventions?"[3] Anishinaabe writer Leanne Simpson wrote, "While it has become the practice of . . . the more liberal and well-meaning segments to condemn racist stereotypes, this group is immobilized with regard to land issues."[4] Resisting racist stereotypes and spending time critiquing cultural appropriation is important, but I think we need to think a bit more critically about what our aim is. So, what is cultural appropriation?

Cultural appropriation is the idea that a dominant group takes, at will, cultural markers from a powerless group, and appropriates them, in unacknowledged ways that ignore the historical roots of said thing and then makes it seem brand new. The "thing" can be appropriating language, clothing, hairstyle, histories—it can be a range of things. Cultural appropriation is nothing more than classic colonialism—taking shit that don't belong to you, repackaging it as your own invention, and then rebranding it. It's like when I saw some white man call *elote* "loaded corn," and my Latinx friends scoffed at this notion. Again, it is easy to discuss cultural appropriation when it comes to white people doing it, but when it comes to Black and Indigenous peoples, it gets trickier.

Cultural appropriation in Black and Indigenous contexts can be defined in terms of minstrelsy and "playing Indian." We also call them "blackface" and "redface." Philip Deloria defines playing Indian as "a persistent tradition in American culture, stretching from the very instant of the national bang into an ever-expanding present and future."[5] Playing Indian happens in the popular cultural realm in the form of non-Indigenous people wearing headdresses, utilizing Indigenous patterns in the fashion world, or what we discuss most: sports mascots. The importance of understanding the links between blackface and redface are simple: the people who believe, for instance, that Native mascots are acceptable, also tend to hold other racist viewpoints. If you're white and you think Indigenous caricatures are cool, then you're likely and unsurprisingly one of those All Lives Matter folks. (Here is your reminder: all lives don't matter because Black lives haven't ever mattered. After centuries of protest and resistance, they still barely matter to white America.) However, as Deloria points out, it is really about power.

Indian play is more than white people defining themselves through Native culture. It reveals how white American political power is rooted in the domination of Indigenous peoples."[6] Playing Indian is an attempt to keep Indigenous peoples and their customs stuck in the past in order to take their land.

Minstrelsy has had a similar trajectory, with some small caveats. We typically think of minstrelsy, or blackface, as something that happened in the nineteenth century, but it continues today. We think of white people performing in front of all-white audiences making fun of Black people, speaking a bastardized version of Black English. Or they show up as college students, paint their faces black, and use the word "nigga" over and over. According to whiteness scholar Dave Roediger, minstrel shows were fundamental expressions of northern white working-class culture across different white ethnicities.[7] Today, blackface performance is even more deeply embedded across all US cultures and races. Nothing represents the pervasiveness of blackness more than music, especially hip-hop.

Anyone who raps is also utilizing Black English. Anyone. If you are a non-Black rapper who utilizes Hip Hop Nation Language, which is also a part of Black English, and you know nothing about Black English(es) and don't respect its West African roots, as well as learning how it developed in the United States (and elsewhere in the diaspora), then you might actually be performing minstrelsy without even knowing it. Or it could be a lazy attempt at appreciating the culture with which you want to engage. I want to reiterate, this ain't all the fault of white people. If you're an Indigenous, Latinx, or Asian rapper out here sayin' the N-word, using Black phrases, nuances, tones, and gestures, if you "sound" Black, and you ain't also out here protesting for Black lives and hanging around Black people, you're a cultural appropriator. It don't matter to me if you out here spittin' liberation theology in your lyrics, if you don't try and understand Black history and Black language, you really need to ask if you're actively contributing to the liberation of Black people. Remember this: without Black people, there would be no rap music. Many, though, support Black lives, so big shout out to them.

Cultural appreciation is the act of engaging respectfully with, and being invested in, the culture *and* the people from which that culture emerges. At an individual level, it is the act of someone who deeply understands the experiences and histories of an oppressed group, consistently hangs around those people, continues to learn from that cultural group, and knows the boundaries ascribed to them. They are also deeply invested in knowing their place and supporting that group—and I mean a real ride-or-die. Now hear me out, my good, liberal white folks: just because you know some underground hip-hop headz, and maybe they vouch for you, that does not mean you have a cultural free pass that applies to, for instance, all Black people. Your cultural license applies to that group who knows you—not to everyone else. Again, the people who are not from this group know their boundaries and accept it. If you can't accept the cultural groups' boundaries that they set upon you, are you more invested in the people or in the culture that you divorce from the people? Let that sink in.

NDN POPULAR CULTURE

In Ralph Ellison's novel *Invisible Man*, the unnamed narrator says, "When they approach me they see only my surroundings, themselves, or figments of their imagination—indeed, everything and anything except me."[8] This aptly defines Indigenous people and NdN popular culture. The use of "NdN" is hard to precisely locate; however, it is a word that is generally used by Native people only, and usually on social media and in texting language as a shorthand for the word "Indian." While my aunties use "Indian," and some Native people on the rez do, Indigenous artists, intellectuals, and millennials and Generation Zers are less likely to use it. In this way, the use of the term "NdN" is a reclaiming of sorts, semantically inverting the meaning of a term to something that Indigenous millennials and Generation Zers identify with. So, my non-NdN peers, outside of a context in which they are quoting something, don't get used to using it without expecting some form of critique.

Before defining NdN popular culture, I want to define popular culture. Popular culture is the culture created by marginalized groups. They make meaning of and produce ideas about their everyday lives through popular cultural mediums such as music, visual art, and other forms of artistic, humanist expression. Although everyday people produce popular culture, it is not divorced from the larger structures of oppression and systems of power that subjugate them.[9] Popular culture for Indigenous people is produced within settler capitalist society. Therefore, whatever they produce has to be understood in that real-world context. Native people produce popular culture out of their experience and relationship to the larger white settler population, and within a society that values Black popular culture for consumption but not Black lives.

So, what is NdN popular culture? It is the use and remix of Indigenous cultures and languages, often blending with other cultures, especially Black American culture and language, and making it one's own. These remixes show up in the form of Indigenous aesthetics and art, writing, social media and memes, and other cultural expressions that attempt to challenge, critique, and disrupt settler ideas of how Indigenous peoples are supposed to act, think, and be in the world.

NdN popular culture is not the idea that some have in their head as to how Indigenous people are supposed to be in the white imagination. It consists of Indigenous people asserting their presence in the world in recognizable and subtle ways. NdN popular culture is similarly not just a response to whiteness. Michael Eric Dyson's thoughts on Black culture reflect a phenomenon parallel to NdN popular culture. As Dyson notes in his book *Reflecting Black*,

> Black culture is not simply formed in the response to forces of oppression. Its purposes do not easily reduce to resisting racism. Although black cultural creativity and agency are profoundly influenced by racist oppression, their rich range of expressions are not exhausted by the preoccupation with such oppression.[10]

Like Black popular culture, Indigenous people's cultural inventiveness is not subjugated to the rules, limits, and blandness of whiteness. Native people seek to produce multiple forms of expressive humanistic culture in order to exist in the world in their fullness. In fact, being occupied with solely dismantling the structures of settler colonialism and racial capitalism that dominate their lives is not the only thing that they do daily, as important as resisting them are. Their continued existence demonstrates their ability to resist. Finally, it is about Indigenous peoples' ability to be themselves in the modern world and create a future where they exist, in a society that has been predicated on their supposed invisibility and continued presence within the white, settler gaze. The subjects of this gaze include racist mascots, dehumanizing stereotypes, and assurances that the idea of Native people remains stuck in the digital and literary imagination. NdN popular culture disrupts these ideas but also goes beyond them, serving as both protest and a part of Indigenous futures.

I think one of the most important persons producing NdN popular culture today is Johnnie Jae. She is an Otoe-Missouria and Choctaw journalist, speaker, podcaster, and entrepreneur. Jae founded A Tribe Called Geek, an "award winning media platform for Indigenous Geek Culture and STEM."[11] For me, her work is the epitome of contemporary Indigenous activism and the possibilities of Indigenous representation of the future. It is not only consumed with challenging racist stereotypes, but crafting a future not rooted in reproduced stereotypes of the warrior Native male who will save us all. Instead, she is creating an Indigenous future rooted in all things nerdy. As someone who grew up a nerd, this is dope and some of the best work of Indigenous modernity going forward. Her work is a powerful illustration of critiquing colonialism and building Indigenous futures.

BLACK WOMEN, INDIGENOUS WOMEN, AND SOCIAL MEDIA

On August 7, 2017, I received numerous messages across social media platforms. One of my white-passing Indigenous homies texted me the message, "Have you seen this?" along with a screenshot, taken from Twitter, of rapper Omerrettà the Great posing in a Pocahontas outfit. My first thought was, "Why do white-looking Natives always send me some shit when it comes to Black folks?! Damn! Can a nigga live?" My second thought was, "Here comes both the antiblackness and anti-Indianness." And sure enough, we saw both.

A self-identified Indigenous woman on Twitter wrote, "If you aren't Native, keep your hands off our culture! We rock our regalia beautifully every single day." In a six-point thread, she explained:

1. Miss Chocolate Pocahontas is sexualizing Native women in that trash regalia.
2. Our sexual assault rates are some of the highest, a lot is caused by our Native women being sexualized.
3. She is using the name Pocahontas with ignorance, not thinking of her ACTUAL (not Disney) history.
4. Yes she is a beautiful Black woman. No she is not the Black Pocahontas.
5. No it is not anti Black to call out cultural appropriation against Native people when done by Black folks.
6. Any of you, including Black folks and poc can be problematic and anti native and I'll call you out just like I would a white person."[12]

Of course, Black women did not sit idly by. One person wrote, "You do NOT get to decide what is anti black or not. If you don't like BW (Black women), just say it. No need to bash this girl for wearing a Disney outfit." Another Black woman wrote, "Black folks need not to be simple minded. This is offensive & I thought it before I even opened it. Yall gotta respect other ppl culture too." Another person wrote, "Thank you for breaking this down and educating that culture appropriating doesn't just happen in the Black community. (I'm also black)."

There are several things happening in these responses. People are upset about antiblackness and Indigenous erasure. Indigenous people are upset that a Black person played Indian. Black people were mad that a Black woman got called out for playing Indian; however, others understood the issue. Indigenous women had the right to be angry. After all, Black lesbian feminist Audre Lorde has made a convincing case for the usefulness of anger when calling out racial insensitivity.[13]

Beyond the specifics of this incident, it demonstrated to me the limits of call-out culture and social media. Social media is a powerful tool. People have used it to organize social movements, including the Movement for Black Lives and recent protests happening at the time of this writing to bring justice for Breonna Taylor and George Floyd. We should ask long-term questions about the role social media plays in our in-person social relationships. Does using social media produce better social relationships, built on a foundation of compassion and love? Does it help us become more invested in people, even when they make mistakes? Leanne Simpson writes of her experience in the Idle No More movement, an Indigenous-led social movement founded in 2012 that calls for the Canadian government to honor the treaties and Indigenous sovereignty and cease environmental deprivation:

> Most of my comrades I had never met in person. While there were small groups of people meeting and strategizing about specific actions and events, we had no mechanism to make decisions as a movement because at this point social media had replaced organizing. Disagreements over analysis occurred online, and because we had shallow cyber relationships, instead of real-world ones, the larger structure fell apart quickly. We tried to build a movement online through social media, and when we needed to trust each other, when we needed to give each other the benefit of the doubt, when we needed empathy and a history together that we could trust, we couldn't.[14]

I believe Simpson is correct. Social media is here to stay and there is no doubt about its powerful use in helping change our conditions.

However, its limitations are glaring when a disagreement happens. What would happen if, instead of talking on social media, we reached out in another way? We are so quick to use Twitter fingers that we rarely think about the fact that we are dealing with people. Finding ways of meeting might be difficult, but we should try.

Later in 2017, more issues emerged when another Black woman rapper engaged in cultural appropriation, and the discourse was even worse. On November 17, rapper Nicki Minaj posted on her Instagram a drawing of herself depicted as three fictionalized versions of Pocahontas, which was used as the cover of *Paper* magazine. The center figure, or the "main Pocahontas," is sitting on a chair with her breasts out and two bling-bling pieces covering her nipples. Her legs are also covered in sparkling knee-high boots. Pocahontas number two is standing, draped over her shoulder, with her right hand touching the middle Pocahontas's nipple; she is also dressed in a short skirt. Pocahontas number three is on her knees, with black knee-high boots, wearing a black bodysuit, appearing to perform oral sex on the middle Pocahontas.

The images of the Disney-themed Pocahontas are disturbing. And Native women did not take too kindly to seeing this. For instance, in a response published in *Bitch Media* by Abaki Beck, who is Blackfeet and European American, she wrote,

> Lest we forget: Pocahontas was a teenage rape victim who was forced to marry older Englishman John Rolfe and died at the age of 20 in England. Thanks to Disney, she is one of the few pop culture representations of Native Americans that most Americans are familiar with. With her post . . . Minaj directly contributed to the sexualization of Native women that continues to put them in danger.[15]

Beck is correct to call Minaj's post ahistorical and problematic. She goes on to cite an important book by Muscogee-Creek law professor Sarah Deer, *The Beginning and End of Rape* (2015), and the data on sexual assault and violence against Indigenous women in Canada and the United States. She also identifies how this form of cultural appropriation contributes to the invisibility of Indigenous people at large. While I don't think Beck's commentary is anti-Black (women), I do think a discussion of intersectionality and positionality is essential.

Intersectionality is used in so many contexts today that it often loses the power of its original intent: to understand how multiple forms of oppression impact the material lives of Black (and other) women of color. Patricia Hill Collins and Sirma Bilge argue that intersectional frameworks do two things. First, they "understand power relations through a lens of mutual construction" and that people's "lives are generally shaped by many factors in diverse and mutually influencing ways."[16] They also contend that "power relations are to be analyzed both via their intersections, for example, of racism and sexism, as well as *across domains of power*, namely structural, disciplinary, cultural, and interpersonal."[17]

Beck's commentary breaks down issues of power, including invisibility and the violence suffered by Indigenous women, but not once does she mention that, in spite of Minaj's celebrity, she is still a Black woman. Yes, Minaj profits off her hypersexuality; yes, she benefits from her celebrity and can have a major impact on others; and yes, celebrities be hella out of touch with the reality of others, but she still deals with sexism and racism because she is a Black woman. (I should put it out there that I am absolutely not a Nicki stan!) Minaj is guilty of utilizing the Disney-created Pocahontas, but she did not create it—Disney did. And as far as the art goes, Beck did not spend that same energy criticizing the artist. The artist, David Salamanca, who is a white-looking Argentinian artist, created the image—where was the rage about him? What about *Paper*? Who is the editor of the magazine? Why were they not the main target of the criticism?

This image represents the complications that Black and Indigenous women's hypersexualization and Indian play in the capitalist media. Nicki Minaj is wrong. The artist is wrong, and has some, perhaps, racist ideas. If playing Indian is also about the creation of a sense of self, this photo doesn't much change Minaj's persona of a Black woman empowered through hypersexualization within the capitalist cultural marketplace—a market that continues to negatively portray Black women. Indeed, as black feminist critic bell hooks notes in her essay "Selling Hot Pussy: Representations of Black Female Sexuality in the Cultural Marketplace,"

> Bombarded with images representing black female bodies as expendable, black women have either passively absorbed this thinking

or vehemently resisted it. Popular culture provides countless examples of black female appropriation and exploitation of "negative stereotypes" to either assert control over the representation or at least reap the benefits of it. Since black female sexuality has been represented in racist/sexist iconography as more free and liberated, many black women singers, irrespective of the quality of their voices, have cultivated an image which suggests they are sexually available and licentious.[18]

Hooks presents for us an opportunity to reflect on how Black women artistically produce sexuality within the culture of capitalism. Minaj posted an image of something she did not draw, which is important. It doesn't absolve her of guilt—she is guilty of contributing to the hypersexualization of a real and imagined person (the historical figure of Pocahontas and the Disney character). But it is clear that the artist's conception should be under equal scrutiny.

However, what if we think about the post in other ways, in addition to its clear Indian play? For instance, look at the eyes of the subjects. They are gazing back at the audience, indicating a power move—one, perhaps, of women directly challenging the gaze of the sexist audience? Through the hypersexualization, perhaps Minaj is also attempting to reclaim, at least in part, the idea of women's sexual empowerment? Again, my aim is not to dismiss the interpretation but to think alongside that critique, and consider other aspects of the image, even how Nicki Minaj looks at her subjects.

The critique of Minaj, as with Omerretta, seems to be based on the premise that as Black women they should know better. Of course, they can do better. But, again, if anyone can reproduce a settler-colonial idea, then even Black people can fuck up. However, it seems that when Black people make (egregious) mistakes, people get a little bit saucier (or bring out a little bit of antiblackness?) in their critiques.

Black and Indigenous solidarity is a difficult task, no matter how hard we might try. Furthermore, solidarity is not inevitable; it requires intensive labor, intentional compassion, and love. We will disagree, but we must work from a position of kindness and patience. We might get upset with one another, we might call each other out, but it should be done through love, and with the larger intention of ending the structural forces of antiblackness and settler colonialism. This work requires patience. We should ask, given that our education system is so broken, when would a non-Indigenous person of color learn about Indigenous erasure? If "playing Indian" and Indigenous erasure is as pervasive as I think it is, how mad can I be when people of color support racist Native imagery? When would they have learned otherwise? You don't know what you ain't never learned. We can assume that they have Google and have read about why something is racist or problematic, but we don't know for sure, and if algorithms work to curate for you what you see on social media and the internet at large, then there is hardly any chance in hell that someone who is ignorant about a subject will learn about it.

As I mentioned above, holding each other accountable is important. But it has to be rooted in liberation and not individualism. It can't replicate the carceral state's goal of punishment. What I'm saying is that we shouldn't be out here snitching on one another, calling out people in public, for some individual pettiness; save that for your private DMs. We have to rely on those with wisdom in our communities, young and old, and find ways to be better human beings. Finally, we need to be patient with one another. If that's not the point of holding people accountable, then what is?

Technology and social media are not going to save us. Only our offline relationships built on a foundation of revolutionary struggle will. If, as Safiya Umoja Noble convincingly argues in her book, *Algorithms of Oppression: How Search Engines Reinforce Racism* (2018), that this form of technology is not neutral, and can reproduce racist and sexist ideas about Black women, then how can we rely on it to order our steps in the fight for social justice and radical transformation?[19] Our liberation is going to come in face-to-face meetings and taking it to the streets.

R*DSK*N/N*GG*R/NIGGA AND THE POWER OF LANGUAGE

In this section, I want to analyze the discourse on blackface and redface, specifically the social use of two words. But first, what is language? Language is an essential component of our everyday lives. It shapes how we think about the world and our place in it. Language is also symbolic, and has many meanings depending on context, time, place, and who is involved. Before expanding, let me share a brief story of being on the rez, my brother and cousins, and a rap battle.

In the summer of 2007, I was with my two cousins and my older brother. My brother and I were on the rez partying it up for a few days, staying at our auntie's crib. My cousins knew of a party happening on the rez, so we went. There was a wide array of people. There were Saginaw Chippewas, Black folks, and some whites. We had a blast. Toward the end of the night, we noticed a commotion and went to see what it was about. Two young men, a Black brotha and a Native brotha, were engaged in a rap battle. I was curious to see how the Native brotha was going to do. The Black brotha went first, getting all up in the Native brotha's grill, spitting out some clunky but decent lines and referring to the Native brotha as "nigga" a few times. The Native brotha came out with some fire. They went for another round. Both rhymers got better. I was struck, however, in the second round, when the Native brotha said something like, "I will destroy you, nigga."

I, having just finished my second year of university and thinking I knew everything, awkwardly looked around (think Issa Rae from the show *Insecure*) to see if my brother or cousins heard it. They continued to watch the battle. I couldn't listen anymore and was bothered. My family was unbothered. I asked them about it later and they seemed to have collectively concluded that *hey, we all niggas!* I thought to myself, *Damn, can this Native nigga actually say "nigga"? Maybe I was the nigga trippin'!*[20] I tell this story to reveal the complexities of the N-word and the politics of who can say it, who has said it, and who might want to think carefully about saying it outside certain community boundaries. To my non-Black folks, I'm not saying don't say it, cause, you know, some Black people are cool with non-Black people saying it. Other people wanna be grown and pretend like the N-word passport allows them entry and usage in every Black group. If you're non-Black and out here slinging the N-word, I would highly recommend you understand that the laying on of hands might come your way—and I ain't talkin' bout the preacher praying for you at church!

According to critical sociolinguist and activist Geneva Smitherman, "Language plays a dominant role in the formation of ideology, consciousness, behavior and social relations; thus contemporary political and social theory must address the role of language in social change."[21] Discourse and language are important factors in oppression, and also liberation. This concept applies to a discussion of the terms "n*gg*r/nigga" and "r*dsk*n." The conversation vexes me.

It baffles me when I hear Indigenous people uncritically assert, "You wouldn't say the N-word, so why would you say the R-word?!" What if I told all my Indigenous peers that Black folks do, in fact, use the N-word? Would that change your question?

Let me break down the uses of the N-word. There are two versions: "n*gg*r" and "nigga." The former is racist; I don't need to explain anything else about it. The latter has some nuance to it. Black people use it in a variety of contexts. Some are okay with it and some are not. There are a variety of opinions about it.

For example, in July 2007, in Detroit, Michigan, at the NAACP's Ninth Annual Convention, a funeral ceremony was held to actually bury the N-word. A march preceded the funeral; led by NAACP chairman Julian Bond and now-disgraced former Detroit mayor Kwame Kilpatrick, hip-hop icon Curtis Blow and R&B legend Eddie Levert, it extended from Cobo Hall to Hart Plaza. Addressing the N-word, Kilpatrick proclaimed, "We don't want to see you around here no more." Even former Michigan Democratic governor Jennifer Granholm participated in the procession, holding forth with some white-woman liberalism, proclaiming, "We can plant the seed to a new word, the 'A' word. All—all our people. We're all in this together." To her credit, Granholm followed that up by suggesting we end forms of structural racism, including predatory lending and the end to affirmative action.[22] Whether she actually believed it, her policies said otherwise. (I don't have much more to say about this, but y'all NAACP niggas need to go on somewhere and go back to your roots!) In other words, Black people hold many opinions about the word.

It can be used positively, negatively, or be neutral. If someone says, "That's my nigga" or an elongated "Myyyyyy nigga," then that is positive. If someone says, "Fuck that nigga," then that is negative. Neutral would be something like, "Niggas is wildin." That could refer to people in general, Black people, white people. I have friends and family who apply "nigga" to a variety of people, regardless of race. The neutrality of "nigga" in the sentence means that if I took it out, the meaning of the sentence—that someone or some people are acting a fool—would not change. "Nigga" is here to stay, and I'm okay with that, even with its pervasiveness.

Black folks use "nigga" as a term of endearment or greeting. The late, great rapper Tupac Shakur stated that "nigga" stood for "Never Ignorant, Getting Goals Accomplished." Again, Geneva Smitherman has long written about the use of "nigga," writing:

> It's a fact that nigga is from the lexicon of the counter language that African Americans have created over the centuries, turning the White man's language upon its head, transforming bad into good. The impact of words depends on who is saying what to whom, under what conditions, and with what intentions. Meanings reside in the speakers of the language.[23]

In spite of this research, there is always an older head who references the history of the N-word and why it should never be used. I'm cool with that. However, that is also not a realistic goal since the fact remains that Black people do use "nigga." As we can see, "nigga" is firmly rooted in the idea of a counter language. This doesn't mean that everyone agrees with it, but it does have a longer history, and one that is widely used in Black communities. Even noted public intellectual Michael Eric Dyson notes that Dr. King once used the term "nigga" to refer to one of his comrades.[24] Furthermore, Black people, as Smitherman notes, don't "call each other nigga," for "call" implies name-calling, a linguistic offense, like "he called me a name," or, in Black Talk, he "called outa my name." Rather, "nigga" is used to address another African American, as a greeting, or to refer to a Brotha or Sista. So, it's semantically inaccurate for someone to critique the everyday, conversational use of "nigga" by complaining that they "call each other nigga all the time."[25]

Black folks can *allow* non-Black people to use it (but, again, I'd be careful 'cause language does have consequences). Black and non-Black people can use it in oppressive ways, too, depending on the context or action involved or the meaning intended. Hip-hop does share *some* of the blame for allowing some non-Black people to use it, but not completely. Non-Black people, especially white people, just want to use it to be cool and probably racist. If hip-hop did not exist, white people would still be using the racist version of the N-word. The R-word, however, is less complicated.

"R*dsk*n," as far as I know, has one, maybe two contexts. It was formerly used as the Washington Football Team's name, accompanied by a racist logo. Shout out to Suzan Harjo, Amanda Blackhorse, and all the people who have been making noise for years. Billionaires may have forced their hand, but your activism was the foundation for them getting rid of that racist image and name. The sports media continue to use it, though. The word is used to dehumanize Indigenous peoples, keeping them in the past. On a few occasions, I have heard some Indigenous youth using "skin" as a term of endearment. I haven't seen the evidence to suggest that Indigenous people use it as pervasively as "nigga." I've also heard of some folks who use the phrase "what up, my Native" instead of "nigga," which, if we wanted to be very critical, is a little too close to "nigga." Regardless, the R-word is just racist, unless it precedes a potato.

No one wants to be a r*dsk*n. It is almost entirely used in a derogatory manner. In general, you don't go up to someone and be like, "What up, my redskin," or "That's my redskin"—unless I've missed something. It just wouldn't happen, because even the most racist white people wouldn't use the term outside of their entangled belief in the Washington Football Team. It is just not a term circulated in everyday discourse. Of course, this is because of settler colonialism and its major goal of erasing any Indigenous presence. Still, the term does not have the same mainstream usage as "nigga."

Over the last several years, I've seen numerous Native people comment on non-Black-Indigenous people using the N-word. The social media version goes something like this: if you're not Afro-Indigenous (here meaning someone who is African American and Native American), then you should not be using the term. A good example is a series of short video interviews initially released in 2015 but that resurfaced in 2019, on Indigenous Peoples' Day (formerly Columbus Day; the only Christopher we now acknowledge is Wallace—the Notorious B. I. G.). On November 26, 2015, the *Daily Mail*, a UK online news source, posted the videos featuring a variety of Native Americans on the topics of Christopher Columbus, Thanksgiving, and the term "r*dsk*n." While the point of the videos was to offer Indigenous voices on these issues, it was perhaps overshadowed by the one on the R-word.

The interviewee is asked about the use of the R-word. Below is the exchange, and it's offensive. Whenever you use the term "nigger" or "redskin" or "whitey" or "ch*nk," it's definitely not a good thing.

> INTERVIEWER: Has anyone ever called you a "redskin" or any-
> thing else insulting?
> RESPONDENT: A "river n****r." I've been called that all through-
> out high school. I was like, 1 out of 4 Native Americans. So, I
> experienced a lot of racism. And I still do. I definitely speak up.
> I definitely, in a good way, let people know that using offensive
> words is not something that will help us progress as a nation.[26]

The issue that people on social media had is her use of the N-word. She is correct in being offended. No one wants to be called a river n****r or a n****r lover or any variation. Although, given the rampant nature of antiblackness, it's hard to know if people are offended because they have been called something racist or simply that it is perhaps the most offensive word in the English language, and so they have been associated with Black people, something that all minorities know not to want to associate with outside of hip-hop. Both the R-word and the N-word are steeped in white supremacy. Arguably, Black folks have more sway in the public sphere in getting attention on issues (owing to the growing sympathies of white people?), and therefore, by comparing the two, Indigenous people could gain more needed exposure. The R-word is racist, demeaning, and, as far as I can tell, Indigenous people generally don't use it as a term of endearment. However, the missing part of the analysis is that, while both are steeped in white supremacy, the N-word is slightly more complicated.

This leads me to ask several questions: Why compare the N-word and R-word? Should we compare them? Who benefits? Do Black and Indigenous people equally benefit from the conversation? At this juncture, I would say yes and no. In addition to Indigenous peoples' long-standing activism and research, the Washington Football Team's decision to remove their racist image and nickname could be attributed to the pressure from the Movement for Black Lives and corporations like Bank of America, FedEx, Nike, and Pepsi.[27] However, the discursive history of the comparison should shed some light on the limits of discursive forms of solidarity.

To highlight the indirect impact that raising awareness about the N-word has had on efforts targeting the R-word is not at all to discount the dogged advocacy of Indigenous peoples. They have long fought for respect and an end to racist imagery through #ChangetheName campaigns and highly visible court cases. In addition, John and Kenn Little made *More Than a Word*, a fantastic documentary released in 2017, on the history of the R-word. Indigenous peoples have some platforms through which to share their voices on issues such as language, including social media. Again, if we take seriously discursive solidarity, we have to consider how Black folks benefit or do not benefit from the comparison.

Another controversial term is "savage." Everybody is a "savage" these days, or something they do is labeled "savage." Damn, things done changed! I don't remember when I first heard the word used this way. I hear "savage" from a lot of young Black people in person and on social media, and it usually refers to someone doing something fearless, beyond belief, even absurdly funny. The use of the term is ubiquitous throughout hip-hop culture and has many contexts. You can go savage on a beat or just be a savage. Hip-hop sensation Megan Thee Stallion has inverted "savage" to mean Black women's empowerment. Over the last four years while giving talks, Native people have asked me, "Why are Black people using the term 'savage'? It's offensive to me!"

It's one of those comments I hear that, as an Afro-Indigenous person, makes me want to pull out the little hair that I have left. Native Americans who now exist in the US have never been the only savages, and also don't have a monopoly on the word "savage." Europeans have called people of African descent "savages" as they have with Indigenous people throughout modern history. If Black people want to use the term, It's fine. We can't be mad at their rhetorical brevity, their ability to semantically invert a word and change the meaning. In fact, changing "bad" to mean good or "savage" to mean something different is hella savage!

I'm not saying that words don't have power, and that they can't also be harmful. Black people have not fully wrested the term "savage" from its white supremacist roots, and probably never will. But they have done a little damage. And depending on who says it, the word is not created equal. For instance, there are probably some young white folks who use the word "savage" among their POC peer groups—I say, have at it. But I wouldn't go around calling Black or Indigenous people a savage, peer or no peer. You may slip up and use it, but your peer may then turn into a "savage," slip up themselves and accidentally show you some tough love. While not everything should be compared, I think solidarity can happen, and has happened in the realm of popular culture.

BLACK PEOPLE CHALLENGING MASCOTS IN THE PUBLIC SPHERE

Black Americans have found many ways to challenge anti-Indigenous racism in the media. For instance, on May 20, 2000, Rev. Dr. Bernice Jackson, a former executive director of the *Civil Rights Journal* of the United Church of Christ Commission for Racial Justice, penned an op-ed in the *Pittsburgh Courier* regarding the need to eliminate the Cleveland Indians' Chief Wahoo symbol. She had been protesting with Indigenous peoples outside the Cleveland Indians stadium for at least a decade before writing the op-ed. While the team, in part, put an end to the use of the symbol in 2019, there is still the need to eradicate the vestiges of Indian play. They need to get rid of the music and the tomahawk chops that are a part of the game experience.

In 2000, Bernice Jackson had already proclaimed that they need to get rid of Chief Wahoo in an op-ed. She began with, "It is so important that as we move into this new millennium that we do not take our old baggage with us."[28] The baggage she referred to was racism, in particular that of the Chief Wahoo logo. She gets right to the heart of the matter about the symbol's overt racism: "Chief Wahoo is a racist stereotype and logo. The bug-eyed, buck-toothed, grinning red figure honors no one. It destroys the self-esteem of Native American children and it mis-educates other children. It teaches them that indigenous people are sports team mascots, not human beings created in the image of God."

She also gives the definition of racism: prejudice plus power. Applying that definition to his case, she remarks, "Chief Wahoo is a racist symbol because those in power—in this case, the sports industry and mainstream media—refuse to hear the voice of the oppressed." Concluding the piece, she writes, "Native-American people are a proud people, as well they should be. They have given many gifts to all of us. Indeed, some might say they gave the greatest gift of all—their land, albeit unwillingly. We have taken much from them and now it is time to give them something back—their dignity. Native-Americans are people, not mascots to our sports industry." Jackson also understood the importance of land to Indigenous struggles. Others have followed in her path, continuing to carry out acts of Black solidarity with Indigenous peoples in the sports industry and mainstream media.

BOMANI JONES AND THE CAUCASIAN T-SHIRT

On April 7, 2016, sports journalist and television personality Bomani Jones, a cohost of ESPN's *High Noon* and formerly *Highly Questionable*, made headlines by wearing a "Caucasian" T-shirt on ESPN's *Mike & Mike* show. The T-shirt was designed by Brian Kirby, through his company Shelf Life Clothing, and intended to raise awareness about and help eliminate the Cleveland Baseball Team's Chief Wahoo logo. Joining the show that day was ESPN anchor Molly Qerim Rose, who asked him what statement he was trying to make. Jones responded, "It's obvious, this is the same thing that goes on with the logo for the Cleveland Indians." He pointed out the hypocrisy of those who refuse to see the logo as anything other than racism. "To have a problem with the logo of this would be to have a problem with the Indians. But if you're quiet about the Indians, and now have something to say about my shirt, I think it's time for introspection."[29]

Importantly, he also hit the nail on the head about the political economy of racist mascots, by pointing out that the reason that the Cleveland Baseball Team—or the Washington Football Team, for that matter—didn't get rid of their mascot is that they make money off it. Jones told the truth. Dan Snyder, the owner of the Washington Football Team, proclaimed as recently as 2013 that he would never change the team name.[30] Even before the removal of the image and mascot, the organization removed the statue of the team's founder, George Marshall, because he was an ardent racist. When it happened,

I wondered, "How can Snyder remove a racist statue but not consider removing the logo?" We know why. For Dan Snyder and other powerful billionaires and corporations, the symbolic support of tackling white supremacy is useful only when it is in fashion.

I'm glad we are taking down other racist iconography and symbols. The logos of Land O' Lakes butter, which features a Native woman, is being removed, as is the Black woman on the face of that diabesity liquid called Aunt Jemima syrup. (I used to excuse the shit out of racism and pile the liquid and butter on some pancakes and waffles!) I'm ecstatic that NASCAR got rid of the Confederate flags. Let's not forget Bree Newsome, who in 2015 scaled a pole to take down the Confederate symbol flag in South Carolina! She still the real MVP!

A point that we often miss or dilute about these symbols and why people are upset is that they aren't just about cultural appropriation. Cultural appropriation means very little unless we frame it under neoliberalism—or perhaps more precisely, under racial capitalism. Corporations, catering to their largely white audiences, earn money by dehumanizing Indigenous peoples. If companies and professional sports teams remove racist imagery, it doesn't necessarily mean that these billionaire corporations suddenly have a conscience; we shouldn't even be that excited about these minor changes. It just means they understand they can no longer make money off racist symbols.

Of course, Twitter exploded with criticism of Bomani Jones, some of whom said he was race-baiting. Kirby, the shirt's designer, stated his support for Jones, "Bomani Jones couldn't have been a more perfect spokesman for the intent of the shirt." Kirby wanted it to be humorous while making a point: "It's just holding up a mirror saying, 'Hey, I'm wearing this and you're broadcasting Indians games with the same kind of imagery. Why is this a problem and that not a problem?' It's about flipping the image on it."[31] This was an important national moment of Black solidarity. Jones did not have to engage in such an act that could have got him disciplined, if not fired. However, in order to change racist imagery, we need supporters both from the marginalized group being targeted and those outside it. Although the Cleveland Baseball Team and the Washington Football Team have changed their names, we also need sportscasters to stop saying the word because they can't help making a racist, Freudian slip. It shouldn't be that hard.

DESUS AND MERO, SATIRE, AND THE CHICAGO HOCKEY TEAM

Desus and Mero is the name of a television show, and also the names of the personalities who host it. It is a mix of comedy, analysis of pop culture, and political satire. These two Black men from the Bronx—Desus (real name: Daniel Baker), born to immigrant Jamaican parents, and the Kid Mero (real name: Joel Martinez), born to Dominican parents—through comedy offer plenty of commentary on politics, calling out racism and offering many other forms of cultural, political, and social critique. One particular rhetorical moment stood out to me that demonstrated their knowledge and commitment to solidarity with Indigenous peoples. They pointed out the issue of racist mascots, and how Black players experience racism in a predominantly white sport.

In February 2018, Desus and Mero did a segment on an incident involving the Chicago Bl*c*h*wks hockey team in which a group of fans taunted a Black player with racist remarks. Desus begins the segment, "A Chicago hockey fan was banned for life after racially taunting a Black player."[32] The fans, seen pointing at Washington Capitals player Devante Smith-Pelly, yelled "basketball" at him while he was sitting in the penalty box. He then confronted them with his stick held high.

Desus sarcastically adds, "How can I be racist if I'm rooting for the Blackhawks?" Mero then quickly chimes in, pointing out the major contradiction, "Also, nobody ever said anything about the Blackhawks logo?" Desus comes back, call-and-response fashion, "It's double layers of racism." The Capitals' coach, Barry Trotz, in an interview later remarked, "There's absolutely no place in the game of hockey or our country for racism. . . . I think it's disgusting, and there's no place for it . . . it just shows ignorance."[33] Desus and Mero also point out the contradictions of Trotz's remark by using another clip, this one a statement by Chicago team captain Jonathan Toews: "We don't support that kind of behavior and in this day and age it's time to start moving past that and realize that we don't want to stoop to those levels." Desus remarks, "You know, you want racial progression? Let's focus on our racist logo first."

Desus and Mero get it! They understand that double layers of racism can exist, and offer the possibility that Black popular culture can also deviate from Black issues and contribute to Indigenous peoples' struggle to put an end to dehumanizing mascots. At the end of the segment, Desus says, "Even the Cleveland Indians like, 'Yo, we gon' chill with that.'"[34] The possibilities are endless, and as we protest dehumanizing mascots, protest out in the streets, let's not forget the joys and possibilities of Black and Indigenous laughter.

They had done a lot of work learning about the issue. Interestingly enough, people had called them out on Twitter, particularly Desus, for wearing a Bl*c*h*wks hat on television in October 2017. They did not take it personally, and they addressed it in this particular segment using critical inquiry. Shout out to them! Black and Indigenous folks can learn from their example! Let's grow together.

The challenges and possibilities of Black and Indigenous solidarity in the realm of popular culture can be fleeting. Formal and informal education about each other's histories is important, but this must all be followed by collective action. We need to support each other. We need to end antiblackness and Indigenous erasure in the public sphere, by all means necessary. As the previous chapters have demonstrated, we have done it before and we can do it again.

In part, what we need is for Black and Indigenous creatives, whether they're poets, visual artists, or singers who help us imagine another world, to collaborate. They can show each of their respective communities what solidarity looks like, and also illustrate the possibilities of our shared futures, and what a holistic humanity can look like. We also need Black and Indigenous artists to collaborate on projects, and create the Afro-Indigenous future we need. We tend to think of our issues as so different that we can't collaborate. If Black comedians, for instance, can stop erasing Indigenous peoples and using jokes that are based on stereotypes of Native people, and if Native people can avoid the pitfalls of appropriating blackness without acknowledgment, then we can get somewhere free. Above all, our conception and use of popular culture should be for expressing ourselves and humanizing ourselves to each other.

Popular culture matters. How we produce it and how we consume it is also important. As we move from cultural appropriation to cultural appreciation to the forms of culture that will emerge in the aftermath of settler colonialism and white supremacy, it is urgent that we learn each other's histories. We must carefully produce popular culture together. Cultural collaboration will be a key part of our evolving society. We need to continue to walk side by side and produce culture that is, in Frantz Fanon's words, "based on the values that inspired the struggle for freedom."[35] In this aftermath moment, our cultures will represent not just struggle, critique, and pain, but the joys of freedom.

CHAPTER EIGHT

THE MATTER OF BLACK AND INDIGENOUS LIVES, POLICING, AND JUSTICE

LIKE MANY PEOPLE who believe in justice, I was angry at the deaths of Breonna Taylor and George Floyd. It reminded me of the continued epidemic of the Missing and Murdered Indigenous Women in Canada and the US.[1] I was also reminded of the killing of Indigenous people like fourteen-year-old child Jason Pero, in November 2017.[2] These murders and systematic violence reminded me of two things: that we live in what Frantz Fanon called "atmospheric violence,"[3] and that policing, a form of surveillance and social control, is intimately tied to US democracy.[3] As Malcolm X once stated about the lack of justice in American courts,

> This is American justice. This is American democracy and those of you who are familiar with it know that in American democracy is hypocrisy. Now if I'm wrong put me in jail, but if you can't prove that democracy is not hypocrisy then don't put your hands on me. Democracy is hypocrisy. If democracy means freedom why aren't our people free? If democracy means justice, why don't we have justice? If democracy means equality why don't we have equality?[4]

The question of whether we can achieve freedom within US democracy, including under its laws and justice system, its economic structure, and whether we can truly take the conceptual principles set out by white slave owners and land stealers and apply them is still up in the air.

We should be outraged but never be surprised. Black and Indigenous peoples will never get justice in the US because it is a police state. The democratic project has been designed to control them/us. You can't have justice in a state built on enslavement and the dispossession of Indigenous land until something new emerges. One of the many challenges is that we often can't see beyond a course of action as simple as say voting. Voting is important but so is changing how elections are financed. We need a political imagination beyond what we can't seem to be able to get.

On June 1, 2020, I tuned into the ESPN show *First Take*, anchored by Stephen A. Smith and Max Kellerman. While I don't usually enjoy Stephen A.'s yelling and sports takes, I do like to see him and Max go back and forth. But on this day, I was concerned about how they would discuss the ongoing rebellions happening throughout US cities. Stephen A., who I consider an ideological liberal at best and only slightly left of being a black conservative—"stay off the weeeed" comes to mind—came with the fire. I told my homie, "He sound like Malcolm X."

While I enjoyed the discussion between the hosts and their guests, what I was really struck by was some of the language exhibited in the signs in ESPN's protest footage. Because protest signs and other visuals are carefully chosen by the media for spectacle, one of them stood out to me. It had the hashtag #holdthepoliceaccountable, which got me thinking about other phrases and ideological suggestions for how we might get free: "End police brutality"; "We need police reform"; "We need a community review board"; "We need police who are a part of our community"; "Defund the police."

Pundits, including CNN's Don Lemon and Black athletes, while offering some critical commentary, also suggest we need white athletes to speak up more. I want us to think about some of these asks. Do we really need more white voices? If history has taught us anything, they almost all refuse to go into the heart of the beast of racism: in their own families and with their friends. White terrorists and supremacists aren't part of some random group of lone radicals; they are the friends and family of our white colleagues, neighbors, friends, and people who provide services on our behalf. Additionally, if you're Black, Indigenous, and Latinx, and you have a family member in the police, you have to deal with an uneasy and complicated choice between your love for your family and your belief in revolutionary justice—to quote N.W.A, it's a matter of Black police, and Indigenous and Latinx police, "showin' out for the white cop" and white supremacy. We can't celebrate police marching with protesters; the people aren't the problem. They need to deal with the racial brutalizing of their peers. What they could do is drop their badges and teach the people how to protect themselves. That would be a revolutionary act.

Now, let me get back to police reform. Let me say this clearly: we cannot reform the police. We cannot hold them accountable. A community review board is cool, but it won't work long term. Hell, Black and Latinx people have been calling for community oversight for decades. I was doing archival research on Detroit and discovered that way back in 1917, Black people were asking for an end to police brutality! Having police be a part of your community might sound good, but then we reduce police brutality to "a few bad apples" and exclusively the result of white individuals. Black and Latinx and Indigenous police officers commit brutality too, because they work on behalf of a system designed to protect the property of the wealthy and control people of color. We can't focus exclusively on ending police brutality. Here is why: a focus on ending police brutality does not, in effect, dismantle the colonial order of policing. Policing—the social, political, and economic control of subjugated people—will continue to exist. We have to work to dismantle the police. Defunding the police is an important step.

The People's Budget LA, a coalition of Black Lives Matter LA and several other Los Angeles–based organizations, have recommended that the city council and mayor of Los Angeles reduce the Los Angeles Police Department budget from 54 percent to 5.7 percent.[5] We can and should defund the police, or at least drastically reduce their funding, at the local level and divert that money to other services that focus on the health of our most vulnerable.[6] As an alternative to the police, the people surveyed by People's Budget LA recommend a "Universal Aid and Crisis Management" funding category. This includes funding for

> long-term housing, renter support and emergency housing, food assistance, support for those seeking work, support for small businesses, providing public health care, offering youth development

programs and supporting youth centers, fighting the impacts of climate change and ensuring our city's environment is protected.[7]

This is an important way to reallocate money. However, another question to ask is, what to do with trained killers? Will they then be turned into "social workers" and cause even more harm? Can they, especially the Black, Indigenous, and Latinx officers, truly be reintegrated into our communities? Would they want to be? Maybe they could return and teach everyday people how to defend themselves.

If budgets are reduced, and liberal governments tell the public that they are reducing the police, will they then contract with private security companies in the name of protecting the people? We've already seen a process like this play out in our public schools.

We should take away police officers' guns. We can strip them of guns, but then we will have to question why police officers need guns in the first place, then deal with the necessity of the Second Amendment, which will lead to a more fundamental question as to why we hold the Constitution as sacrosanct. I know we are not all ready for these conversations!

Another reason why we can't reform the police is policing is a fundamental part of US democracy. As I mentioned in the first few chapters, the architects of the US democratic project not only designed their political program to protect themselves against factions (such as the Africans and the Indigenous nations) and the will of the majority but to also control Indigenous peoples and land. They tried to ignore the issue of slavery. Black and Indigenous Lives didn't matter then; they still don't matter. There are other entities that also need to be held accountable and directly confronted.

Guns aren't the only weapon of choice for police officers. We must ask this question: Where do police officers learn their techniques that lead to the violent brutalization and death of Black, Indigenous, and Latinx peoples? The martial arts community. When we see a police officer mounting a Black person and controlling their wrists and legs, holding them in a chokehold, putting their knee on someone's neck, you know where they learned that from? A martial artist. They learn chokeholds from Brazilian jujitsu experts. They learn disarmament maneuvers from many types of martial arts. I recall one photo of police officers—I believe in Los Angeles—holding Kali rattan sticks.

These are sticks used in Filipino martial arts, which uses sticks and knives. If you've ever practiced with the Kali sticks and accidentally get hit by your sparring partner, it stings. Imagine being a protester and getting hit with them! In this regard, we also have to hold the martial arts community accountable.

The martial arts experts who are teaching police forces need to sever their relationships with them and no longer accept training contracts. I've been to at least a few gyms in my life and always see someone who has all the signs of a white supremacist. Don't train them. I understand you have bills to pay and deserve to be paid for your labor, but you are actively teaching people who commit violence against Black and Indigenous people. If you want to help someone, actively recruit and train the people who are suffering from police violence in order that they can defend themselves.

BLACK LIVES MATTERS AND NATIVE LIVES MATTER, AND THE PROBLEM OF NAMING

I appreciate the many Indigenous voices who have expressed their solidarity for the movement against police brutality, including the Metropolitan Urban Indian Directors, which consists of thirty or so organizations focused on Indigenous issues in the Twin Cities in Minnesota. They condemned the murder of George Floyd. They also highlighted the history of the Minneapolis Police Department's violent actions, pointing out that the reason the American Indian Movement was founded in 1968 in the first place was because of police brutality. "No more," they proclaimed. "We demand action and improvement, nothing less."[8] I appreciate their solidarity and that they underscored the systemic issue of police violence against Indigenous peoples. We should not forget that Indigenous peoples are also targeted by the police, and it's not just in border towns. Mainstream society ignores the fact that the majority of Native people live in cities. So, being non-white, they of course will suffer from police violence there. However, they often found some solace in asserting that they don't need to be erased, that Indigenous lives also matter.

Black Lives Matter was founded by three Black women organizers, Alicia Garza, Patrisse Khan-Cullors, and Opal Tometi, two of whom identify as queer. It began as a slogan in response to the acquittal of

George Zimmerman, the murderer of Trayvon Martin. Popular use of the #BlackLivesMatter hashtag across social media is, in the words of the founders, "an ideological and political intervention in a world where Black lives are systematically and intentionally targeted for demise. It is an affirmation of Black folks' humanity, our contributions to this society, and our resilience in the face of deadly oppression."[9] They were also concerned with dealing with the invisible, vulnerable population of Black queer, trans, and non-conforming folks. They wanted to make all Black lives matter.[10] BLM is a decentralized movement that continues to be involved in a variety of tactics and struggles, from Black immigrant rights and prison abolition to strategic forms of getting Black people to vote. They desire to bring light to the invisibility of what Black public intellectual Marc Lamont Hill calls "nobodies."[11]

The phrase "Black Lives Matter" has a clear herstory and ideological foundation. There is a genealogy. Similarly, Native Americans began to use the phrases "Native Lives Matter" to highlight that, they, too, were murdered by the police and continued to suffer all sorts of violence related not just to racism but the ongoing forms of dispossession they experience every day. Indeed, Native Americans have died disproportionately more from police violence than any other group. According to a CNN review of CDC data, between 1999 and 2015, for every 1 million people, an average 2.9 Native people died as a result of a "legal intervention," and the majority of those deaths were police shootings; Black Americans during that period were killed at a rate of 2.6 people per million, which means the mortality rate was 12 percent higher for Native people than for Black folks.[12] I do not highlight this to create division between Black and Indigenous peoples, and it should be obvious at this point that is not my intention. However, we have to come to terms with the fact that Native Americans cannot be forgotten when it comes to police brutality. Still, it is difficult to trace the genealogy of Native Lives Matter, and it is difficult to distinguish between the ways this sociolinguistic and social media construction is useful and the ways it merely coopts the movement that inspired its name.[13] If Black Lives Matter was created by queer Black women to assert the humanity of Black people in a country where their lives don't actually matter, is it cool that non-Black people apply it to their own movement? It's just like the hashtag #SayHerName, created by

Black women in response to the murder of Black women, in particular the tragedy of Sandra Bland's death.[14] Should, for instance, Indigenous or Latinx women use it? I will leave the question there, but if cultural appropriation has taught us anything, it is that as soon as you take something out of its original context, it becomes something different, and might even become a caricature.

Native people's use of tropes, slogans, and sayings taken from Black protest language is not new. For instance, we didn't see the emergence of "Red Power" until after Stokely Carmichael proclaimed "Black Power." We saw Native men and women use the Black Power fist as a signal of solidarity, and that they had power. To be clear, there was nothing wrong with adopting slogans and modes of protest. Many young Native people felt empowered by the more radical elements of the Black Freedom Movement. As I demonstrated in the previous chapters, they often worked together. The American Indian Movement was founded in Minneapolis, Minnesota, in order to stop police violence. The Red Power movement has its ideological roots in Black Power and further developed with the Native people's protest, for the purposes of asserting their sovereignty. In fact, the use of Red Power in this context is not at all radical—and that includes the call for the US government to honor the treaties. Native people wanted the US to simply do what it said it was going to do.

Native Lives Matter is rooted in the ideological genealogy of Black Power language, Red Power protest, and an assertion of Native sovereignty. I would further define it as an attempt to sociolinguistically construct an Indigenous reality that highlights the fact that Native people, too, suffer from police violence, even disproportionately, and their voices should be heard. Some Black folks might see Native people using "Lives Matter" as a form of cooptation that decenters the unique issues facing Black people, and, depending on whether those Indigenous people respect Black struggle, that might be correct. Black folks can't continue to erase Native people on whose land they now exist. Even using the chant "Whose streets? Our streets!" and not thinking about how that might contribute to Indigenous erasure is a problem. Black folks shouldn't uncritically except the narrative that the US can be reformed, that we can effect change by simply holding our leaders' feet to the fire. Where do Native people fit into this discussion? We need to foster forms of connection and move beyond the narrowness of "focusing on ourselves" first. As Black feminist prison abolitionist Angela Davis notes,

> I think we need to be more reflective, more critical and more explicit about our concepts of community. There is often as much heterogeneity within a black community, or more heterogeneity, than in cross-racial communities. . . . What is problematic is the degree to which nationalism has become a paradigm for our community-building processes.[15]

I see Native Lives Matter as an attempt to create Black and Indigenous public dialogue and an expression of solidarity. Native Lives Matter can hopefully shape a politics that leads to "a world that accommodates Indigenous nationhood, Indigenous ontologies, and Indigenous political practices."[16] After all, if Black lives matter on Turtle Island, then Native lives and land have to matter too. If, in moments like the murder of George Floyd and Breonna Taylor, Black folks desire and appreciate Indigenous solidarity, they also have to show up and show out for Native people murdered, like Leroy Martinez and all of the Indigenous women killed and gone missing.

Finally, we need to recognize that the *slogan* of Black Lives Matter might be compromised. Given how the corporate media and corporations are now paying money for anti-racism training, and major sports leagues, like the National Basketball Association, have even placed "Black Lives Matter" on the hardwood court, the slogan—not the movement or its ideological significance—has lost some of its luster. Here, we can learn a lesson from history. Stokely Carmichael may have used the phrase "Black Power" to promote his idea of Black capitalism, a strategy of Black economic empowerment that promoted a segregated economy to further improve the life chances of the Black community (a strategy even President Richard Nixon supported).[17] However, this was a far cry from overthrowing the racist capitalist system. I want to be very clear that I ain't throwing any shade at the founders of the movement. But we as people in struggle can't ignore that fact that the state—a combination of the corporate media, corporations, and the US government—adapts accordingly in order to appease the masses. We don't have to give up the work, but we have to adapt just as quickly.

THE POSSIBILITIES FOR
AFRO-INDIGENOUS FUTURES

We might think of Indigenous futurism as an even broader
social project, as one that we and our people have co-produced
for centuries. There is of course the artistic-theoretical
component of this project . . . but there is also a mundane facet
to this: the hard and less glamorous work of survival and care
for one another, which always has a future-bearing energy to it.

— BILLY-RAY BELCOURT (Driftpile Cree Nation)[1]

IN THIS BOOK, I have tried to demonstrate the history of the United States through the lens of Afro-Indigenous histories, relationships, and people. I have tried to show that the relationship between settler colonialism and white supremacy has been a defining feature of the United States, and that these political and material categories continue to shape our everyday lives. I want to end with a note, if you will, on why Black and Indigenous people need each other. In particular, we need to come together to liberate ourselves, all of us.

However, I must say that I often feel vexed—as a Black and Indigenous person—when this topic comes up. I'm forced to choose—between being Black or Indigenous but not both. I do believe that there is a natural possibility of coalition between Black and Indigenous communities. Although they are different, that difference does not mean that they cannot come together for radical transformation. I now want to turn to Black lesbian feminist Audre Lorde to frame my thoughts and also offer some advice, with love.

I used the words of Cree queer poet Billy-Ray Belcourt in this chapter's epigraph to show how we might proceed forward in creating the shared future that we want. He uses two key terms to describe our futures: "survival" and "care." Black and Indigenous survival after centuries of violence has been about creating a future. Survival has never been passive. It has been a sustained creation of possibility for living in a white supremacist world. Caring for one another is the only way we can actually imagine and then envision the society that we actually want to live in. This will not be easy.

We can't assume that our coalition based on survival and care for our future will be easy. As Audre Lorde notes in her essay "Learning from the 60s," "Any future vision which can encompass all of us, by definition, must be complex and expanding, not easy to achieve."[2] This quote should remind us that we will not figure things out right away. Liberation takes work; it takes compassion, love, and patience. It requires that we embrace our differences. To achieve such unity, again returning to Lorde, it "implies the coming together of elements which are, to begin with, varied and diverse in their particular natures."[3]

I think we clearly recognize the differences among each other. We fight over who has it worse, Blacks or Indigenous people. We talk emphatically that the defining feature of Indigenous peoples is the treaty relationship—which is true—but don't consider similarities. At all.

WHERE TO BEGIN?

First, we have to realize that, for the most part, we can't rely on most white people. It is a recurring historical truth. Sure, there are white exceptions who are antiracist and want liberation, but they are rare. I am glad to see a large number of white people in the streets protesting on behalf of Black lives. I remain cautious, though. I have seen countless videos of white millennials escalating out-of-control situations when we know that Black and Brown people are going to experience the brunt of white supremacy's force. I'm still struggling with the video footage of a young white woman yelling in the face of Black police officers, including a Black woman, that "they are the problem" and telling the Black woman to "smile for Breonna Taylor."[4] While I do believe the police need to be abolished, this white woman was more engaging in an act of whiteness than one of genuine protest. She might have sincerely believed in police abolition and desire justice for Breonna Taylor, but she must not forget that she is white, and even though Black police officers can show out for their white officer peers, and they are working for the state, it still doesn't sit right by me. Just because you are anti-police, that does not necessarily mean that your whiteness has disappeared or that anti-Black racism is gone. Remember what James Baldwin told us, "White Americans find it as difficult as white people elsewhere do to divest themselves of the notion that they are in possession of some intrinsic value that black people need, or want."[5] Even Dr. King—yes, the one that even conservatives love to tout as the content-of-your-character caricature—argued that he was disappointed in the "white moderate" who "is more devoted to 'order' than to justice; who prefers a negative peace which is the absence of tension to a positive peace which is the presence of justice . . . who paternalistically believes he can set the timetable for another man's freedom."[6] White liberals are who we should be concerned about. Of course, Malcolm X warned us to be aware of the fox and the wolf—by which he meant that white liberals would try and be your friend in order to take advantage of you, but the wolf would always make clear its intentions and commit an act of violence. Finally, let's not forget the words of South African and Black Consciousness movement freedom fighter Steve Biko, who wrote of white liberals:

> Instead of involving themselves in an all-out attempt to stamp out racism from their white society, liberals waste lots of time trying to prove to as many blacks as they can find that they are liberal. This arises out of the false belief that we are faced with a black problem. There is nothing the matter with blacks. The problem is WHITE RACISM and it rests squarely on the laps of the white society.[7]

History has shown us that, for the most part, white liberals can't be trusted. Of course, that isn't every white person, but if you grow up in a privileged society for centuries, it has to be hard to not only accept a possible uprooting of society but also an active dismantling of those structures that is led by others. And I'm not just referring to white men. I'm also talking to white women, the Beckies and Karens, who weaponize racism and call the police on Black people for simply living their lives. We shouldn't be surprised by them, though: their forbears participated in the slavery of this country.[8] I am pessimistic, but until they really listen and take heed of Black folks' understanding about how society works, they won't free themselves of their own white womanness, and truly be free.

It seems that Indigenous peoples often have a hard time dealing with Black people and their historical experiences. As I've alluded to elsewhere in the book, instead of thinking about Black people only through the lens of enslavement—though that is the fundamental source of their oppression—how about we think of them the way Cedric Robinson thought of them? How about we consider that they are a part of a longer historical legacy of (African) Indigenous peoples forcibly removed from their homeland? Why not? We do this for Cherokees forcibly removed to Indian territory, and they are still considered Indigenous even though they were removed from their homeland. I think this will require that we think long and hard about our commitment to the national boundaries of the United States, and think more globally—which of course means to also include Africans and the descendants of the enslaved.

I know that some people are going to proclaim that Black people are settlers and even have settler privilege. I will concede—based upon history—that some Black folks have contributed to settler colonialism by doing things on behalf of the settler state. For instance, I'm thinking here of the Buffalo Soldiers engaging in the western expansion of the US nation-state. However, they were not settlers. As Zoé Samudzi and William Anderson argue in their book *As Black as Resistance* (2018), the descendants of enslaved Africans today have tried to reconcile their past, recover their roots, and also create a home space within the US.[9]

There are Indigenous folks actively working to assert Indigenous sovereignty by engaging with Black folks on Turtle Island. I think Anishinaabe scholar Leanne Simpson has some important thoughts about this, particularly in her reflections during the aftermath of Missouri prosecutor Robert McCulloch's decision not to pursue charges against police officer Darren Wilson, who murdered Michael Brown in Ferguson, Missouri. Speaking out of solidarity and love, Simpson wrote, "I was reminded over and over this week that Black and Indigenous communities of struggle are deeply connected through our experiences with colonialism, oppression and white supremacy. . . . To me, Ferguson, is a call not only to indict the systems that create and maintain the forces of Indigenous genocide and antiblackness. I have a responsibility to make space on my land for those communities of struggles, to center and amplify Black voices and to co-resist."[10] While I think Black and Indigenous solidarity is important, we also have to include all people, especially other people of color, who want to engage in the struggle for freedom. While my particular focus is on Black and Indigenous liberation, I also realize that those struggles are connected to other struggles for undocumented rights (don't forget the Central American, Asian, Afro-Latinx, and African immigrants). But until we study and uproot the ongoing legacies of dispossession and enslavement, we ain't really gonna get nowhere!

KINSHIP AS SOLIDARITY

I had the great fortune of hearing one of my favorite scholars, Kim TallBear, give a talk at the University of Alberta, as part of the Creative Economies workshop hosted by my homies, Alex Da Costa and Dia Da Costa. TallBear's talk was, of course, brilliant. I was most struck by her discussion of kinship, and how Indigenous people, indeed all of us, need to restore more just relationships between non-Indigenous human and non-human forms. For Black Americans, kinship is essential. This will require Black folks to continue to come to terms with the trauma of antiblackness that they suffer from. In search of freedom dreams and a homeland, Black folks continue to suffer the trauma of enslavement and the lack of a home. To be sure, many do consider this place their home; however, they cannot forget that they are on Indigenous land. Each Indigenous nation must think about ways to be inclusive to their Indigenous homelands, based upon their laws, with the hopes of creating new ones for the future.

THE YEAR AGAINST RACISM, RACIAL DISCRIMINATION, AND XENOPHOBIA

Two decades ago, the United Nations declared 2001 as the year against racism and xenophobia. From August 31 to September 8, delegates from around the world met in Durban, South Africa, to discuss the history and ongoing consequences of racism and xenophobia, as well as a future free of it. It was significant that the government of South Africa, then led by President Thabo Mbeki, hosted the conference. With the new South Africa having just emerged from de jure apartheid only seven years earlier, it was essential to demonstrate the importance of ending racial discrimination.

In the opening remarks on August 31, President Mbeki declared, "Our common humanity dictates that as we rose against apartheid racism, so must we combine to defeat the consequences of slavery, colonialism and racism," which for him, "continue to define the lives of billions of people who are brown and black, as lives of hopelessness."[11] Mbeki knew firsthand the ongoing consequences of apartheid, both racism and colonialism. The official declaration published by the United Nations referred to colonialism and Indigenous peoples, recognizing that the conference was taking place in the "International Decade of the World's Indigenous People," which "presents a unique opportunity to consider the invaluable contributions of indigenous peoples to political, economic, social, cultural and spiritual development throughout the world to our societies, as well as the challenges faced by them, including racism and racial discrimination."[12] In addition, the declaration included language that explored the connections between racism and colonialism, and how people of African descent, people of Asian descent, and Indigenous peoples suffered colonialism:

> We acknowledge the suffering caused by colonialism and affirm that, wherever and whenever it occurred, it must be condemned and its reoccurrence prevented. We further regret that the effects and persistence of these structures and practices have been among the factors contributing to lasting social and economic inequalities in many parts of the world today.[13]

The relationship between colonialism and racism, and their ongoing consequences, remain crucial for understanding Afro-Indigenous relationships. But the work must be global. If settler colonialism is global, and it is linked with racism—even while considering the specificity of its operation—understanding connections with other peoples is crucial for liberation going forward. As Black radical Angela Davis contends, "I think movements . . . are most powerful when they begin to affect the vision and perspective of those who do not necessarily associate themselves with those movements."[14] We can learn from Davis here, and also, recall that some Indigenous peoples in the US have forged close relationships with people of African descent.

CHEROKEE PRINCIPAL CHIEF WILMA MANKILLER
AND THE POLITICS OF BLACKNESS

On November 14, 2001, at the Fifth-Seventh Annual Session of the National Congress of American Indians, principal chief of the Cherokee Nation, Wilma Mankiller moderated a panel session titled "Exploring the Legacy and Future of Black/Indian Relations." She was joined by a distinguished set of people, including Dr. Willard Johnson, professor emeritus of political science at Massachusetts Institute of Technology; Daniel F. Littlefield, professor of history at the University of Arkansas at Little Rock; Dr. Patrick Minges, director of publications at Human Rights Watch; Ms. Deborah Tucker, director of community outreach and cultural activities at Wayne State University; and Dr. David Wilkins, professor of American Indian Studies at the University of Minnesota. The talk was sponsored by the Kansas Institute for African American and Native American Family History, with support from the Freedom Forum.

Chief Mankiller stated that she actually became interested in Black and Indigenous relationships through her reading of Chinua Achebe's *Things Fall Apart*, and that she was also slightly influenced by the South African struggles against apartheid:

> I knew there were a lot of political organizations, but I really didn't put it together until I read Achebe's story about an individual family, an individual community, and the destruction of the people. The situation was strikingly similar to what has happened to Native People in this country. It is almost as if the colonizers had "a little black book" that they used to colonize the people, as they went around the world. They took away the leaders, destroyed their medicines, destroyed their governmental system, sent the kids away to distant schools and, in the case of Africa, to French and other European schools, and in our case, to government boarding schools, the native boarding school. That piqued my interest and I have been interested in these issues since that time.[15]

Achebe's book is taught in high schools around the US but exclusively as African literature. What if it was taught as an Indigenous book in a global Indigenous studies course? Again, would that help us think differently about Black Americans? Would it help us think carefully about Black and Indigenous relationships today and going forward? Mankiller offered four reasons why it is important to discuss these relationships, the first being that it is necessary to build coalitions with Black Americans, even though she often believes that at times their issues, especially during the civil rights movement, are different. She argued, "I had a great deal of trouble explaining to my friends who were working in the Civil Rights Movement that while the civil rights movement tried to help people gain entry into the system, we were fighting to understand our different issues here."[16] Though I think that is a simplification of Black freedom struggles, it is a common belief.

The second reason she offered is the rampant antiblackness in US society. She illustrated her point by touching on the issue of white-looking Native people being easily accepted as Natives by whites, remarking, "If you meet someone who says I am half white and half Yakama, or half white and half Oneida, or whatever, people tend to accept those people. But, if you find someone who says I am half black and half Oneida, Yakama, or Cherokee, people have more difficulty with that."

The third reason she gave, related to the previous one, was the antiblackness within Indian Country. Namely, she spoke specifically about the Seminole Nation's 2000 expelling of Freedmen, whom she explicitly referred to as citizens. She commented that this raised several issues, including "the tribal right, which tribes have fought for since the beginning of contact, to determine who is their membership" and "the civil and human rights of the Freedmen, and to bring together these very different issues—they are sort of at a juncture, and I think that we are going to see these issues arise more often." Finally, she ended her remarks with the fourth reason: the importance of kinship and connection. She stated that she could look at Black folks and say, "That person is Creek, or that person is Cherokee," which made her think about the lost connections and possibility of reconnecting those people of African descent to their US Indigenous roots.

Chief Mankiller, who passed in 2010, was a fantastic leader of the Cherokee Nation and well respected in Indian Country. She also tried her best to acknowledge the importance of Black and Indigenous relations, and she even offered some perspective on changing the narrative on Black and Native relations—a future, perhaps. She also offered a way to think about these connections outside of enslavement—even as that remains an important priority. We can learn a lot from her perspective when thinking about the future of Black and Indigenous relationships. Chief Mankiller's example should be a message to all of us: that Indigenous peoples exist throughout the world, and we can learn a great deal from others, including from the African continent.

"WHO'LL PAY REPARATIONS FOR OUR SOULS?" BLACK REPARATIONS ON INDIGENOUS LAND

In the great Gil Scott-Heron's "Who'll Pay Reparations on My Soul?," he asks: Do we really even want any reparations or compensation from this government? Do we really want to be associated with this government and so-called democracy? Will it heal our souls? We have to ask, what would it look like to prepare for and then actually implement reparations? Law professor Alfred L. Brophy notes in *Reparations: Pro and Con* (2006) that implementing reparations could happen in a four-step plan for correcting past injustice for a better future. The first step "involves truth commissions and apologies." This, he argues, is "inexpensive, and its low costs are spread across a wide group." The second step "involves Civil Rights legislation that gives additional rights of action to victims of race discrimination." The third step would involve "community-based reparation payments for slavery." And the final step would require "direct cash payments to individuals."[17] Do we even want to accept an apology for a settler-colonial, white supremacist state? It might be possible, but, as Anishinaabe legal scholar Sheryl Lightfoot argues regarding state apologies to Indigenous peoples, "official apologies to Indigenous peoples have the potential to play a meaningful role within a larger program of Indigenous-state reconciliation only if such apologies are employed in a way that moves beyond rhetoric and helps reset the relationship between the state and Indigenous peoples away from hierarchical and colonial power relations and toward one grounded in mutual respect."[18] In other words, the settler state has to be sincere. Lightfoot further contends that a state apology "must, first, fully and comprehensively acknowledge the wrongs of the past and/or the present. Second, the state must make credible commitment to do things differently, to make substantial changes in its policy behavior, in the future."[19] We have to think in the short term and long term about what an apology could do, including its benefits and potential harms.

On July 14, 2020, the city of Asheville, North Carolina, passed a resolution supporting reparations for the Black community. The city council members apologized, on behalf of themselves and the city, for the enslavement, segregation, and incarceration of Black people. They highlight all of the systemic forms of racism that have impeded Black peoples' advancement in society. They also offer nine points that they hope would lead to some form of systemic change.[20]

In discussing the merits of this resolution, I don't want to come off as a hater (well, a little bit!). The resolution, while important, also highlights some of the challenges of reparations discourse and practice. The focus on homeownership and the possibilities of building wealth might help in the short term, but what if capitalism is the problem? Are homeownership and other opportunities to build wealth the goal? It's too early to tell what might come of it, though William Darity Jr. and A. Kirsten Mullen's book *From Here to Equality* (2020) offers a practical guide to get the reparations plan rolling, including a recommendation of $15–$20 trillion in total funding.[21]

That brings up another question regarding reparations—the actual dollar amount that qualifies as compensation? Black activists and scholars have since the nineteenth century attempted to call for reparations for Africans enslaved.[22] But what, really, is just compensation? Historian Daina Ramey Berry argues that a variety of white people, from slave masters to doctors who wanted to use Black bodies for experiments, valued enslaved Africans in life and death.[23] Yes, there is a value to labor, but how much are Black bones worth? Again, I know that's not what reparations advocates are seeking, but Black death must be a part of the calculations, and there is no price for that.

Should we really desire to get compensation from a system built on Indigenous dispossession and Indigenous genocide? I don't think so. Even if we did get reparations, we don't want to then become neocolonialists, engaging in all sorts of unspeakable human atrocities because we continued a capitalist way of life.

I believe that the descendants of enslaved Africans deserve reparations. The conversation around reparations is simplistic, however. For instance, in Ta-Nehisi Coates's fantastic article on reparations published in *The Atlantic* in 2014, he notes:

And so we must imagine a new country. Reparations—by which I mean the full acceptance of our collective biography and its consequences—is the price we must pay to see ourselves squarely. The recovering alcoholic may well have to live with his illness for the rest of his life. But at least he is not living a drunken lie. Reparations beckons us to reject the intoxication of hubris and see America as it is—the work of fallible humans.[24]

This passage is beautifully written. My immediate question though, is, what about Native people upon whose land this conversation is being held? My point is not to decenter the real, structurally racist obstacles that have impeded Black progress. But we must ask, how much should we really be invested in the white supremacist project of US democracy, built on Native dispossession and genocide and African enslavement? Can we imagine something different, more just?

It is still very difficult—even taboo for some—to really think about reparations for the descendants of African slaves. I appreciate the effort of the Asheville city council. In November 2019, the city council of Evanston, Illinois, passed a resolution to fund reparations efforts through a cannabis tax.[25] Big shout out to them. It is indisputable, though, that the colonization and exploitation of Africans on the continent and enslavement of Africans in the US and the exploitation of their labor were fundamental to the development of modern capitalism.

The connection between enslavement and the modern forms of capital development were rooted in Indigenous dispossession. After all, those Africans had to work on someone's dispossessed land, and it wasn't theirs. I want to briefly discuss something that offers a point of departure for discussing Black belonging and what the US "owes" to these folks, and that is the recent example of constructing Black belonging known as ADOS—American Descendants of Slavery.

Founded by Yvette Carnell, a writer and media pundit, and Antonio Moore, a Los Angeles–based lawyer, ADOS believes that Black is not a good identity for the descendants of enslaved peoples in the US because it obscures the particularities of enslavement within this country. Moreover, members argue that ADOS deserves reparations for enslavement and the suffering during the Jim Crow era. An overview of ADOS reads, "Codified by government and exploited by private actors, the creation of an ADOS underclass served as the financial engine of a nation that never recognized the debt it owed the group as a result. As such, the ADOS movement is underpinned by the demand for reparative justice in making the group whole." Furthermore, "through federally-supported, discriminatory practices like redlining, black presence literally made wealth disappear in communities, all while American whites—and more recently, immigrants—enjoy advantage in a land of apparently equal opportunity that was in fact manufactured on the back of black failure."[26]

The grievances of ADOS are rooted in three centuries' worth of Black nationalist commentary on what the US owes Black people for enslaving them and exploiting their labor. While some sought to leave the US, others believed that the US should give them land that they deserved. We should ask questions of ADOS, and demonstrate some empathy. First, are there any benefits of the ADOS movement and the questions it is asking? Second, although the project is centered on the United States, I would ask, how does the ADOS movement relate to other nation-state-based movements for belonging in other non-Black countries? Not that ADOS has to expand its philosophy, but making such comparisons is always helpful in theory, if not always fruitful in practice.

However, there are limits. Beyond history, time periods, and the facts of how the US developed, ADOS has an "Indigenous problem." Indeed, its rhetoric curiously leaves out Indigenous peoples, upon whose land the ancestors of the American Descendants of Slavery worked. To be clear, I do support reparations. But in the long term, I believe that a fundamental rupture with capitalism needs to happen. We cannot thrive under capitalism; and in the long run, receiving trillions of dollars from a country that does, in fact, owe us will not end racial capitalism. We need to simultaneously think of the current and long-term situation of Black people, and whether we even want to be a part of a despicable system such as capitalism.

What many people, such as Ta-Nehisi Coates and the founders of ADOS, fail to consider is, how can we justifiably give Black folks reparations without also considering how we offer reparations to Indigenous peoples? We can and should do both. We need to imagine how we can get freedom together. We need to think big, too. I don't want to hear what is not possible. Our imaginations, coupled with radical love, knowledge of our ancestors' freedom dreams, and resistance, will carry us home. The US and Europe owe us some checks, and we need to take them and cash them! This won't be easy, and remember: it took a bloody civil war to end enslavement. People really believed that slavery was never going to end, and then it did.

It is difficult to have a reparations conversation within the context of a capitalist system. This system of exploitation has, I think, constricted the public discourse about what is owed. Radical change under capitalism won't work. We can't have radical change or what Leanne Simpson calls a radical resurgence until capitalism is gone. It is a racist system rooted in the history of slavery and dispossession, and currently based upon imperialism, militarism, and the exploitation of workers.[27] We cannot get rid of racism without also uprooting its capitalist base. The modern capitalist system is based upon the exploitation of Black and Brown people around the globe. Indeed, the term "transatlantic slave trade" signifies the global nature of this historical sin and its permanent consequences for people today. Below, I outline just a few ways in which we might think about reparations, at least at the level of discourse.

LAND. In order to have the right conversation about reparations, we have to include Indigenous peoples, and we have to center a discussion of land. We know that the US government has participated in the dispossession of Black people's land. A 2001 investigation by the Associated Press confirms this to be true. In one case, stolen land became a country club; and in another, an oil field.[28] That history is unjust and racist. It shows that dispossession has long been a part of antiblackness in this so-called democracy. However, that dispossession occurred first with Native peoples. We cannot forget that. This was and remains their land. How do we come to terms with this conversation? We must return land to Indigenous people. To do so, the United States, as it currently exists, must radically transform. How this happens is up to the oppressed. However, as Dr. Martin Luther King Jr. told us a long time ago, we need a "revolution of values." We have to rethink the concept of land, we have to rethink the concept of land ownership, and no longer in terms of a capitalist logic. Land can no longer be a commodity used for capitalist excavation. For example, even if the settler governments return land, can we still survive off poisonous land and water? No. And let's not forget that Indigenous

Black South Africans are trying to reclaim land *without* offering any compensation to white landowners. That might seem extreme, but that is justice. When the Afrikaners created the Natives Land Act of 1913, they stripped Indigenous South Africans from their land and didn't allow them to own land. Now imagine you owned land, and someone took it from you, occupied it, made money off it at your detriment, and then had the nerve to argue that their actions were justified? Reports indicate that if there is no compensation, then the South African economy would be decimated.[29] Good. If Indigenous peoples and those committed to the cause of Black and Indigenous freedom want justice, then maybe the economy should collapse so we can remake society and root it in the possibilities of being human, free from exploitation and dispossession.

MODERN FINANCIAL INSTITUTIONS. The banks, insurance companies, and all of the modern financial institutions that were built off Black people's labor and the land speculation that contributed to the rapid dispossession of Indigenous land need to recompense those groups. Morally and materially, how can institutions that built the foundations of their wealth this way continue to exist?[30] Even the UK press admitted in an article in the *Independent* that after abolition, slave owning families were paid handsomely for losing their "property." Those families continue to benefit today.[31] To put it simply, you don't have massive development and wealth without great inequality and underdevelopment.[32]

BLACK AND INDIGENOUS CONVERSATIONS. Black and Indigenous peoples need to have real conversations about what the world is going to look like after the US ceases to exist the way it does. These groups need to form partnerships and radically imagine how to create new relationships—even treaties—with one another, about how are they going to share the land and how are they going to create new ways of living that are not built on the exploitation of land and peoples.

HOUSING. If you want to discuss how the modern real estate industry has impacted African American peoples, be sure to check out Keeanga-Yamahtta Taylor's award-winning book, *Race for Profit*.[33] It is excellent. Reparations should require the state to provide decent and adequate housing to people of African descent. I don't know how they are going to pay for it, but it can't be that difficult to make affordable and accessible housing for the poor and the houseless.

This housing should also be afforded to Native people. Again, returning land would be an essential piece to this. For instance, if there are vacant plots of land that exist in major urban centers, they should automatically be given to the Indigenous peoples and caretakers of that land. And the federal government should pay for them to build on that land. It could be used for housing, for ceremony—however those people want to use that land. But it should be returned.

RECOVERING OUR ROOTS. Malcolm X taught us, "Of all our studies, history is best qualified to reward our research." We need to recover our histories, which were taken away from us by Europeans. Western states that are fundamentally rooted in the enslavement of Africans should provide resources to help people throughout the diaspora find their roots. This is the least that they could do so that people of African descent, as much as possible, learn their African histories. Working in true partnership with African nations, which will also mean the end of predatory International Monetary Fund loans and other neoliberal policies that have kept these nations broke, Western states should also ensure descendants the opportunity to visit Africa and learn about their roots. This is not a call for people of African descent to assert themselves as colonizers of different African nations. We could borrow from Ghana's "Year of Return" and figure out other ways to offer citizenship to people of African descent in the diaspora.[34] While the traumas of the slave trade have erased the unique Indigenous African roots of people in the diaspora, we can still create new meanings of what it means to be an African today.

We also need a revolution in values. One of the people putting this into practice is Rev. Dr. William J. Barber II, founder of Repairers of the Breach and Moral Mondays. Based in North Carolina, Repairers of the Breach works with a variety of groups to "advance a moral agenda that uplifts our deepest constitutional and moral values of love, justice, and mercy."[35] In 2016, the organization produced a document titled the "Higher Ground Moral Declaration," based upon five principles advocating for several priorities: economic justice, the end of war, universal healthcare, immigrant rights, LGBTQA+ rights, voting rights, fair labor practices, and fighting for the dignity of all oppressed people. He and his organization represent a moral imperative, rooted in justice, and are engaged in the moral and ethical work, rooted in protest, that we need to continue to engage in.

Nothing will happen without struggle. We need to remember that the enslavement of Africans did not end because white people felt guilty, or the state that was making billions of dollars off the labor of African peoples all of a sudden wanted to give up its wealth. It took a civil war. I am not advocating for a violent civil war; I value human life. However, if we are going to get liberation, then we need to think strategically and carefully about the world in which we want to live, and what it will take to get there. I am not committed to a violent "democracy" that continues to exploit and murder Black and Indigenous peoples. So, voting is cool, at least in certain moments for temporary conditions, but it has not saved us and never will. Yes, our Black ancestors died just so future generations could vote, but today Black people continue to die, even sitting in the house, minding their own business. While I'm at it, nonviolent direct action and appealing to the moral conscience of those invested in the subjugation of Black, Indigenous, and people of color isn't the hill any of us should die on either, but that's another subject for another time. We need reparations, and we need them now. What follows are nine steps that I think we might take to move forward in the push for change. How we figure this out will have to come from us, because if billionaires are upset about a wealth tax, what will they and those who hold power do when we come to cash the check and take back what's ours?

1. I think the first thing we should recall is that the Africans kidnapped, beaten, and tortured from their homes were Indigenous. Are Indigenous. And Indigenous people do not just lose their indigeneity—or sense of culture and belonging. We wouldn't say that about Indigenous people here, so why would we think differently about people of African descent? These cultural remnants remain, including the use of Black English, Black sayings, customs, religious practices, and so on. We must un-archive those things. In addition, because enslavement made them make a way outta no way, of course people of African descent created new ideas of what it means

to be African, or Indigenous, and that aspect of the culture should be acknowledged.

2. You know how Indigenous Nations in North America could assert their sovereignty and right to self-determination? They can make new agreements, arrangements, treaties—whatever you want to call it—with Black people and other people of color. They can reimagine sovereignty. Begin finding ways to incorporate Black folks into their spaces and cultures. I'm not sure how this would look nation to nation, but we can look at the very small example of how the Standing Rock Sioux engaged with NBA basketball star Kyrie Irving (and his sister) by formally reconnecting them. For those who might be skeptical, ask yourselves this question: what do we have to lose? I think it has the potential to end antiblackness in Native communities and end Indigenous erasure in Black communities. Given the nature of patriarchy, it might be best that Indigenous and Black femmes, non-gender-conforming people, or more precisely, Black/Indigenous femmes and non-gender-conforming people, meet and negotiate how this might work.[36]

3. If tribal nations recreate new relationships, even political arrangements with Black folks, they might also consider further rethinking the nature of treaties within the context of US liberal democracy. If liberal democracy is an ongoing project that continues to fail (can we really redeem the soul of this nation or is it like Lucifer, the fallen angel?), then the treaties need to take on a new meaning, and we need to imagine how treaties will look in the aftermath of colonialism. Treaties are important, even sacrosanct to many tribal nations. They are a product of the sustained US genocide against Indigenous nations. Tribal nations might consider them sacred, but the US government sure doesn't, and the majority were created with a power imbalance in mind. The treaties have to be honored by both groups, and since the US government has violated every single one, are they, in fact, sacred anymore? From the get-go, the US Constitution has more authority than a treaty, as that is considered the supreme law of the land.[37] Treaties are entangled with US liberal democracy. The US government has

shown it can't be trusted. Indigenous scholars such as Glen Coulthard (Yellowknives Dené) and Audra Simpson (Mohawk) have helped us further think about how we might reject colonial land and political arrangements, so maybe we need to rethink our relationship to treaties, or at least how they relate to US democracy. Finally, I don't believe that treaties are the only thing that define tribal nations; that is shortsighted. If we want radical transformation, we should not be wedded to the idea that the US will continue business as usual; it can't.

4. The Five Tribes, formerly the Five Civilized Tribes, or Five-Former-Slave-Owning Tribes need to carefully affirm that Black Lives Matter. We know the history of many of those tribes and that only a few mixed blood elites enslaved Africans. That remains a sore spot, and a foundational reason as to why antiblackness, including Black removal of citizens continues to happen. For many Black folks, they may not know the intricate details of Indigenous dispossession and enslavement in Indian Country, but they know it happened, and that it was the Five Tribes who did it.

5. If we create these new arrangements, we also need to think about the question of land. How do we all relate to this land? This will require that we are honest about history, and the conflicts between different tribal nations, before, during, and especially after colonization. This work is painful. We need to think about how we all live and relate to particular places, and this can't just include people, but plants, water, the air—we really have to rethink Indigenous conceptions of place.[38]

6. An immediate and practical action we can take is to write a history about Indigenous and African enslavement. For analytical purposes, I focused in this book on Indigenous dispossession and African enslavement and their aftermaths. However, Andrés Reséndez's book *The Other Slavery* (2016) challenges us to think through the histories of enslavement for both groups, how they ran parallel and how they diverged, and how uncovering and comparing these histories can help us move forward in our collective liberation.

7. Decentering white Indians. We really need to deal with whiteness in our Indigenous communities. When I bring this up, I

hear many positive things, and I appreciate those. But there is always a troubling tendency for white-looking Native people to say something like, "I carry the trauma of my ancestors within me." My response to that is, "That's cool, see a therapist." While there are perhaps a few scenarios in which such people could be physically harmed, antiblackness has its own issues. I am treated like a Black person in the world—how are they treated? We should instead center the voices of Afro-Indigenous peoples and Latinx-Indigenous peoples.

8. We need to imagine a new politics. We need abolition. Abolition posits that prisons and all of the other manifestations of social control cannot be reformed. We also need to not just defund the police but completely dismantle all such forms of violently racist and classist organization. Abolition asks us to think more broadly about the potentials of social transformation outside of what actually exists. It requires a new language to explain the world we actually want. Plenty of activists, organizations, and individuals have ideas. There are too many to name. But we should listen to the most vulnerable, the so-called inarticulate, those who might not speak the way you want, those whose voices quiver with anger and fear, because they have a lot to say about transforming a world that hates them.[39]

9. Finally, to paraphrase Tupac Shakur, there will never be peace until we are all free!

We have work to do. But we can do it. Antiblackness and Indigenous dispossession have to end. Let's do it together.

SOVEREIGNTY AND CITIZENSHIP: THE CASE OF THE FIVE TRIBES AND THE FREEDMEN

W. E. B. DU BOIS asked in his 1903 classic, *The Souls of Black Folk*, "How does it feel to be a problem?" A better question might be, how does one become a problem in the first place? This is the question that the Freedmen of the Five Tribes are asking today. To offer a brief summary of the Freedmen, they are connected to the Five Tribes (Cherokee, Chickasaw, Choctaw, Creek, and Seminole). They are the descendants of Africans and mixed Afro-Indigenous peoples who were enslaved by the Five Tribes during the nineteenth century, and when the US government removed the tribes during the nineteenth century to Indian Territory (present-day Oklahoma), the Freedmen remained under the tribes' control.

Given this history, the Freedmen want to know, how did the Five Tribes construct them as a problem, as people who don't belong among them as citizens? I will get to that below. But first, in discussing the ongoing saga of the Freedmen, it is imperative to get at the heart of the matter: the relationship between, on the one hand, tribal sovereignty, and on the other, Freedmen (second-class and non-) citizenship, the legacy of the Five Tribes' enslaving practices, and the matter of (anti-)blackness.

In this situation, we can cut through the legal jargon of treaties and Indian law, the so-called complications of tribal sovereignty, and any other excuses that Indigenous people use to explain why the Five Tribes have refused to do the right thing. As Afro-Indigenous people and Black people know all too well, race and racism are facts of our lives. We can't get out of this hell and neither can any non-Black people. Antiblackness and anti-Indigenousness are not so different as to say one is worse than the other, but in this case, there is a clear case of injustice.

When I first conceptualized this book, I hesitated to write about the Freedmen issue for a few reasons. First, I'm not related to the Five Tribes. It just isn't my experience, and many of those folks are out there fighting to receive or maintain their citizenship. Respect. This is their history and I didn't want to overstep my boundaries. The story of the Five Tribes and the Freedmen dominates discussions of what it means to be an Afro-Indigenous person. Whenever I mention Afro-Indigenous history, the case of the Freedmen (and the Mardi Gras Indians; I still ain't touched that one!) is brought up, and I've spent my writing career letting others write about it. I figured I didn't have anything new to say. Frankly, I also want people to appreciate other facets of Black and Indigenous histories. Nevertheless, here we are. With some gentle nudging from the publishing game's best editor and also current events, and given the topic of the book, I might as well offer my two cents here as a postscript.

The case of the Freedmen and the Five Tribes is an issue based on political and moral questions of sovereignty, citizenship, and racism. I will state my position clearly: I support the Freedmen across all Five Tribes receiving their due citizenship. It is the right thing to do. Those tribes enslaved them and they owe their ancestors for creating the condition of Freedmen bondage, a harm that cannot be properly repaid. For those who were not enslaved but are now hardly citizens because of their blackness, the Five Tribes owe them something too. The scarlet letter of Freedmen, their blackness, is now associated with their citizenship.

I am not comparing Indigenous genocide and African enslavement in the sense that one is worse than the other; I don't mean to ignore Indigenous genocide. They are two different but equally irreparable forms of ongoing terror that continue to shape the lives of Afro-Indigenous, Black, and Indigenous peoples. Nevertheless, as the Choctaw and Chickasaw Freedmen Twitter account has accurately noted, throughout the period of enslavement individual Natives assisted in recapturing Africans who had escaped their captivity.

For example, the 1791 Treaty of Holston, between the United States government and the Cherokee Nation, bears the signature of a person named Sawntteh, or "Slave Catcher." I'm uncertain who this person was, but their name represented their job, to catch slaves.[1] It is also important to remind people that the US government created treaties with some tribal nations and explicitly stated in them that those nations must return enslaved Africans. For example, Article VII of the Treaty with the Florida Tribes of Indians (1823) stated that they would not harbor enslaved Africans, and had to exert all of their will to apprehend them. The agent assigned to them would compensate them for expenses incurred retrieving enslaved Africans.[2] These arrangements were also included in a Treaty with the Delawares (1778). Again, if we demand that the US government honor the treaties and respect tribal sovereignty, does that mean every article of those treaties? I would hope not. I can't recall tribal nations for whom capturing slaves was in their treaties mentioning this. The particular legacy of capturing enslaved Africans and returning them to their enslavers for money ain't nothing but bondage money. I wonder how much these tribes were paid to commit these acts? I guess Black bondage was the price of admission to civilization for those tribes.

Another significant subject of conversation regarding this topic is the question of racism, and the argument that because tribes are not a race, any accusation of racism is irrelevant, even distracting. As those in support of the Five Tribes' sovereignty and the expulsion of the Freedmen argue, the Five Tribes don't want the inclusion of the Freedmen not because they are Black, but because they were not citizens, and the US government forced them to adopt them. They further argue that this is a matter of sovereignty, not Black civil rights.[3] And Natives, even some of y'all's favorite scholar's favorite scholar, jump through a lot of hoops to emphasize this point. If that ain't no anti-Black discourse! Let me offer a brief, summative history as to why they enslaved Africans in the first place.

The Five Tribes all enslaved Africans to demonstrate that they were "civilized." Who were they trying to prove their civility to? White America. Why? To halt the US from encroaching further on their land. I think this is only a part of the reason. I believe that some of those elite members of the Five Tribes wanted to adopt American capitalism. They wanted money, and they understood that enslaving and exploiting Africans would help them earn wealth, and therefore would allow them to at least be civilized and connected to whiteness, if not become fully civilized.

During the Civil War, some of the Five Tribes signed treaties with the Confederacy. Yes, some did so reluctantly, and yes, there were factions, but here we are. Yes, they brokered deals with the "country" that wanted to maintain African enslavement. For nations who participated in the bondage and exploitation of Africans, this made sense. They wanted to maintain their way of life. They also believed they could keep their land. The Five Tribes were in a hard spot, and chose the better of two evils. Of course, the most vulnerable in this scenario, were the enslaved.[4]

Below is a timeline that includes some key facts regarding treaties signed by the Five Tribes. My aim is not to offer a comprehensive analysis of these treaties for each individual tribe. The timeline's dates contain important decisions in history that differentiated between those who were of African descent and those who weren't, under the guise of notions of "legitimate" citizenship.

1866: The US government signs treaties with the Five Tribes, impressing upon them to end enslavement and that they have to adopt the formerly enslaved Africans and people of African descent as citizens.

1896: The Dawes Commission creates land plots and determines who are citizens based on how they look.

1906: The Dawes Commission designates members of the Five Tribes under separate categories, thus creating separate rolls for Freedmen and those considered members of the Five Tribes by blood.

1970: Congress passes the Principal Chiefs Act, requiring the Five Tribes to secure approval for their voting laws for the selection of the principal chief. They had to meet three conditions, one of which required that voter qualifications be broad enough to include enrolled Cherokee Freedmen.

1975: The Cherokee Nation Judicial Appeals Tribunal rules that the Cherokee Freedmen are entitled to citizenship. The Creek

Nation submits a constitution that strips Creek Freedmen of their rights.

2003: The Cherokee Nation ratifies a new constitution that removes the necessity for the Department of the Interior and the Bureau of Indian Affairs to approve amendments to the Cherokee Nation constitution. The nation's argument is that it seeks to enact sovereignty, a rationale that, in theory and mostly in practice, I agree with. The illegally elected chief, Chad Smith, appoints two more judges, and they rule, in a 3–2 decision, that the Cherokee Nation can hold a vote on the status of the Freedmen.

2007: In March, the Cherokee Nation holds a vote with less than 4 percent of the total population participating, and they vote to remove the Cherokee Freedmen "not on the Dawes blood rolls from the nation." Again, this signaled out those who were not considered blood. In May, the Cherokee Nation determines that it will allow registered Freedmen to vote in the June 2007 election for tribal officers. They could vote, but their rights were restricted to second-class citizenship.

There are more details that would further fill out the picture, but I wanted to lay out all of that to highlight how the dispute developed. The current dilemma involves a web of interests for tribes, Freedmen, and the federal government, and they go something like this: the Five Tribes maintain that it is an incursion on their sovereignty for the US to force them to include the Freedmen as citizens, and that the US forced them to sign those treaties. The Freedmen believe that the Five Tribes should simply honor the treaty that they signed with the US in 1866. The US government, led by Black congresspeople, believe that the Five Tribes' exclusion of the Freedmen is simply an act of antiblackness. All three of these perspectives are true. In their own vulnerability, the Five Tribes' blatant discrimination perpetuates the one thing that continues to hinder Black freedom: a lack of belonging, or a place to call home. Black people are hardly full citizens in a white supremacist country, not all Black people whose ancestors are rooted in the soil of the US can return to Africa, and on top of that, their Indigenous relatives don't want them. Where are they supposed to go? This is where I think current Native congresspeople could step in and make a small contribution to Black humanity.

The Freedmen Twitter account has critiqued former representative and now secretary of the interior Deb Haaland (Laguna Pueblo) for her stances against the Freedmen. Although I read carefully through her sponsored bills for clues, I couldn't glean her stance on the Freedmen issue. The Freedmen opposed to her likely believe that her stances in support of tribal sovereignty are an affront to them. By extension, perhaps they think she might be anti-Black? However, she has supported other bills that benefit African Americans.

I do believe that Haaland deserves to be secretary of the interior. I actually like her record. However, tribal sovereignty should not be used to be anti-Black. Of course, sovereignty means much more than issues relating to the Freedmen. However, as secretary of the interior, she should not bow to the pressure of the Five Tribes and perhaps Indian Country at large. She should be on the moral side of history and assert that the Freedmen should be treated as free, full citizens.

The question people always ask is, what can be done? In my estimation, as a non-citizen of any of the Five Tribes, the most basic thing they could do is simply embrace the Freedmen as equal citizens. I don't agree with the language of proposed congressional bills stating that the government would "sever" ties with the Five Tribes if they don't restore the Freedmen's citizenship. That is reactionary and hypocritical because, in general, the US has stayed out of tribal issues related to citizenship. This is why I would like to see the Five Tribes exercise sovereignty on their own. If Indigenous sovereignty means anything, it is not only a foundation to nationhood but also a moral code for respecting human (Black people!) and non-human relations. It is also an attempt to put into practice a better approach to living free than US liberal democracy. For the Five Tribes, ending a direct form of anti-Black racism is certainly in the top five best things to do. Until this is completed in a proper way, everyday Black people who don't know the complexities of this history will continue to ask a question that I hate answering: "Didn't the Indians own slaves though?" I would love to be able to tell them, "Yes, they did, but they have done everything they could to make right their historical blunder."

Months after writing this section, the Cherokee Nation did the right thing. On February 22, 2021, the Cherokee Nation Supreme Court ruled that the tribe's constitution remove the phrase "by blood" so that the Freedmen could be enrolled as citizens.[5] I am glad they are doing this. It is one step in the right direction. I hope the other Four Tribes do the same.

ACKNOWLEDGMENTS

YOU DON'T WRITE a book like this without some love. I first have to give a shout out to the best editor in the game: Gayatri Patnaik. The editor of the ReVisioning American History series at Beacon Press, she believed in this project from the beginning. I appreciated her criticisms and feedback—she da best! Thank you to Maya Fernandez, Ruthie Block, and the entire Beacon team for your work on this project. Much love.

I also want to thank Paul Ortiz and Roxanne Dunbar-Ortiz, both with whom I had early conversations about this project and are also authors in the ReVisioning American History series. You should check them out. They helped me think about the larger history of Black and Indigenous struggle and to carefully imagine what this history could look like in a book format.

I'd like to thank my mother for doing her part as a single mother to raise five children. Thank you to my siblings Twin, YaYa, Shaun, and J for always supporting me and showing me love. They always keep my grounded and remind me that I'm not as cool and important as I think I am. Thank you to my nieces and nephews: RJ, Brandon, Hayden, Cherish, Makiah, and J.J. You are part of the future generation that is going to continue challenging American democracy.

I have to give a big shout to my mentors and Fam: Dr. G (Geneva Smitherman), AJ Rice, Austin Jackson, David E. Kirkland, Jeffrey Robinson, H. Samy Alim, and Ashley Newby. No one has influenced me more in the academy than my academic mama, Dr. G. She has mentored me and always demanded that I honor my ancestors and do work on behalf of the future generations. I gotta give a big shout out to AJ. We been brothas since our first experience during the Ronald E.

McNair Program. I appreciate you being there and I know you got my back. Thank you all for your laughs over food and general companionship over the years. As many writers and academics know, this experience can be lonely and take you away from your blood relatives, but I developed a set of relatives who have my back through thick and thin. Thank you to Fred and Holly Hoxie. Fred was my dissertation chair, but more than that, Holly and Fred treat me like a son. Robert Warrior, who was a co-chair, helped me think through some of these questions early on during my graduate school years.

Thank you to my brothas Bryce Henson, Kevin Whalen, and "E" Eduardo Coronel. You all have been down like four flat tires through everything. I have to thank my Los Angeles family: Liseth Amaya, Mama Millie, Rafael Leonor, Marvin and Jessica Amaya, Lesly Flores, Liz and Isabella "BellaMafia" Wright, Kat and Emma, Joel and Susean Ruiz, Jennifer Carrillo, Victer and Edwin, Martin, Yoli, and Camila May Jauregui. Big shout to Martin. Though he's a USC Trojan, he read some of the manuscript and gave good advice. I always enjoy the BBQs, random get-togethers, and whiskey drinking. Gracias to Mama Coronel and Señor Coronel for always letting me stay at the crib when I've visited. And the food. Damn, she make some good food! I also have to say thank you to my Chicago family, Mike Staudenmaier, Anne Carlson, Sophia, Nico, and Malcolm. I am grateful for you all and am glad I always have a home in Chicago!

Thank you to my colleagues at UCLA. Thank you to Robin D. G. Kelley, who has been a brilliant mentor. Robin's commitment to excellence and unwavering belief in radical transformation has been an inspiration to me, and I'm glad to have been able to learn from him. Thank you to the UCLA staff: Eboni Shaw, Elliott Delgado, and Tricia Park. Thank you to my UCLA colleagues: Randy Akee, Julian Anesi, Bryonn Bain, Karida Brown, Scot Brown, Keith Camacho, Jessica Cattelino, Erin Debenport, Ugo Edu, Aisha Finch, Lorrie Frasure, Mishuana Goeman, Sarah Haley, Kelly Lytle Hernández, Peter Hudson, Marcus Hunter, Gaye Theresa Johnson, Cheryl Keyes, Ben Madley, Uri McMillan, Safiya Umoja Noble, Jemima Pierre, Shana Redmond, Desi Rodriguez-Lonebear, SA Smythe, Shannon Speed, Angela Riley, and Ananya Roy, and Brenda Stevenson. In ways small or large, directly or indirectly, you all have helped me think differently about scholarship and the world.

I completed the bulk of this project during my time as a Mellon Mays Fellow at the James Weldon Johnson Institute on Race and Difference at Emory University. Thank you to the director, Andra Gillespie, and the assistant director, Rhonda Patrick, for providing space and affording me the opportunity. Thank you to my fellow Mays fellows, Shanté Paradigm Smalls and Yami Rodriguez. I also want to thank the students in the class that I taught. They were fantastic and helped me think through some of this work.

Many people have influenced this work in small and large ways. Thank you to Leanne Betasamosake Simpson, Tiffany King, Dave Roediger, Dan Cobb, Keith Richotte Jr., Shanya Cordis, Zoé Samudzi, Shay-Akil McLean, Zoe Todd, Jessica Vasquez, Antoinette Burton, Mary-Ann Winkelmes, Veronica Mendez, Adam Banks, and a host of other activists and intellectuals who have helped me think through my ideas over the years. I appreciate you.

Many universities have sponsored me and allowed me to speak and work through these ideas on their campus or virtually. Thank you to the University of Texas, Austin; the University of California, Berkeley; Dartmouth College; the University of Florida; James Madison College at Michigan State; Princeton University; the University of Michigan; the University of Alberta; the Autry Museum; the California Museum of African American History; and a host of other places.

I would like to thank Kristen Martinez, who worked as my research assistant. She is doing a dope project on Indigenous metal and punk rock. Keep up the good work. Big shout to other students who've impacted me: Annie Mendoza, Jessica Newby, Aaron Montenegro, Shalene Joseph, Kylie Gemmell, Mari Nobre, Kaelyn Grace Apple, Darnay Holmes, Kristopher Barnes, Adarius Pickett, Kassie Sakar, Angelica Castillo, Wiyaka Bear Eagle, and all of the students I've had in classes. Keep up the fight and as I always say, "Read!"

Finally, I would like to thank my cat and dog, El Don and ChiChi, who, during a global pandemic and quarantine, held me down.

Any errors of interpretation or research are my own. If anything, I hope that people will take this work, expand upon it, challenge it, and help end the horrors of anti-Black racism and Indigenous genocide. We must demand our freedom, together.

NOTES

AUTHOR'S NOTE

1. For a history of Medicine Bear American Academy, see Kyle T. Mays, *City of Dispossessions: African Americans, Indigenous People, and the Creation of Modern Detroit* (Philadelphia: University of Pennsylvania Press, forthcoming).

INTRODUCTION

1. Jack D. Forbes, *Africans and Native Americans: The Language of Race and the Evolution of Red-Black Peoples* (Urbana: University of Illinois Press, 1993), 1. It is fitting to begin with a quote from Jack Forbes. He, in addition to being a pioneer in Native studies, was also an important contributor to Afro-Indigenous studies.

2. For a discussion on labels, see Robert Keith Collins, "What Is a Black Indian? Misplaced Expectations and Lived Realities," in *IndiVisible: African-Native American Lives in the Americas*, ed. Gabrielle Tayac (Washington, DC: Smithsonian Institution, National Museum of the American Indian, 2009), 183–95.

3. There are a host of books on Afro-Indigenous history, especially covering the nineteenth century. This is not an exhaustive list but just a handful that have influenced me: Kendra Taira Field, *Growing Up with Country: Family, Race, and Nation After the Civil War* (New Haven, CT: Yale University Press, 2018); Tiya Miles, *The House on Diamond Hill: A Cherokee Plantation Story* (Chapel Hill: University of North Carolina Press, 2010); Arica L. Coleman, *That the Blood Stay Pure: African Americans, Native Americans, and the Predicament of Race and Identity in Virginia* (Bloomington: Indiana University Press, 2013); David Chang, *The Color of the Land: Race, Nation, and the Politics of Land Ownership in Oklahoma, 1832–1929* (Minneapolis: University of Minnesota Press, 2010); James F. Brooks, ed., *Confounding the Color Line: The (American) Indian-Black Experience in North America* (Lincoln: University of Nebraska Press, 2002); Sharon P. Holland and Tiya Miles, eds., *Crossing Waters, Crossing Worlds: The African Diaspora in Indian Country* (Durham, NC: Duke University Press, 2006); Sharon P. Holland and Tiya Miles, "Afro-Native Realities," in *The World of Indigenous North America*, ed. Robert Warrior (New York: Routledge, 2015), 524–48; Tiya Miles, *Ties That Bind: The Story of An Afro-Cherokee Family in Slavery and Freedom* (Berkeley: University of California Press, 2005); Celia E.

Naylor, *African Cherokees in Indian Territory: From Chattel to Citizens* (Chapel Hill: University of North Carolina Press, 2009).

4. John Nankivell, *Buffalo Soldier Regiment: History of the Twenty-Fifth United States Infantry* (Lincoln: University of Nebraska Press, 2001); William Leckie and Shirley A. Leckie, *The Buffalo Soldiers: A Narrative of the Black Calvary in the West* (Norman: University of Oklahoma Press, 2003).

5. Patrick Wolfe, *Traces of History: Elementary Structures of Race* (London: Verso, 2016), 2.

6. Carter G. Woodson, "The Relations of Negroes and Indians in Massachusetts," *Journal of Negro History* 1, no. 5 (1920): 45; J. H. Johnston, "Documentary Evidence of the Relations of Negroes and Indians," *Journal of Negro History* 14, no. 1 (1929): 21–43.

7. Sharon P. Holland and Tiya Miles, "Afro-Native Realities," in *The World of Indigenous North America*, ed. Robert Warrior (New York: Routledge, 2015), 524–48.

8. William A. Galston, "The Populist Challenge to Liberal Democracy," *Journal of Democracy* 29, no. 2 (2018): 9–10.

9. David Orr, "Does Democracy Have a Future?," in *Democracy Unchained: How to Rebuild Government for the People*, ed. Orr et al. (New York: New Press, 2020), 2–11.

10. See, for instance, chapter 5, "Slavery Takes Command," in Sven Beckert, *Empire of Cotton: A Global History* (New York: Vintage Books, 2014), 98–135. See also Edward E. Baptist, *The Half Has Never Been Told: Slavery and the Making of American Capitalism* (New York: Basic Books, 2016).

11. Claudio Saunt, "Financing Dispossession: Stocks, Bonds, and the Deportation of Native Peoples in the Antebellum United States," *Journal of American History* 106, no. 2 (2019): 316.

12. Andrés Reséndez, *The Other Slavery: The Uncovered Story of Indian Enslavement in America* (New York: Houghton Mifflin, 2016), 5.

13. Reséndez, *The Other Slavery*, 10.

14. Reséndez, *The Other Slavery*, 9.

15. J. Kēhaulani Kauanui, "Tracing Historical Specificity: Race and the Colonial Politics of (In)Capacity," *American Quarterly* 69, no. 2 (2017): 257–65.

16. Theodore Allen, *The Invention of the White Race: The Origins of Racial Oppression in Anglo-America* (New York: Verso, 1997), 239. Historian and whiteness scholar David Roediger offers a brief explanation in *How Race Survived U.S. History* (London: Verso, 2008), 5–6. See also Aileen Moreton-Robinson, *The White Possessive: Property, Power, and Indigenous Sovereignty* (Minneapolis: University of Minnesota Press, 2016). Moreton-Robinson has contributed significantly to this conversation centering the link between whiteness and Indigenous dispossession.

17. Vincent Harding, *There Is a River: The Black Struggle for Freedom in America* (New York: Harcourt Brace Jovanovich, 1981), 30. See also the debate between Kauanui, "Tracing Historical Specificity," and Robin D. G. Kelley, "The Rest of Us: Rethinking Settler and Native," *American Quarterly* 69, no. 2 (2017): 267–76. The debate between scholars is that Bacon's rebellion was

solely about Indigenous removal. Kelley and Harding, writing many years before, don't dispute that. They argue, however, that Africans likely had their own reasons, including seeking freedom from hardened racial lines. I fall on the side of Kelley because Kauanui, like Wolfe, ignores the fact that Africans were Indigenous in some capacity. In other words, they have to answer the question: When did these Africans participating in Bacon's rebellion lose their Indigenous roots? While Kauanui offers a righteous critique of Afro-pessimists, she in some ways reiterates the point of them having little agency or desire for freedom that was not so easily aligned with whites.

18. Roxanne Dunbar-Ortiz, *An Indigenous Peoples' History of the United States* (Boston: Beacon Press, 2014), 3.

19. Sidney J. Lemelle and Robin D. G. Kelley, "Imagining Home: Pan-Africanism Revisited," in *Imagining Home: Class, Culture and Nationalism in the African Diaspora*, ed. Lemelle and Kelley (London: Verso, 1994), 2.

20. Cedric J. Robinson, *Black Marxism: The Making of the Black Radical Tradition* (1983; repr., Chapel Hill: University of North Carolina Press, 2000), 121–22.

21. Judith Carney, *Black Rice: The African Origins of Rice Cultivation in the Americas* (Cambridge, MA: Harvard University Press, 2001), 2.

22. Cheryl Harris, "Whiteness as Property," *Harvard Law Review* 106, no. 8 (1993): 1710–91.

23. Robin D. G. Kelley, *Race Rebels: Culture, Politics, and the Black Working Class* (New York: Free Press, 1994), 4–5. Kelley develops a conceptual way to understand Black working-class resistance through the work of James C. Scott's work on "hidden transcripts." James C. Scott's, *Weapons of the Weak: Everyday Forms of Peasant Resistance* (New Haven, CT: Yale University Press, 1985).

24. Robin D. G. Kelley, "'We Are Not What We Seem': Rethinking Black Working-Class Opposition in the Jim Crow South," *Journal of American History* 80, no. 1 (1993): 78.

25. For a history of birthright citizenship before the Fourteenth Amendment, see Martha S. Jones, *Birthright Citizens: A History of Race and Rights in Antebellum America* (Cambridge: Cambridge University Press, 2018). Throughout the nineteenth century, there were Black nationalists, especially Martin Delany, who advocated for a "nation within a nation." For primary sources and a brief biography of Delany, see Robert S. Levine, ed., *Martin R. Delany: A Documentary Reader* (Chapel Hill: University of North Carolina Press, 2003).

26. Robin D. G. Kelley, *Freedom Dreams: The Black Radical Imagination* (Boston: Beacon Press, 2002), 17. Furthermore, Kelley contends that Exodus in the Black experience meant "dreams of black self-determination, of being on our own, under our own rules and beliefs, developing our own cultures, without interference."

27. Carole E. Goldberg et al., *American Indian Law: Native Nations and the Federal System: Cases and Materials*, 7th ed. (New Providence, NJ: LexisNexis, 2015); Keith Richotte Jr., *Federal Indian Law and Policy: An Introduction* (St. Paul, MN: West Academic Publishing, 2020).

28. Gerald Vizenor, "Aesthetics of Survivance: Literary Theory and Practice," in *Survivance: Narratives of Native Presence*, ed. Vizenor (Lincoln: University of Nebraska Press, 2008), 1.

29. Leanne Simpson, *Islands of Decolonial Love: Stories and Songs* (Winnipeg, Manitoba: ARP Books, 2013), 85.

30. Audre Lorde, "The Uses of Anger," *Women's Studies Quarterly* 25, nos. 1–2 (Spring–Summer 1997): 278–85.

CHAPTER 1. INDIGENOUS AFRICANS AND NATIVE AMERICANS
IN PREREVOLUTIONARY AMERICA

1. "The 1619 Project," *New York Times*, August 14, 2019, https://www.nytimes.com/interactive/2019/08/14/magazine/1619-america-slavery.html.

2. Nikole Hannah-Jones, "The 1619 Project," *New York Times Magazine*, August 18, 2019, 16.

3. "President Trump Remarks at White House History Conference," C-SPAN, September 17, 2020, https://www.c-span.org/video/?475934-1/president-trump-announces-1776-commission-restore-patriotic-education-nations-schools&fbclid=IwAR0wO3SiOhn5exWm48-hZ-eKsKdS5iP5d2SwbsZFsxi9CVaqqxGo2nytgdU.

4. Natalie Diaz, Twitter, August 15, 2019.

5. Terri Hansen, "How the Iroquois Great Law of Peace Shaped U.S. Democracy," December 17, 2018, PBS, "Native America," https://www.pbs.org/native-america/blogs/native-voices/how-the-iroquois-great-law-of-peace-shaped-us-democracy.

6. Philip Deloria, *Playing Indian* (New Haven, CT: Yale University Press, 1998), 185.

7. See for instance, Hortense J. Spillers, "Mama's Baby, Papa's Maybe: An American Grammar Book," *Diacritics* 17, no. 2 (Summer 1987): 64–81. Spillers offers a classic example of how Black scholars have thought about the changes that Black people experienced from the continent through the transatlantic slave trade. She calls this "an American grammar." However, what is often missing from Black studies and also Native studies is the recognition that these were Indigenous peoples with cultures, homeland, and community. Spillers writes, "The massive demographic shifts, the violent formation of a modern African consciousness, that take place on the sub-Saharan Continent during the initiative strikes which open the Atlantic Slave Trade in the fifteenth century of our Christ, interrupted hundreds of years of black African culture" (p. 69).

8. W. E. B. Du Bois, *Black Reconstruction in America* (1935; repr., Millwood, NY: Kraus-Thomson, 1976), 4.

9. Sterling Stuckey, *Slave Culture: Nationalist Theory and the Foundations of Black America* (New York: Oxford University Press, 1987), 3.

10. Vincent Carretta, *Equiano, the African: Biography of a Self-Made Man* (New York & London: Penguin Books, 2005), 8.

11. Manisha Sinha, *The Slave's Cause: A History of Abolition* (New Haven, CT: Yale University Press, 2016), 126. Sinha also writes, "The identity of displaced Africans was highly malleable and subject to arbitrary categorization by European authorities. Carretta's evidence, in short, is not definitive."

12. Chima J. Korieth, ed., *Olaudah Equiano and the Igbo World: History, Society, and Atlantic Diaspora Connections* (Trenton, NJ, and Asamara, Eritrea: Africa World Press, 2008), 7.

13. Maureen N. Eke, "(Re)Imagining Community: Olaudah Equiano and the Re(Construction) of Igbo (African) Identity," *Olaudah Equiano and the Igbo World*, 24.

14. Eke, "(Re)Imagining Community," 36.

15. Olaudah Equiano and Vincent Carretta, *The Interesting Narrative and Other Writings: Revised Edition* (New York: Penguin Classics, 2003), 60.

16. Equiano and Carretta, *The Interesting Narrative*, 56.

17. Robinson, *Black Marxism*, 309.

18. Sinha, *The Slave's Cause*, 29.

19. Henry Louis Gates Jr., *The Trials of Phillis Wheatley: America's First Black Poet and Her Encounters with the Founding Fathers* (New York: BasicCivitas Books, 2003), 20. For an analysis of the French and Indian War, see Richard White, *The Middle Ground: Indians, Empires, and Republics in the Great Lakes Region, 1650–1815* (New York: Cambridge University Press, 2011), chapter 5, "The Clash of Empires," 222–68.

20. Vincent Carretta, *Phillis Wheatley: Biography of a Genius in Bondage* (Athens: University of Georgia Press, 2011), 8–10.

21. Phillis Wheatley, "On Being Brought from Africa to America," Poetry Foundation website, https://poets.org/poem/being-brought-africa-america (accessed November 20, 2019).

22. Sinha, *The Slave's Cause*, 31.

23. For the letter, see "Letter to Reverend Samson Occum," *Connecticut Gazette*, March 11, 1774, https://www.pbs.org/wgbh/aia/part2/2h19t.html, accessed March 22, 2021.

24. Stuckey, *Slave Culture*, 24.

25. Walker, "In Search of Our Mothers' Gardens," 404.

26. Caryn E. Neumann, "Prince, Lucy Terry," in *Encyclopedia of African American History, 1619–1895: From the Colonial Period to the Age of Frederick Douglass*, ed. Paul Finkelman, Oxford African American Studies Center (New York: Oxford University Press, 2008), http://www.oxfordaasc.com/article/opr/t0004/e0460.

27. "Bars Fight," Africans in America, PBS, https://www.pbs.org/wgbh/aia/part2/2h1592t.html.

28. Josiah Gilbert Holland, *History of Western Massachusetts* (Springfield, MA: Samuel Bowles and Company, 1855).

29. Sharon M. Harris, "Lucy Terry: A Life of Radical Resistance," in *African American Culture and Legal Discourse*, ed. Lovalrie King and Richard Schur (New York: Palgrave Macmillan, 2009), 107–10.

30. Ibram X. Kendi, *Stamped from the Beginning: The Definitive History of Racist Ideas in America* (New York: Nation Books, 2016), 10.

31. Henry Louis Gates Jr. "Who Led the First Back-to-Africa Effort?," *The African Americans: Many Rivers to Cross*, https://www.pbs.org/wnet/african-americans-many-rivers-to-cross/history/who-led-the-1st-back-to-africa-effort, accessed July 15, 2019.

32. Lamont D. Thomas, *Rise to Be a People: A Biography of Paul Cuffe* (Urbana: University of Illinois Press, 1986), 3.

33. See, for instance, Woodson, "The Relations of Negroes and Indians in Massachusetts," 45–57. Woodson wrote on the variety of tribal nations who interacted with Black folks in the eighteenth and nineteenth centuries. However, he accepts the belief that Native people then disappeared. See also Johnston, "Documentary Evidence of the Relations of Negroes and Indians," 21–43.

34. Jean M. O'Brien, *Dispossession by Degrees: Indian Land and Identity in Natick, Massachusetts, 1650–1790* (Cambridge: Cambridge University Press, 1997).

35. "The Brig Traveller, Lately Arrived at Liverpool, from Sierra Leone, Is Perhaps the First Vessel Ever," *Times*, August 2, 1811.

36. Sinha, *The Slave's Cause*, 162–63. Sinha writes that Cuffe's wife, Alice Pequit, a Wampanoag, like his mother, "had refused to relocate to Africa" (163). It made sense because that was not her homeland. While she had her reasons, it also reveals, perhaps, another conflict: that she could not fathom the antiblackness that Cuffe experienced throughout his life.

37. Thomas King, *The Inconvenient Indian: A Curious Account of Native People in North America* (Minneapolis: University of Minnesota Press, 2013), 3.

38. Mitch Kachun, *First Martyr of Liberty: Crispus Attucks in American Memory* (New York: Oxford University Press, 2017), 8. Kachun does a wonderful job of explaining how a variety of actors have used and memorialized the life of Attucks, from the American Revolution to the New Negro and up into the present.

39. Kachun, *First Martyr of Liberty*, 227–28.

40. Kachun, *First Martyr of Liberty*, 15.

41. "Boston Massacre Engraving by Paul Revere," Paul Revere Heritage Project, http://www.paul-revere-heritage.com/boston-massacre-engraving.html (accessed May 28, 2020).

42. Cheryl Harris, "Whiteness as Property," *Harvard Law Review* 106, no. 8 (1993): 1710–91.

CHAPTER 2. ANTIBLACKNESS, SETTLER COLONIALISM, AND THE US DEMOCRATIC PROJECT

1. Harris, "Whiteness as Property," 1720.

2. Harris, "Whiteness as Property," 21.

3. Aziz Rana, *The Two Faces of American Freedom* (Cambridge, MA: Harvard University Press, 2010), 3.

4. Rana, *The Two Faces of American Freedom*, 3.

5. House Concurrent Resolution 331, 100th Cong., 2nd Sess. (1988).

6. Robin DiAngelo, *White Fragility: Why It's So Hard for White People to Talk About Racism* (Boston: Beacon Press, 2018), 2.

7. Nawal Arjini, "Ishmael Reed Tries to Undo the Damage 'Hamilton' Has Wrought," *The Nation*, June 3, 2019, https://www.thenation.com/article/archive/ishmael-reed-haunting-of-lin-manuel-miranda-hamilton-play-review.

8. "The Federalist Papers: No. 24," The Avalon Project, Yale Law School, https://avalon.law.yale.edu/18th_century/fed24.asp.

9. US Declaration of Independence, http://www.ushistory.org/declaration/document/ (accessed September 3, 2019).

10. Anthony F. C. Wallace, *Jefferson and the Indians: The Tragic Fate of the First Americans* (Cambridge, MA: Belknap Press of Harvard University, 1999), viii.

11. Wallace, *Jefferson and the Indians*, 18.

12. Thomas Jefferson, "Thomas Jefferson First Inaugural Address," March 4, 1801, https://avalon.law.yale.edu/19th_century/jefinau1.asp (accessed May 23, 2020).

13. Thomas Jefferson, *Notes on the State of Virginia*, ed. William Peden (Chapel Hill: University of North Carolina Press, 1982), v.

14. Jefferson, *Notes on the State of Virginia*, 138.

15. Jefferson, *Notes on the State of Virginia*.

16. Jefferson, *Notes on the State of Virginia*.

17. Jefferson, *Notes on the State of Virginia*, 139.

18. Jefferson, *Notes on the State of Virginia*.

19. Jefferson, *Notes on the State of Virginia*, 140.

20. Gates, *The Trials of Phillis Wheatley*, 40.

21. David Walker, *David Walker's Appeal: To the Coloured Citizens of the World, but in Particular, and Very Expressly, to Those of the United States of America* (1829; repr., New York: Hill and Wang, 1965), 27.

22. Alvin B. Tillery Jr., "Tocqueville as Critical Race Theorist: Whiteness as Property, Interest Convergence, and the Limits of Jacksonian Democracy," *Political Research Quarterly* 62, no. 4 (December 2009): 639–52. Tillery Jr. writes, "Tocqueville's belief that social relations and the law are the source of racial differences is the first place where there are similarities between his ideas and the critical race theorists. Tocqueville also shares the criticalists' positions that white privilege is endemic in American culture and that both the laws and outcomes in democratic theory politics are functions of this social reality. Moreover, Tocqueville joins the critical race theorists in positing that the American race system generates negative externalities for whites. Finally, Tocqueville's analysis of the manumission laws shows that he developed a nascent conception of the interest convergence theory" (640). I would be curious to know how critical race theorists like Derrick Bell and Kimberlee Crenshaw would view this comparison. I do agree that Tocqueville offers a solid analysis of US social relations, democratic theory, and the political, cultural, and social function of white supremacy.

23. Alexis de Tocqueville, *Democracy in America* (New York: Bantam Dell, 2004), 385.

24. Tocqueville, *Democracy in America*, 385.

25. Tocqueville, *Democracy in America*, 385.

26. Geneva Smitherman, *Talkin and Testifyin: The Language of Black America* (Detroit: Wayne State University Press, 1986), 2.

27. Tocqueville, *Democracy in America*, 387.

28. Tocqueville, *Democracy in America*, 387.

29. Tocqueville, *Democracy in America*, 340.

30. Tocqueville, *Democracy in America*, 432–33.

31. Tocqueville, *Democracy in America*, 438.

CHAPTER 3. ENSLAVEMENT, DISPOSSESSION, RESISTANCE

1. Du Bois, *Black Reconstruction in America*, 727.

2. Jervis Anderson, "Ralph Ellison Goes Home: The Author of 'Invisible Man' Revisits His Oklahoma Childhood," *New Yorker*, November 15, 1976, https://www.newyorker.com/magazine/1976/11/22/going-to-the-territory (accessed March 2021).

3. Joe Gioia, *Guitar and the New World: A Fugitive History* (Albany: SUNY Press, 2014), 99.

4. For a wonderful history of land ownership and Black and Indigenous histories, see Chang, *The Color of the Land*.

5. Eric Foner, *Forever Free: The Story of Emancipation and Reconstruction* (New York: Vintage Books, 2006), 122–23.

6. Scott, *Weapons of the Weak*, xvi–xvii.

7. Sinha, *The Slave's Cause*, 5.

8. Du Bois, *Black Reconstruction in America*, 57.

9. Claud Anderson, *Black Labor, White Wealth: The Search for Power and Economic Justice* (Bethesda, MD: PowerNomics Corporation of America, 1994), 77.

10. Miles, *Ties That Bind*, 5.

11. Lisa Ford, *Settler Sovereignty: Jurisdiction and Indigenous People in America and Australia, 1788–1836* (Cambridge, MA: Harvard University Press, 2010), 36. Ford goes as far as to say that the way the Cherokees constructed an idea of race, as one tied to their sovereignty, was similar to how settlers constructed race in the state of Georgia.

12. For a history of the Seminole nation, especially people of African descent, see Kenneth Porter, *The Black Seminoles: A History of Freedom-Seeking People* (Gainesville: Florida University Press, 1996). Another perspective includes the work of Susan A. Miller. For instance, see Susan A. Miller, "Seminoles and Africans Under Seminole Law: Sources and Discourses of Tribal Sovereignty and 'Black Indian' Entitlement," *Wicazo Sa Review* 20, no. 1 (Spring 2005): 23–47. While Miller believes that the Seminole Nation were forced into accepting people of African descent with the treaty of 1866 following the Civil War, she does acknowledge that they have other "indigenous roots" based in Africa. Miller contends that Africans cannot "be both Indigenous Maroons and assimilated Americans, however, so their indigenous identity is at play in this transaction. From an American Indian studies perspective, the Freedmen retain the indigenous status of their African forbears, and therefore, the United States owes them recognition as an Indigenous people" (44). See also Susan A. Miller's, *Coacoochee's Bones: A Seminole Saga* (Lawrence: University Press of Kansas, 2003).

13. "Jackson Criticizes Oakland Schools' 'Ebonics' Decision," *Los Angeles Times*, December 23, 1996, https://www.latimes.com/archives/la-xpm-1996-12-23-mn-11966-story.html.

14. "Print the Legend: Writing the Screenplay for *Harriet*," Focus Features, https://www.focusfeatures.com/article/interview_screenwriter_gregory-allen-howard, accessed July 27, 2020.

15. Alaina E. Roberts, "How Native Americans Adopted Slavery from White Settlers," *Al Jazeera*, December 26, 2018, https://www.aljazeera.com/indepth /opinion/native-americans-adopted-slavery-white-settlers-181225180750948.html.

16. *Harriet*, directed by Kasi Lemmons (Los Angeles: Focus Features, 2019).

17. Miles, *The House on Diamond Hill*, 24. Miles notes that James Vann, owner of the Diamond Hill Vann plantation, was a tyrant and could be exceptionally cruel.

18. Peter Cozzens, *Tecumseh and the Prophet: The Shawnee Brothers Who Defied a Nation* (New York: Penguin Random House, 2020), xiii.

19. Cozzens, *Tecumseh and the Prophet*, 197.

20. Cave A. Alfred, *Prophets of the Great Spirit: Native American Revitalization Movements in Eastern North America* (Lincoln: University of Nebraska Press, 2006), 91–139.

21. Cozzens, *Tecumseh and the Prophet*, xvii.

22. Roxanne Dunbar-Ortiz, *An Indigenous Peoples' History of the United States* (Boston: Beacon Press, 2014), 84–85.

23. Shawnee Chief Tecumseh Address to General William Henry Harrison, probably delivered in 1810, at Vincennes in the Indiana Territory, https://www .americanrhetoric.com/speeches/nativeamericans/chieftecumseh.htm (accessed December 20, 2019).

24. Tecumseh Address to Harrison.

25. Tecumseh Address to Harrison.

26. Tecumseh Address to Harrison.

27. While Parker describes her name as "the sound the stars make rushing through the sky," Margaret Noori, a scholar of Anishinaabemowin, translates this slightly differently in a review of Parker's book. See Margaret Noori, "The Complex World of Jane Johnston Schoolcraft," *Michigan Quarterly Review* 47, no. 1 (Winter 2008), http://hdl.handle.net/2027/spo.act2080.0047.121.

28. Robert Dale Parker, ed., *The Sound the Stars Make Rushing Through the Sky: The Writings of Jane Johnston Schoolcraft* (Philadelphia: University of Pennsylvania Press, 2007), 6. For other histories of Johnston's work, see Tammrah Stone-Gordon, "Woman of the Sound the Stars Make Rushing Through the Sky: A Literary Biography of Jane Johnston Schoolcraft" (master's thesis, Michigan State University, 1993).

29. Parker, *The Sounds the Stars Make*, 2.

30. Parker, *The Sounds the Stars Make*.

31. Scott Richard Lyons, *X-Marks: Native Signatures of Assent* (Minneapolis: University of Minnesota Press, 2010), 3.

32. Julius H. Rubin, *Perishing Heathens: Stories of Protestant Missionaries and Christian Indians in Antebellum America* (Lincoln: University of Nebraska Press, 2017), 174.

33. Robert Warrior, *Tribal Secrets: Recovering American Indian Intellectual Traditions* (Minneapolis: University of Minnesota Press, 1995), 124. Warrior calls this intellectual sovereignty.

34. Jane Johnston Schoolcraft, "Invocation, to My Maternal Grand-Father on Hearing His Descent from Chippewa Ancestors Misrepresented," in Parker, *The Sound the Stars Make*, 99–103.

35. Parker, *The Sound of the Stars Make*, 100.

36. "Missouri's Dred Scott Case, 1846–1857," State Archives, Missouri, https://www.sos.mo.gov/archives/resources/africanamerican/scott/scott.asp, accessed March 23, 2021.

37. Dred Scott v. Sandford, 60 U.S. 393 (1856), accessed March 23, 2021.

38. *Dred Scott v. Sandford.*

39. *Dred Scott v. Sandford.*

40. Brandon R. Byrd, *The Black Republic: African Americans and the Fate of Haiti* (Philadelphia: University of Pennsylvania Press, 2020), 2. To be clear, the argument of the book is not about white people's views of Haiti but those of African Americans.

41. Byrd, *The Black Republic.*

42. Byrd, *The Black Republic*, 163.

43. Claude Clegg, *The Price of Liberty: African Americans and the Making of Liberia* (Chapel Hill: University of North Carolina Press, 2004), 5, 6. See also Howard Temperley, "African-American Aspirations and the Settlement of Liberia," *Slavery & Abolition* 21, no. 2 (August 2000): 67–92. Temperley suggests that there were twelve thousand who settled in Liberia.

44. Sinha, *The Slave's Cause*, 160.

45. Sean Wilentz and David Walker, "Introduction: The Mysteries of David Walker," in *David Walker's Appeal: To the Coloured Citizens of the World, but in Particular, and Very Expressly, to Those of The United States of America* (New York: Hill and Wang, 1995), vii–xxiii.

46. Walker, *David Walker's Appeal*, 62–63.

47. Jean M. O'Brien, *Firsting and Lasting: Writing Indians Out of Existence in New England* (Minneapolis: University of Minnesota Press, 2010). As O'Brien notes in this book, Native people were written out of the history of New England.

48. Michelle Obama, "Remarks by the First Lady at the Sojourner Truth Bust Unveiling," April 28, 2009, Office of the First Lady, Washington, DC.

49. Nell Irvin Painter, *Sojourner Truth: A Life, a Symbol* (New York: W. W. Norton, 1996), 4.

50. Painter, *Sojourner Truth.*

51. bell hooks, *Ain't I A Woman: Black Women and Feminism* (London: Pluto Press, 1982), 2.

52. Reverend Marius Robinson, "Women's Rights Convention," *Anti-Slavery Bugle* (New-Lisbon, OH), June 21, 1851.

53. Cheryl Harris, "Finding Sojourner's Truth: Race, Gender, and the Institution of Property," *Cardozo Law Review* 18, no. 309 (November 1996): 2–88, 2.

54. Amy Kaplan, "Manifest Domesticity," *American Literature* 70, no. 3 (September 1998): 581–606. Kaplan argues that "if domesticity plays a key role in imagining the nation as home, then women, positioned at the center of the home, play a major role in defining the contours of the nation and its shifting borders with the foreign" (582).

55. Frederick Douglass, *Narrative of the Life of Frederick Douglass: An American Slave, Written by Himself*, ed. David W. Blight (Boston: Bedford/St. Martin's, 2003), 97.

56. David W. Blight, *Frederick Douglass: Prophet of Freedom* (New York: Simon & Schuster, 2018), xix.

57. Frederick Douglass, *Life and Times of Frederick Douglass, Written by Himself*, rev. ed. (Boston: De Wolfe & Fiske, 1892), http://hdl.handle.net/2027 /nco1.ark:/13960/t75t4qt9v, 355.

58. *National Anti-Slavery Standard* (New York, NY), May 29, 1869.

59. Donal F. Lindsey, *Indians at Hampton Institute, 1877–1923* (Urbana: University of Illinois Press, 1994), 23.

60. Booker T. Washington, *Up from Slavery* (1901; repr., CreateSpace Independent Publishing Platform, 2018), 45.

61. Blight, *Frederick Douglass*, 486.

62. Frederick Douglass, "'Composite Nation' Lecture in the Parker Fraternity Course, Boston," Library of Congress, 1867 Manuscript/Mixed Material, Folder 2 of 3, https://www.loc.gov/item/mfd.22017.

63. Douglass, "'Composite Nation' Lecture."

64. Douglass, "Composite Nation' Lecture."

65. Douglass, "'Composite Nation' Lecture."

66. Du Bois, *Black Reconstruction in America*, 708.

67. C. Joseph Genetin-Pilawa, *Crooked Paths to Allotment: The Fight over Federal Indian Policy after the Civil War* (Chapel Hill: University of North Carolina Press, 2012), 92–93. Historian Genetin-Pilawa calls the Indigenous activists that helped shape these activities "political entrepreneurs," who, he argues, "seize moments of opportunity to shape political debates, frames issues, and influence agendas. They create and often transform policies and institutions" (5).

68. "Ely Parker's Implementation of the Peace Policy," PBS, http://www.pbs .org/warrior/content/timeline/hero/1869peace.html.

CHAPTER 4. BLACK AND INDIGENOUS (INTER)NATIONALISMS DURING THE PROGRESSIVE ERA

1. Rayford W. Logan, *The Negro in American Life and Thought: The Nadir, 1877–1901* (New York: Dial Press, 1954), 52.

2. Glenda Gilmore, ed., introduction, *Who Were the Progressives?* (New York: Bedford/St. Martin's, 2002), 3.

3. David Chang, "Enclosures of Land and Sovereignty: The Allotment of American Indian Lands," *Radical History Review* 109 (2011): 108.

4. For an analysis of the links between incarceration, gender, and modernity during Jim Crow, see Sarah Haley, *No Mercy Here: Gender, Punishment, and the Making of Jim Crow Modernity* (Chapel Hill: University of North Carolina Press, 2016), 3.

5. Keisha N. Blain, *Set the World on Fire: Black Nationalist Women and the Global Struggle for Freedom* (Philadelphia: University of Pennsylvania Press, 2018), 105.

6. Paul C. Rosier, *Serving Their Country: American Indian Politics and Patriotism in the Twentieth Century* (Cambridge, MA: Harvard University Press, 2009), 7. Though Rosier refers to the years after the World Wars and Vietnam, I do think this book serves as an instructive point of comparison for understanding Black and Indigenous internationalism in different periods.

7. Frederick E. Hoxie, ed., *Talking Back to Civilization: Indian Voices from the Progressive Era* (New York: Palgrave Macmillan, 2001), 3.

8. Andrew Woolford, *This Benevolent Experiment: Indigenous Boarding Schools, Genocide, and Redress in Canada and the United States* (Winnipeg: University of Manitoba Press, 2015); Kevin Whalen, *Native Students at Work: American Indian Labor and Sherman Institute's Outing Program, 1900–1945* (Seattle: University of Washington Press, 2016). Woolford argues that the experiences of Indigenous youth at the boarding schools amount to genocide, according to United Nation's definition. Whalen analyzes the relationship between labor and the boarding schools, and how Indigenous students at the Sherman Boarding School utilized the outing program in order to make money and to see places like Los Angeles.

9. Society of American Indians, *Constitution and By-Laws*, 3–4.

10. Arthur Parker, "Certain Important Elements of the Indian Problem," *Quarterly Journal of the Society of American Indians* 3, no. 1 (1913): 26.

11. Parker, *Quarterly Journal of the Society of American Indians*, 30–31.

12. Laura Cornelius Kellogg, "Some Facts and Figures on Indian Education," *Quarterly Journal of the American Indian* 1, no. 1 (1913): 36.

13. Kellogg, "Some Facts and Figures on Indian Education," 37.

14. Blain, *Set the World on Fire*, 14–16.

15. Robert Hill, ed., *The Marcus Garvey and Universal Negro Improvement Association Papers*, vol. 1, *1826–August 1919* (Berkeley: University of California Press, 1983), 67.

16. Tony Martin, *Race First: The Ideological and Organizational Struggles of Marcus Garvey and the Universal Negro Improvement Association* (Westport, CT: Greenwood Press, 1976), 7–10.

17. Martin, *Race First*, 11.

18. Hill, *The Marcus Garvey and Universal Negro Improvement Association Papers*, 257.

19. UNIA Declaration of Rights of the Negro Peoples of the World, New York, August 13, 1920, in Robert Hill, ed., *The Marcus Garvey and Universal Negro Improvement Association Papers*, vol. 2, *August 1919–August 1920* (Berkeley: University of California Press, 1983), 571–80.

20. Erez Manela, *The Wilsonian Moment: Self-Determination and the International Origins of Anticolonial Nationalism* (New York: Oxford University Press, 2007), 5.

21. Manela, *The Wilsonian Moment*.

22. UNIA Declaration of Rights of the Negro Peoples.

23. UNIA Declaration of Rights of the Negro Peoples.

24. Kelley, "The Rest of Us," 269.

25. UNIA Declaration of Rights of the Negro Peoples.

26. UNIA Declaration of Rights of the Negro Peoples.

27. Marcus Garvey, "An Appeal to the Soul of White America," https://teachingamericanhistory.org/library/document/an-appeal-to-the-soul-of-white-america, accessed March 24, 2021.

28. Garvey, "An Appeal to the Soul of White America."

29. Cyril Briggs, Hubert Harrison, and W. A. Domingo were Black radicals who initially admired Garvey, but all three eventually grew disenchanted with

his perspective, which they decided was rooted in imperialism and an attempt to conquer Africa. See Minkah Makalani, *In the Cause of Freedom: Radical Black Internationalism from Harlem to London, 1917–1939* (Chapel Hill: University of North Carolina Press, 2011), 60–69.

30. Manning Marable, "Blackness Beyond Boundaries: Navigating the Political Economies of Global Inequality," in *Transnational Blackness: Navigating the Global Color Line*, ed. Manning Marable and Vanessa Agard-Jones (New York: Palgrave Macmillan, 2008), 4.

31. Frederick Hoxie, *This Indian Country: American Indian Political Activism and the Place They Made* (New York: Penguin Books, 2012), 225.

32. Hoxie, *This Indian Country*, 231.

33. See Ida B. Wells-Barnett, *On Lynchings* (Mineola, NY: Dover Publications, 2014).

34. Equal Justice Initiative, *Lynching in America: Confronting the Legacy of Racial Terror* (Montgomery, AL: Equal Justice Initiative, 2017), 4.

35. Gustav Spiller, ed., *Papers on Interracial Problems* (1911; repr., New York: Arno, 1969), 4, 23.

36. *The Crisis* 1, no. 2 (1910).

37. *The Crisis* 1, no. 2 (1910).

38. *The Crisis* 1, no. 6 (1911): 23.

39. Richard Henry Pratt, "The Advantages of Mingling Indians with Whites," in *Americanizing the American Indians: Writings by the "Friends of the Indian," 1880–1900*, ed. Francis Paul Prucha (Cambridge, MA: Harvard University Press, 1973), 260–61.

40. Charles A. Eastman to Richard Henry Pratt, January 27, 1911, Papers of Richard Henry Pratt, Box 3, Folder 85.

41. Raymond Wilson, *Ohiyesa: Charles Eastman, Santee Sioux* (Urbana: University of Illinois Press, 1983), 150.

42. Charles A. Eastman, *From the Deep Woods to Civilization* (Boston: Little, Brown, 1916), 192–93.

43. Eastman, *From the Deep Woods to Civilization*, 187.

44. *The Crisis*, 1 no. 2 (1910).

45. The URC sent out press releases and wrote to educational secretaries in countries around the world so that they might adopt the URC's stance on race and enlightenment.

46. The URC's proposed second Congress did not occur because of World War I.

47. Spiller, *Proceedings*, 5.

48. Spiller, *Proceedings*, 348.

49. Spiller, *Proceedings*, 351.

50. Spiller, *Proceedings*, 353.

51. Spiller, *Proceedings*, 368.

52. Spiller, *Proceedings*, 369.

53. Kiara M. Vigil, *Indigenous Intellectuals: Sovereignty, Citizenship, and the American Imagination, 1880–1930* (Cambridge: Cambridge University Press, 2015), 50.

54. Vigil, *Indigenous Intellectuals*, 374.

55. Vigil, *Indigenous Intellectuals*, 360.

56. Vigil, *Indigenous Intellectuals*, 376.

57. W. E. B. Du Bois, "The Souls of White Folk," in *Darkwater: Voices from Within the Veil* (New York: Harcourt, Brace, 1921), 49.

58. Eastman, *From the Deep Woods to Civilization*, 189.

CHAPTER 5. BLACK AMERICANS AND NATIVE AMERICANS IN THE CIVIL RIGHTS IMAGINATION

1. "Says Indians on Bottom," *Chicago Defender*, December 10, 1949.

2. Vine Deloria Jr. and Clifford Lytle, *The Nations Within: The Past and Future of American Indian Sovereignty* (New York: Pantheon Books, 1984), 158–59. Deloria Jr. and Lytle offer a fantastic analysis of modern tribal governments and a variety of policies that have impacted Native nations.

3. Colleen Doody, *Detroit's Cold War: The Origins of Postwar Conservatism* (Urbana: University of Illinois Press, 2013), 49.

4. Ira Katznelson, *When Affirmative Action Was White: An Untold History of Racial Inequality in America* (New York: W. W. Norton, 2006), 23.

5. Douglas K. Miller, *Indians on the Move: Native American Mobility and Urbanization in the Twentieth Century* (Chapel Hill: University of North Carolina Press, 2019), 9.

6. Malinda Maynor Lowery, *The Lumbee Indians: An American Struggle* (Chapel Hill: University of North Carolina Press, 2018), 137.

7. Lowery, *The Lumbee Indians*, 137–39.

8. Langston Hughes, "Simple, Indians, and the K.K.K.," *Chicago Defender*, February 1, 1958.

9. Robert F. Williams, *Negroes with Guns* (New York: Alexander Street Press, 1962), 58.

10. National Congress of American Indians, "Mission and History," http://www.ncai.org/about-ncai/mission-history (accessed April 30, 2020).

11. Daniel Cobb, "Talking the Language of the Larger World: Politics in Cold War (Native) America," in *Beyond Red Power: American Indian Politics and Activism since 1900* (Santa Fe: School for Advanced Research Press, 2007), 162–63.

12. James Baldwin, *The Fire Next Time* (New York: Vintage International, 1993), 85.

13. James Cone, *Martin and Malcolm: A Dream or a Nightmare* (Maryknoll, NY: Orbis Books, 1992), 4.

14. Peniel E. Joseph, *The Sword and the Shield: The Revolutionary Lives of Malcolm X and Martin Luther King Jr.* (New York: Basic Books, 2020), 16–17.

15. Sam Wineburg and Chauncey Monte-Sano, "'Famous Americans': The Changing Pantheon of American Heroes," *Journal of American History* 94, no. 4 (2008): 1186–202.

16. Jeanne Theoharis, *A More Beautiful and Terrible History: The Uses and Misuses of Civil Rights History* (Boston: Beacon Press, 2018), ix–x.

17. Paul Gray, "Required Reading: Nonfiction Books," http://content.time.com/time/magazine/article/0,9171,988496,00.html, accessed March 25, 2021.

18. Ta-Nehisi Coates, *Between the World and Me* (New York: Spiegel & Grau, 2015), 36.

19. John Dittmer, *Local People: The Struggle for Civil Rights in Mississippi* (Urbana: University of Illinois Press, 1994), 12, 127.

20. Martin Luther King Jr., *Why We Can't Wait* (1964) (Boston: Beacon Press, 2010), 141.

21. King, *Why We Can't Wait* (New York: Signet Books, 1964), 119.

22. *Why We Can't Wait* (Signet), 120.

23. *Why We Can't Wait* (Signet), 120.

24. David J. Garrow, *Bearing the Cross: Martin Luther King, Jr., and the Southern Christian Leadership Conference* (New York: William Morrow, 1986), 564.

25. Garrow, *Bearing the Cross,* 556.

26. Martin Luther King Jr., *Where Do We Go from Here: Chaos or Community?* (1968; repr., Boston: Beacon Press, 1986), 84–85.

27. Jodi Byrd, *The Transit of Empire: Indigenous Critiques of Colonialism* (Minneapolis: University of Minnesota Press, 2011), xiii.

28. King, *Where Do We Go from Here?,* 141.

29. Kay Mills, *This Little Light of Mine: The Life of Fannie Lou Hamer* (1993; repr. Lexington: University Press of Kentucky, 2007), 7.

30. Mills, *This Little Light of Mine,* 10.

31. Belinda Robnett, *How Long? How Long? African-American Women in the Struggle for Civil Rights* (New York: Oxford University Press, 1997), 193. Robnett argues that African American women used bridge leadership to connect the local people and those coming from other parts of the US to fight for social justice.

32. Fannie Lou Hamer, "We're on Our Way," speech before a mass meeting held at the Negro Baptist School in Indianola, Mississippi, September 1964, https://voicesofdemocracy.umd.edu/hamer-were-on-our-way-speech-text, accessed March 25, 2021.

33. Malcolm X, *The Autobiography of Malcolm X* (with the assistance of Alex Haley) (New York: Ballantine Books, 1992), 254.

34. *The Autobiography of Malcolm X,* 95.

35. *The Autobiography of Malcolm X.*

36. Leanne Betasamosake Simpson, "The Place Where We All Live and Work Together: A Gendered Analysis of 'Sovereignty,'" in *Native Studies Keywords,* ed. Stephanie Nohelani Teves, Andrea Smith, and Michelle Raheja (Tucson: University of Arizona Press, 2015), 19.

37. Mishuana Goeman, "Land as Life: Unsettling the Logics of Containment," in Teves, Smith, and Raheja, *Native Studies Keywords,* 72–73.

38. *The Autobiography of Malcolm X,* 363.

39. *The Autobiography of Malcolm X.*

40. *The Autobiography of Malcolm X,* 362.

41. *The Autobiography of Malcolm X.*

42. Hazel Hertzberg, *The Search for an American Indian Identity: Modern Pan-Indian Movements* (Syracuse, NY: Syracuse University Press, 1971), l; Kyle T. Mays, "Transnational Progressivism: African Americans, Native Americans, and the Universal Races Congress of 1911," *American Indian Quarterly* 37, no. 3 (Summer 2013): 243–61.

43. Abdul Alkalimat, "The Paradigmatic Agency of Malcolm X: Family, Experience, and Thought," in *Malcolm X's Worldview: An Exemplar for Contemporary Black Studies*, ed. Rita Kiki Edozie and Curtis Stokes (East Lansing: Michigan State University Press, 2015), 44.

44. Alkalimat, "The Paradigmatic Agency of Malcolm X."

45. Malcolm X, *Malcolm X on Afro-American History* (New York: Pathfinder Press, 1990), 87.

46. Malcolm X, "Message to the Grassroots," in *Malcolm X Speaks: Selected Speeches and Statements*, ed. George Breitman (1965; repr., New York: Grove Press, 1994), 7.

47. Carl Husemoller Nightingale, "The Global Inner City: Toward a Historical Analysis," in *W. E. B. Du Bois, Race, and the City: The Philadelphia Negro and Its Legacy*, ed. Michael Katz and Thomas Sugrue (Philadelphia: University of Pennsylvania Press, 1998), 217–58.

48. Steve Clark, ed., *February 1965: The Final Speeches* (New York: Pathfinder Press, 1992), 86.

49. Clark, *February 1965*.

50. Clark, *February 1965*.

51. Malcolm X, *The Autobiography of Malcolm X*, "The Negro," Folder 1/2, box 5, p. 4, Schomburg Center for Black Culture and Research.

52. Malcolm X, "The Ballot or the Bullet," April 3, 1964, https://sites.psu.edu/jld5710/2012/10/02/1964-the-american-nightmare, accessed August 29, 2019. The speech was delivered at Cory Methodist Church, Cleveland, Ohio, on April 3, 1964.

53. Malcolm X, *The Autobiography of Malcolm X*, "The Negro," Folder 2/2.

54. Malcolm X, *The Autobiography of Malcolm X*, "The Negro," Folder 2/2, p. 4.

55. Malcolm X, "The Negro," Folder 2/2, p. 6.

56. Malcolm X, "The Negro," Folder 2/2, p. 21.

57. "Back to the Farm Project for Negroes Is Mapped," *Chicago Defender*, April 1, 1967.

58. Baldwin, *The Fire Next Time*, 8.

59. Christina Sharpe, *In the Wake: On Blackness and Being* (Durham, NC: Duke University Press, 2016), 21.

60. "Has the American Dream Been Achieved at the Expense of the American Negro?," James Baldwin and William Buckley debate at the Cambridge Union, February 18, 1965, https://www.youtube.com/watch?v=VOCZOHQ7fCE.

61. Roxanne Dunbar-Ortiz and Dina Gilio-Whitaker, *"All the Real Indians Died Off": And 20 Other Myths About Native Americans* (Boston: Beacon Press, 2016), 8.

62. To read more about this particular debate, see Nicholas Buccola, *The Fire Is Upon Us: James Baldwin, William F. Buckley Jr., and the Debate over Race in America* (Princeton, NJ: Princeton University Press, 2019). See especially chapters 6 and 7.

63. James Baldwin, *Notes of a Native Son* (Boston: Beacon Press, 1955), 25.

64. Baldwin, *Notes of a Native Son*, 28.

65. Baldwin, *Notes of a Native Son*, 43.

CHAPTER 6. BLACK POWER AND RED POWER, FOR FREEDOM AND SOVEREIGNTY

1. "The Third World," *Black Scholar* 7, no. 9 (June 1976), cover page.

2. "The Third World."

3. Jeffrey O. G. Ogbar, *Black Power: Radical Politics and African American Identity* (Baltimore: Johns Hopkins University Press, 2004), 188.

4. Bradley Shreve, *Red Power Rising: The National Indian Youth Council and the Origins of Native Activism* (Norman: University of Oklahoma Press, 2011). See chapter 5, "'The Time Comes When We Must Take Action!': The Fish-In Campaign and the Rise of Intertribal Direct Action," 119–38. For a brief history of women's roles in Red Power, see Donna Langston, "American Indian Women's Activism in the 1960s and 1970s," *Hypatia* 18, no. 2 (Spring 2003): 114–32.

5. Paul Chaat Smith and Robert Warrior, *Like a Hurricane: The American Indian Movement from Alcatraz to Wounded Knee* (Boston: South End Press, 1995), 135.

6. Smith and Warrior, *Like a Hurricane*.

7. For a history of the term "Black Power" and the movement, see Peniel Joseph, "The Black Power Movement: A State of the Field," *Journal of American History* 96, no. 3 (December 2009): 751–76.

8. Joseph, "The Black Power Movement," 755.

9. Stokely Carmichael and Charles Hamilton, *Black Power: The Politics of Liberation* (New York: Vintage Press, 1992), 44.

10. Vine Deloria Jr., *Custer Died for Your Sins: An Indian Manifesto* (New York: The Macmillan Company, 1969), 172.

11. Deloria, *Custer Died for Your Sins*, 174.

12. Deloria, *Custer Died for Your Sins*, 180.

13. Deloria, *Custer Died for Your Sins*, 194.

14. Deloria, *Custer Died for Your Sins*, 198.

15. Simpson, "The Place Where We All Live and Work Together," 19.

16. Donald P. Baker and Raul Ramirez, "Officials, Indians Parley on Protest," *Washington Post*, November 5, 1972.

17. Key Martin, *Workers World*, December 10, 1998, http://www.hartford -hwp.com/archives/45a/474.html.

18. "Wounded Knee," *New York Times*, March 23, 1973.

19. Jack Burdock, "Angela Davis Hails Young Election, STRESS Abolition," *Detroit News*, February 25, 1974.

20. Emily F. Gibson, "Our Guardian Angels Is Black to the Bone," *Los Angeles Sentinel*, April 5, 1973.

21. Reverend Curtis E. Burrell Jr., "The Black Indian," *Chicago Defender*, April 5, 1973.

22. Imari Abubakari Obadele, *Free the Land! The True Story of the RNA-11 in Mississippi and the Continuing Struggle to Establish an Independent Black Nation in Five States of the Deep South* (Washington, DC: House of Songhay, 1984), 11.

23. Milton R. Henry, "An Independent Black Republic in North America," in *Black Separatism and Social Reality: Rhetoric and Reason*, ed. Raymond L. Hall (New York: Pergamon Press, 1977), 35.

24. The Cherokee Nation is one of the most studied Indigenous nations. I will not recount that familiar story. But it is important to acknowledge that there are also Black-Cherokee relations that Henry does not acknowledge, especially the subject of Cherokees enslaving Blacks. See Miles, *Ties That Bind*; Miles, *House on Diamond Hill*; Naylor, *African Cherokees in Indian Territory*; Faye Yarborough, *Race and the Cherokee Nation: Sovereignty in the Nineteenth Century* (Philadelphia: University of Pennsylvania Press, 2008).

25. Henry, "An Independent Black Republic," 33.

26. For histories on this termination and relocation, see Donald Fixico, *Termination and Relocation: Federal Indian Policy, 1945–1960* (Albuquerque: University of New Mexico Press, 1986); James B. LaGrand, *Indian Metropolis: Native Americans in Chicago, 1945–1975* (Chicago: University of Illinois Press, 2002).

27. Henry, "An Independent Black Republic," 33.

28. Henry, "An Independent Black Republic," 36–37.

29. Hoxie, *This Indian Country*.

30. Henry, "An Independent Black Republic," 39.

31. Henry, "An Independent Black Republic," 36.

32. "Dr. King Says He Is Confident of Support on His Drive for Poor," *New York Times*, March 15, 1968.

33. Gordon K. Mantler, *Power to the Poor: Black-Brown Coalition and the Fight for Economic Justice, 1960–1974* (Chapel Hill: University of North Carolina Press, 2013), 108–10.

34. For a queer analysis of the Poor People's Campaign, see Christina Juhász-Wood, "Assembling the Poor People's Campaign (1968): Queer Activism and Economic Justice," master's thesis, University of New Mexico, 2011.

35. Daniel Cobb, *Native Activism in Cold War America: The Struggle for Sovereignty* (Norman: University of Oklahoma Press, 2008), 2. See also Paul McKenzie-Jones, *Clyde Warrior: Tradition, Community, and Red Power* (Norman: University of Oklahoma Press, 2015).

36. Cobb, *Native Activism in Cold War America*, 4.

37. Southern Christian Leadership Conference, "State of Demands for Rights of the Poor Presented to Agencies of the U.S. Government by the Southern Christian Leadership Conference and Its Committee of 100," April 29–30 and May 1, 1968, https://www.crmvet.org/docs/6805_ppc_demands.pdf, accessed June 4, 2020.

38. See Glen Coulthard, *Red Skin, White Masks: Rejecting the Colonial Politics of Recognition* (Minneapolis: University of Minnesota Press, 2014). As Coulthard argues, "In situations where colonial rule does not depend solely on the exercise of state violence, its reproduction instead rests on the ability to entice Indigenous peoples to *identify*, either implicitly or explicitly, with the more profoundly *asymmetrical* and *nonreciprocal* forms of recognition either imposed on or granted to them by the settler state and society" (25).

39. Cobb, *Native Activism in Cold War America*, 183–84. Cobb quotes Vine Deloria Jr., who asserted that the work of the National Congress of American Indians was essential because it was forced to work with the US government, and not confront them in the way that young people were doing at the time:

"Anyone can get into the headlines by making wild threats and militant statements," remarked Deloria, but "it takes a lot of hard work to raise an entire group to a new conception of themselves. And that is the difference between the nationalists and the militants" (183). Cobb also covers Tillie Walker's challenge of the antiblackness of Native people (169).

40. Ben A. Franklin, "Non-Negro Units Hit March Chiefs; Charge They Are Ignored and 'Abused' by Black Militants," *New York Times*, May 26, 1968.

41. Gabriel Chrisman, "The Fish-in Protests at Franks Landing," https://depts.washington.edu/civilr/fish-ins.htm, accessed March 25, 2021.

42. Poor People's Campaign, Supreme Court Building Confrontation, American Indians, May 9, 1968, Larry Lichenstein 1083: Southern Christian Leadership Conference Records, Side A, Duration: 33 minutes, 2 seconds.

43. Cobb, *Native Activism in Cold War America*, 187.

44. "Petition Planned for U.N. Accuses U.S. of Genocide," *New York Times*, June 21, 1970.

45. Carol Anderson, *Eyes Off the Prize: The United Nations and the African American Struggle for Human Rights, 1944–1955* (Cambridge: Cambridge University Press, 2003), 5.

46. For the history of Native people and the United Nations, see Sheryl Lightfoot, *Global Indigenous Politics: A Subtle Revolution* (New York: Routledge, 2016).

47. William H. McClendon, "The Black Scholar Interviews: Dennis Banks," *Black Scholar* 7, no. 9 (June 1976): 28–66.

48. McClendon, "The Black Scholar Interviews," 33.

49. McClendon, "The Black Scholar Interviews."

50. Jane Rhodes, *Framing the Black Panthers: The Spectacular Rise of a Black Power Icon* (New York: New Press, 2007); Jama Lazerow and Yohuru Williams, eds., *In Search of the Black Panther Party: New Perspectives on a Revolutionary Movement* (Durham, NC: Duke University Press, 2006); Ashley D. Farmer, *Remaking Black Power: How Black Women Transformed an Era* (Chapel Hill: University of North Carolina Press, 2019).

51. David Hilliard, ed., "Stop the Extradition of Dennis Banks," in *The Black Panther Intercommunal News Service, 1967–1980* (New York: Atria Books, 2007), 124–29.

52. Tina Griego, "Cuba Still Harbors One of America's Most Wanted Fugitives. What Happens to Assata Shakur Now?" *Washington Post*, December 20, 2014, https://www.washingtonpost.com/news/storyline/wp/2014/12/20/cuba-still-harbors-one-of-americas-most-wanted-fugitives-what-happens-to-assata-shakur-now.

53. Stephen Ward, "The Third World Women's Alliance: Black Feminist Radicalism and Black Power Politics," in *The Black Power Movement: Rethinking the Civil Rights–Black Power Era* (New York: Routledge, 2006), 119–44. Ward argues that the TWWA was founded in direct response to patriarchy. While true, Ashley Farmer's *Remaking Black Power* attempts to give nuance to this perspective, arguing, "Many female activists did critique this aspect of Black Power organizing and formed independent women's or feminist organizations during the early 1970s. Others challenged sexism and pushed for multifaceted

ideas of blackness from *within* Black Power groups. Whichever avenue these activists chose, they were typically addressing sexist *interpretations* of black nationalist philosophies and principles rather than a given ideology itself." Farmer, *Remaking Black Power*, 17.

54. Assata Shakur, "To My People," *Triple Jeopardy* 3, no. 2 (November–December 1973): 10, https://voices.revealdigital.com.

55. Blain, *Set the World on Fire*, 10.

56. Peniel Joseph, *Stokely: A Life* (New York: Basic Civitas, 2014), 326.

57. Stokely Carmichael, "Pan-Africanism—Land and Power," *Black Scholar* 1, no. 1 (1969): 39.

58. Carmichael, "Pan-Africanism-Land and Power," 283–85.

59. Kwame Nkrumah, *Class Struggle in Africa* (London: Panaf Books, 1970), 87.

60. Nkrumah, *Class Struggle in Africa*.

61. Nkrumah, *Class Struggle in Africa*, 87–88.

62. Stokely Carmichael, *Stokely Speaks: From Black Power to Pan-Africanism* (Chicago: Chicago Review Press, 2007), 200.

63. Carmichael, *Stokely Speaks*, 225.

64. Nkrumah, *Class Struggle in Africa*, 88.

65. Nkrumah, *Class Struggle in Africa*.

66. https://aaprp-intl.org/historical-origins-of-the-a-aprp/ (accessed November 6, 2019). On its website, the organization states, "The A-APRP emerges from and heralds an intensification of the African and larger worldwide struggles for democratic rights, for national independence and unity; and for scientific socialism. At the same time, it uncompromisingly and unceaselessly fights for the inevitable destruction of capitalism, imperialism, racism, Zionism, apartheid and neo-colonialism."

67. Randy Furst, "Recalling the Past, Planning the Future," *Minneapolis Star*, June 12, 1981.

68. Brown remains a member of the AAPRP. He has also written *Slavery and the Slave Trade Were and Are Crimes Against Humanity* (African Diaspora Publishing Corporation, 2004), and has edited an edition of *Stokely Speaks: From Black Power to Pan-Africanism*.

69. White Earth Reservation Land Settlement, 1985, https://whiteearth.com /assets/files/welsa/whiteearthlandsettlementact.pdf.

70. Simon Anekwe, "Fight for Ancestral Lands: ANC Supports Indians," *New York Amsterdam News*, May 10, 1986.

71. Anekwe, "Fight for Ancestral Lands."

72. While I think we need more historical information on solidarity and tensions, it is clear that African scholars have thought about and compared settler colonialism in the United States, Canada, Australia and New Zealand, and in South Africa. Prominent among them is Bernard Magubane. Though, along with similarities, he found significant differences between South Africa and those abovementioned places. See Bernard Magubane, "The Political Economy of the South African Revolution," *African Journal of Political Economy* 1, no. 1 (1986): 1–28. Magubane writes, "However, unlike the United States, Canada, Australia and New Zealand, i.e., countries that the Europeans claim as part of

the West, South Africa remains an African country and therefore part of the Third World. What makes South Africa the country of the African is not the fact that Blacks constitute the majority of the population; nor even that they are the indigenous inhabitants. After all, remnants of the indigenous peoples of America, Australia and New Zealand are still there, but clearly their lands, except for reservations which they have been confined no longer belongs to them; more they are clearly fugitives in their native countries" (1). While we might disagree with the polemical nature of Magunabe's laying out of the key differences, he might be on to something. Still, connecting African settler colonialism to that of the US, especially bringing together disparate histories, assuming they exist as indicated in the ANC's statement of solidarity, is a project worth exploring outside of the realm of theory.

73. "Gaddafi Prize in Human Rights, November 9, 1991," YouTube, https://www.youtube.com/watch?v=iqrgqNFfzYM&t=1982s, accessed March 25, 2021.

74. Patrick Howe, "Bellecourt Seeks Mandela's Intervention," *Argus-Leader*, November 22, 2000.

75. For a history of the trials that many Native people suffered, see Peter Matthiessen, *In the Spirit of Crazy Horse* (New York: Penguin Books, 1991).

CHAPTER 7. BLACK AND INDIGENOUS POPULAR CULTURES IN THE PUBLIC SPHERE

1. Lauren Michele Jackson, *White Negroes: When Cornrows Were in Vogue . . . and Other Thoughts on Cultural Appropriation* (Boston: Beacon Press, 2019).

2. Kendi, *Stamped from the Beginning*, 10.

3. Stuart Hall, "What Is This 'Black' in Black Popular Culture?," in *Black Popular Culture*, ed. Gina Dent (Boston: New Press, 1998), 29.

4. Leanne Simpson, *As We Have Always Done: Indigenous Freedom through Radical Resurgence* (Minneapolis: University of Minnesota Press, 2017), 113.

5. Deloria, *Playing Indian*, 7.

6. Deloria, *Playing Indian*, 191.

7. David Roediger, *The Wages of Whiteness: Race and the Making of the American Working Class* (New York: Verso, 1991), 115, 118.

8. Ralph Ellison, *Invisible Man* (New York: Vintage International, 1995), 3.

9. John Fiske, *Reading the Popular* (New York: Routledge, 1989), 11–13.

10. Michael Eric Dyson, *Reflecting Black: African-American Cultural Criticism* (Minneapolis: University of Minnesota Press, 1993), xvii.

11. Johnnie Jae, "About," https://johnniejae.com/about/ (accessed August 7, 2020).

12. Kiersten Wells, "Debate Emerges After Native Woman Tells Black Woman to 'Keep Hands Off Our Culture,'" *Atlanta Black Star*, August 9, 2017.

13. Audre Lorde, "The Uses of Anger," *Women's Studies Quarterly* 25, no. 1/2 (Spring–Summer 1997): 278–85.

14. Simpson, *As We Have Always Done*, 223.

15. Abaki Beck, "Rendered Invisible: Pocahontas Is Not a Sex Symbol," *Bitch Media*, November 20, 2017, https://www.bitchmedia.org/article/nicki -minaj-pocahontas-is-not-a-sex-symbol.

16. Patricia Hill Collins and Sirma Bilge, *Intersectionality (Key Concepts)* (Cambridge: Polity, 2016), 26.

17. Collins and Bilge, *Intersectionality (Key Concepts)*, 27.

18. bell hooks, "Selling Hot Pussy: Representations of Black Female Sexuality in the Cultural Marketplace," in *Black Looks: Race and Representation* (Boston: South End Press, 1992), 65. Interestingly enough, the cover of the original edition features a photo of a Native person, used by permission from William Loren Katz, author of *Black Indians: A Hidden Heritage*.

19. Safiya Umoja Noble, *Algorithms of Oppression: How Search Engines Reinforce Racism* (New York: New York University Press, 2017), 17.

20. David E. Kirkland, "Black Masculine Language," in *The Oxford Handbook of African American Language* (2015), ed. Jennifer Bloomquist, Lisa J. Green, and Sonja Lanehart, https://doi.org/10.1093/oxfordhb/9780199795390 .013.43.

21. Geneva Smitherman, "'A New Way of Talkin': Language, Social Change, and Political Theory," in *Talkin That Talk: Language, Culture, and Education in African America* (New York: Routledge, 1999), 94.

22. NAACP, "The 'N' Word Is Laid to Rest by the NAACP," press release, July 9, 2007, https://www.naacp.org/latest/the-n-word-is-laid-to-rest-by -the-naacp.

23. Geneva Smitherman, *Word from the Mother: Language and African Americans* (New York: Routledge, 2006), 51.

24. Cornel West, Tavis Smiley, and Michael Eric Dyson, *N Word, Never Forget: A Journey of Revelations* (Hidden Beach Recordings, 2007).

25. Smitherman, *Word from the Mother*, 52.

26. Erica Tempesta and Valerie Siebert, "Native American Men and Women Respond to 'Thanksgiving,' 'Redskin,' and Christopher Columbus," *Daily Mail*, November 26, 2015, https://www.dailymail.co.uk/femail/article-3334208 /It-massacre-Native-Americans-reveal-REALLY-feel-Thanksgiving-stereotypes -branding-Christopher-Columbus-terrorist-America.html.

27. John Keim, "How the Events of 2020 Forced the Washington NFL Team's Name Change," ESPN.com, July 14, 2020, https://www.espn.com/nfl /story/_/id/29460299/how-events-2020-forced-washington-nfl-team-name -change.

28. Bernice P. Jackson, "Chief Wahoo Must Go," *New Pittsburgh Courier*, May 20, 2000.

29. Alex Reimer, "The Story Behind Bomani Jones' 'Caucasians' Shirt," *Forbes*, April 7, 2016, https://www.forbes.com/sites/alexreimer/2016/04/09/the -story-behind-bomani-jones-caucasian-shirt/#6853d83c4e26.

30. Erik Brady, "Daniel Snyder Says Redskins Will Never Change Name," *USA Today*, May 9, 2013, https://www.usatoday.com/story/sports/nfl/redskins /2013/05/09/washington-redskins-daniel-snyder/2148127.

31. Brady, "Daniel Snyder Says Redskins."

32. Desus and Mero, "Racist Blackhawks Fan," YouTube, February 21, 2018, https://youtu.be/t7EE3PPUHP8, accessed March 25, 2021.

33. Tarik El-Bashier, "Blackhawks Fans Tossed After Directing Racist Remarks at Washington's Smith-Pelly," NBC Sports, February 18, 2018, https://www.nbcsports.com/washington/capitals/blackhawks-fans-tossed-after-directing-racist-remarks-washingtons-smith-pelly.

34. Desus and Mero, "Racist Blackhawks Fan."

35. Frantz Fanon, *The Wretched of the Earth* (New York: Grove Press, 2004), 179.

CHAPTER 8. THE MATTER OF BLACK AND INDIGENOUS LIVES, POLICING, AND JUSTICE

1. Carolyn Smith-Morris, "Addressing the Epidemic of Missing and Murdered Indigenous Women and Girls," *Cultural Survival*, March 6, 2020, https://www.culturalsurvival.org/news/addressing-epidemic-missing-murdered-indigenous-women-and-girls.

2. Eliza Racine, "Native Lives Matter: The Overlooked Police Brutality Against Native Americans," *Lakota Law Project*, November 21, 2017, https://www.lakotalaw.org/news/2017-11-21/native-lives-matter-the-overlooked-police-brutality-against-native-american.

3. Frantz Fanon, *The Wretched of the Earth* (New York: Grove Press, 2004), 31. The important point here is that violence encompasses the entire existence of Black and Indigenous peoples.

4. Rishma Dhaliwal, "Knowledge Session: Democracy Is Hypocrisy," *Iamhiphopmagazine*, March 21, 2015, https://www.iamhiphopmagazine.com/knowledge-session-democracy-is-hypocrisy-by-malcolm-x.

5. "The People's Budget LA: Los Angeles 2020–2021," https://peoplesbudgetla.files.wordpress.com/2020/05/peoplesbudgetreport_may26.pdf.

6. Sam Levin, "What Does 'Defund the Police' Mean? The Rallying Cry Sweeping the US—Explained," *The Guardian*, June 6, 2020, https://www.theguardian.com/us-news/2020/jun/05/defunding-the-police-us-what-does-it-mean. This article documents several organizations who try other methods of public safety intervention instead of using the police.

7. "The Peoples Budget LA," 2.

8. Metropolitan Urban Indian Directors, "MUID Statement Regarding the Police Killing of George Floyd," May 27, 2020, https://muidmn.org/georgefloyd.

9. "Herstory," Black Lives Matter website, https://blacklivesmatter.com/herstory, accessed June 6, 2020. See also Patrisse Khan-Cullors, asha bandele, and Angela Davis, *When They Call You a Terrorist: A Black Lives Matter Memoir* (New York: St. Martin's Press, 2018).

10. Barbara Ransby, *Making All Black Lives Matter: Reimagining Freedom in the Twenty-First Century* (Oakland: University of California Press, 2018), 3–4. As Ransby points out, this movement is decidedly different from those of the past. It centers intersectionality and highlights the voices of Black queer, trans, and women as central to the movement.

11. Marc Lamont Hill, *Nobody: Casualties of America's War on the Vulnerable, from Ferguson to Flint and Beyond* (New York: Atria Books, 2016). Hill

argues that "to be Nobody is to be vulnerable" (xvii) and "abandoned by the state" (xix).

12. Elise Hansen, "The Forgotten Minority in Police Shootings," CNN, November 13, 2017, https://www.cnn.com/2017/11/10/us/native-lives-matter /index.html.

13. For a report on Native Americans and police brutality see the Lakota People's Law Project, https://s3-us-west-1.amazonaws.com/lakota-peoples-law /uploads/Native-Lives-Matter-PDF.pdf. Although they don't offer a genealogy of the phrase, they detail the police violence experienced by Native people and offer some recommendations for change.

14. African American Policy Forum, "#SayHerName," https://aapf.org /sayhername (accessed July 22, 2020).

15. Angela Y. Davis and Elizabeth Martinez, "Coalition Building Among People of Color," in *The Angela Y. Davis Reader*, ed. Joy James (Malden, MA: Blackwell, 1998), 299.

16. Lightfoot, *Global Indigenous Politics*, 200.

17. See Mehrsa Baradaran, "The Decoy of Black Capitalism," in *The Color of Money: Black Banks and the Racial Wealth Gap* (Cambridge, MA: Harvard University Press, 2017), 187–214.

CONCLUSION: THE POSSIBILITIES FOR AFRO-INDIGENOUS FUTURES

1. Billy-Ray Belcourt and Lindsay Nixon, "What Do We Mean by Queer Indigenous Ethics?," *Canadian Art*, May 23, 2018, https://canadianart.ca/features /what-do-we-mean-by-queerindigenousethics.

2. Audre Lorde, "Learning from the 60s," in *Sister Outsider* (Berkeley, CA: Crossing Press, 2007), 136.

3. Lorde, "Learning from the 60s."

4. Frances Mulraney, "White Female Protester Says Black Cops 'Are Part of the Problem,'" *Daily Mail*, June 25, 2020, https://www.dailymail.co.uk/news /article-8457467/White-female-protester-tells-black-cops-problem.html.

5. Baldwin, *The Fire Next Time*, 94.

6. Martin Luther King Jr., "Letter from a Birmingham Jail." April 16, 1963, https://www.africa.upenn.edu/Articles_Gen/Letter_Birmingham.html.

7. Steve Biko, "Black Souls in White Skins?," in *I Write What I Like*, ed. Aelred Stubbs, C. R. (New York: Harpers & Row, 1978), 23.

8. Stephanie E. Jones-Rogers, *They Were Her Property: White Women as Slave Owners in the American South* (New Haven, CT: Yale University Press, 2019).

9. Zoé Samudzi and William C. Anderson, *Black as Resistance: Finding the Conditions for Liberation* (Chico, CA: AK Press, 2018), 24.

10. Leanne Betasamosake Simpson, "Indict the System: Indigenous & Black Resistance," November 29, 2014 (accessed 5 February 2020).

11. "World Conference Against Racism Opens in Durban," Department of Public Information, News and Media Services Division, August 31, 2001, https://www.un.org/WCAR/pressreleases/rd-d13.html.

12. World Conference Against Racism, Racial Discrimination, Xenophobia, and Related Tolerance, 2001, https://www.un.org/WCAR/durban.pdf.

13. World Conference against Racism, Racial Discrimination, 7.

14. Angela Y. Davis, *Freedom Is a Constant Struggle: Ferguson, Palestine, and the Foundations of a Movement*, ed. Frank Barat (Chicago: Haymarket Books, 2016), 47.

15. Willard R. Johnson, "Wilma Mankiller Introductory Remarks," in *Exploring the Legacy and Future of Black/Indian Relations* (St. Paul, MN: 57th Annual National Congress of American Indians, 2001), 1.

16. Johnson, "Wilma Mankiller Introductory Remarks," 1.

17. Alfred L. Brophy, *Reparations: Pro and Con* (Oxford: Oxford University Press, 2006), 169–70. To be clear, Brophy clearly offers detailed arguments regarding how reparations may or may not work. For instance, how do we actually come to know who deserves reparations? As far as truth commissions, how do we collectively determine what is the "truth"?

18. Sheryl Lightfoot, "Settler State Apologies to Indigenous Peoples: A Normative Framework and Comparative Assessment," *NAIS Journal* 2, no. 1 (2015): 17.

19. Lightfoot, "Settler State Apologies to Indigenous Peoples."

20. "Resolution Supporting Community Reparations for Black Asheville," https://drive.google.com/file/d/1WKialVISWzu72mhasyy9SslDbVGMSj5U/view, accessed March 26, 2021.

21. William A. Darity Jr. and A. Kirsten Mullen, *From Here to Equality: Reparations for Black Americans in the Twenty-First Century* (Chapel Hill: University of North Carolina Press, 2020). See chapter 13, "A Program for Black Reparations," 256–70.

22. Darity and Mullen, *From Here to Equality*. See chapter 1, "A Political History of Black America's Reparations Movement," 9–27.

23. Daina Ramey Berry, *The Price for Their Pound of Flesh: The Value of the Enslaved, from Womb to Grave, in the Building of a Nation* (Boston: Beacon Press, 2017), 4–5.

24. Ta-Nehisi Coates, "The Case for Reparations," *The Atlantic*, June 2014, https://www.theatlantic.com/magazine/archive/2014/06/the-case-for-reparations/361631/?utm_source=share&utm_campaign=share.

25. https://www.cityofevanston.org/home/showdocument?id=54614.

26. "About ADOS," https://ados101.com/about-ados (accessed March 5, 2020).

27. Charisse Burden-Stelly, "Modern U.S. Racial Capitalism: Some Theoretical Insights," *Monthly Review* (blog), July 1, 2020, https://monthlyreview.org/2020/07/01/modern-u-s-racial-capitalism.

28. Todd Lewan and Dolores Barclay, "When They Steal Your Land, They Steal Your Future," *Los Angeles Times*, December 2, 2001, https://www.latimes.com/archives/la-xpm-2001-dec-02-mn-10514-story.html.

29. Rural Development Land Reform, *Land Audit Report* (Pretoria: Rural Development and Land Reform, February 2018), https://cisp.cachefly.net/assets/articles/attachments/73229_land_audit_report13feb2018.pdf.

30. Peter J. Hudson, *Bankers and Empire: How Wall Street Colonized the Caribbean* (Chicago: University of Chicago Press, 2017). Although Hudson discusses the Caribbean, we could easily apply his analysis to Africans throughout the

diaspora. Banks and insurance companies in the US and the United Kingdom were developed through African enslavement and various forms of structural racism.

31. Sanchez Manning, "Britain's Colonial Shame: Slave-Owners Given Huge Payouts After Abolition," *Independent*, February 13, 2013, https://www .independent.co.uk/news/uk/home-news/britains-colonial-shame-slave-owners -given-huge-payouts-after-abolition-8508358.html.

32. Walter Rodney, *How Europe Underdeveloped Africa* (Washington, DC: Howard University Press, 1982). Rodney writes, "The operation of the imperialist system bears major responsibility for African economic retardation by draining African wealth and by making it impossible to develop more rapidly the resources of the continent." While he puts much of the responsibility for African underdevelopment on Western European capitalists, he acknowledges that "in recent times, they were joined, and to some extent replaced, by capitalists from the United States" (27).

33. Keeanga-Yamahtta Taylor, *Race for Profit: How Banks and the Real Estate Industry Undermined Black Homeownership* (Chapel Hill: University of North Carolina Press, 2019).

34. Bukola Adebayo, "Ghana Makes 126 People from the Diaspora Citizens as Part of Year of Return Celebrations," CNN World, November 29, 2019, https://www.cnn.com/2019/11/29/africa/ghana-foreign-nationals-citizenship /index.html.

35. Repairers of the Breach, "About Us," https://www.breachrepairers.org /mission (accessed July 22, 2020).

36. For a few examples, see Charlene Carruthers, *Unapologetic: A Black, Queer, and Feminist Mandate for Radical Movements* (Boston: Beacon Press, 2018); Keeanga-Yamahtta Taylor, *From #BlackLivesMatter to Black Liberation* (Chicago: Haymarket Books, 2016); Billy-Ray Belcourt, *This Wound Is a World* (Minneapolis: University of Minnesota Press, 2019). These books, taken together, offer a wide range of ways to view history, inclusively organize, and imagine a new world.

37. Stephen L. Pevar, *The Rights of Indians and Tribes*, 4th ed. (New York: New York University Press, 2004), 46.

38. Simpson, "The Place Where We All Live and Work Together," 19.

39. Gilmore, *Change Everything*. At the time of this writing, this book has not yet been published. However, Gilmore has long been an advocate of abolishing not just the carceral state but also building something new. For example, see Rachel Kushner, "Is Prison Necessary? Ruth Wilson Gilmore Might Change Your Mind," *New York Times Magazine*, April 17, 2019, https://www.nytimes .com/2019/04/17/magazine/prison-abolition-ruth-wilson-gilmore.html. See also Eddie S. Glaude Jr., *Democracy in Black: How Race Still Enslaves the American Soul* (New York: Broadway Books, 2016), particularly the chapter "Democracy in Black," 229–36; Alex S. Vitale, *The End of Policing* (London: Verso, 2017); Maya Schenwar and Victoria Law, *Prison by Any Other Name: The Harmful Consequences of Popular Reforms* (New York: New Press, 2020). Schenwar and Law argue, "The entire system must be ended and replaced with resources and supports that genuinely meet people's needs, as well as strategies that effectively address and reduce harm and violence."

POSTSCRIPT

1. "Treaty with the Cherokee: 1791," https://avalon.law.yale.edu/18th _century/chr1791.asp, accessed December 10, 2020.

2. "Treaty with the Florida Tribes of Indians, 1823," in *Indian Affairs: Laws and Treaties*, vol. 2, ed. Charles J. Kappler (Washington, DC: Government Printing Office, 1904), 204.

3. Circe Sturm, "View of Race, Sovereignty, and Civil Rights: Understanding the Cherokee Freedmen Controversy," *Cultural Anthropology* 29, no. 3 (2014): 576–77.

4. There is a host of scholarship on the Five Tribes and their slaveholding. Daniel F. Littlefield wrote a series of books on the different tribes and their relationship to the Freedmen, including specific volumes on the Chickasaw Freedman and the Cherokee Freedmen. Jodi A. Byrd, "'Been to the Nation, Lord, but I Couldn't Stay There,'" *Interventions* 13, no. 1 (2011): 31–52, https://doi.org /10.1080/1369801X.2011.545576.

5. Cherokee Nation, "Cherokee Nation Supreme Court Issues Decision That 'by Blood' Reference Be Stricken from Cherokee Nation Constitution," *Cherokee Nation One Feather*, February 22, 2021.

PHOTO CREDITS

INDEX

Abernathy, Ralph, 113–14, 118, 120–21
abolitionism, 32, 44–54, 106, 185. *See also* prison abolitionism; slavery
Abolition of the Slave Trade (Clarkson), 14
accountability, 134, 146, 160–65. *See also* reparations
Achebe, Chinua, 173
Acoli, Sundiata, 125
Adams, Hank, 118, 119
Adams, Samuel, 15
Adler, Felix, 68, 69
affirmative action, 77–78, 148
African Americans. *See* Afro-Indigenous Americans; Black Americans; enslaved Africans
African American Vernacular English (or Black English), 27, 35, 137–38. *See also* language
African immigrant community in US, 171
African National Congress (ANC), 130–31
Africans in US. *See* Black Americans; enslaved Africans; Indigenous Africans
Afro-Indigenous Americans: Burrell on, 113–14; Paul Cuffe, 12–14; on cultural appropriation, 141–42; Freedmen of the Five Tribes, 186–92; history of, xiii–xiv, xxi–xxiii; as term, xiii, 150. *See*

also Indigenous Africans; *names of specific persons*
Afro-Latinx community, 171
Afro-Native, as term, xiii. *See also* Afro-Indigenous Americans; Black Americans; Native Americans
Afro-pessimism, 198n17
"Ain't I a Woman?" (Truth), 46–47
Albany Plan, 19–20
Alcatraz Island protest (1969–71), 109. *See also* resistance
Alexander, Michelle, 56
Algorithms of Oppression (Noble), 146
Alkalimat, Abdul, 93
All-African People's Revolutionary Party (AAPRP), 112, 128–31, 215n66
"All Lives Matter," 137
American Anti-Slavery Society (AASS), 50, 52
American Colonization Society (ACS), 43–45
American Descendants of Slavery (ADOS), 177–78
American Dream, 104–5
American Indian Conference, 80, 118
American Indian Movement (AIM), 80, 109, 112, 122, 132, 165. *See also* Native Americans; resistance
American Revolution (1775–83), 8, 10, 15–16, 37, 96, 97, 201n38
Anderson, Claud, 33

Anderson, Larry, 130
Anderson, William, 170
Angelou, Maya, 35
anger, xxiii, 21, 101, 142, 185. *See
    also* fear
Anishinaabe, 39–41, 130, 132, 136,
    170
Anishinaabe, Michi Saagiig, 92
antiblackness: Baldwin on, 101;
    Cuffe and, 13; experienced by
    author, xi; Harris on, xviii–xix;
    by Jefferson, 23; King on, 85–86;
    by Native Americans, 174; negro,
    as term, 22; "n*gg*r," as term,
    147–48, 151; Tocqueville on, 28;
    ubiquity of, 187. *See also* police
    violence; racism
anti-Indigenous: in Declaration of
    Independence, 22–23; "playing
    Indian," 84, 134, 137, 153–54;
    R-word, 84, 150–52; sports team
    mascots, 3, 84, 137, 140,
    153–54, 156–57; ubiquity of, 187.
    See also racism
anti-racism, 111, 168
apartheid, 104, 130–31, 169,
    171–72, 215n72
"An Appeal to the Soul of White
    America" (Garvey), 65
Aquinnah Wampanoag, 12
Armstrong, Samuel C., 51
As Black as Resistance (Samudzi
    and Anderson), 170
Ashanti, 12, 13
Asheville, North Carolina, 176
Asian American community, 53,
    108, 123, 135, 138, 171, 172
assassinations: of Black Panthers,
    124; of King, 118; of Malcolm X,
    96, 104, 114, 122
assimilation, 60, 111. *See also*
    boarding schools; erasure
Assiniboine, 118
Atlanta "Braves," 84
The Atlantic (publication), 176–77
atmospheric violence, 159. *See also*
    police violence
Attucks, Crispus, 5, 14–16, 201n38
Aunt Jemima, 155

author's positionality, ix–xii, 76,
    187
The Autobiography of Malcolm X
    (Malcolm X), 82, 90–91, 92–93,
    98

Baamewaawaagizhigokwe, 39–41
"Back to Africa" bill, 57
Bacon, Nathaniel, xvi
Bacon's Rebellion (1676), xvi–xvii,
    197n17
Baldwin, James, 81, 100–107, 169
banking, 180, 220n30. *See also*
    capitalism
Bank of America, 152
Banks, Dennis, 109, 122–23, 124
Barber, William J., II, 181
"Bars Fight" (Terry), 11
baseball team mascots, 84. *See also*
    sports team mascots
Beck, Abaki, 143, 144
The Beginning and End of Rape
    (Deer), 143
Belcourt, Billy-Ray, 167–68
Bellecourt, Clyde, 109, 112–13, 133
Bellecourt, Vernon, 112, 130, 131,
    132
belonging: of Black Americans,
    xix–xx, 28–29, 92–99, 177–78;
    Cuffe on, 13–14; Garvey and
    UNIA on, 61–66; of Native
    Americans, xxi, 91–92; of white
    people, xviii–xix, 18–19. *See also*
    citizenship; identity
Bennett, Robert L., 119
Berkeley, William, xvi
Berry, Daina Ramey, 176
Between the World and Me (Coates),
    82–83
Big Mountain, Arizona, 130
Biko, Steve, 169
Bilbo, Theodore, 57
Bilge, Sirma, 144
birthright citizenship, xx, 5, 102,
    113. *See also* citizenship; Freed-
    men of the Five Tribes
Bitch Media (publication), 143
Black Americans: ACS on, 43–45;
    belonging of, xix–xx, 28–29,